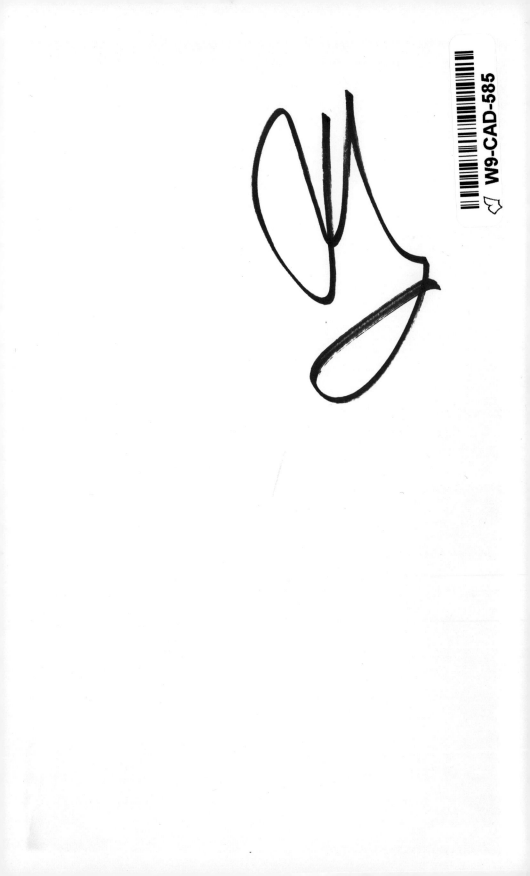

The Biology
of Crabs

Above The mangrove crab *Goniopsis cruentata* in a Jamaican mangrove swamp. Size, about 50 mm carapace width.

Below A large male spider crab *Maia squinado* on a sandy sea-bed in the English Channel. Size, about 170 mm carapace width.

The Biology of Crabs

G.F. WARNER

Lecturer in Zoology, University of Reading

VAN NOSTRAND REINHOLD COMPANY
NEW YORK   CINCINNATI   ATLANTA   DALLAS   SAN FRANCISCO
LONDON   TORONTO   MELBOURNE

First published in Great Britain 1977 by
Paul Elek (Scientific Books) Ltd., London

Van Nostrand Reinhold Company Regional Offices:
New York   Cincinnati   Atlanta   Dallas   San Francisco

Van Nostrand Reinhold Company International Offices:
London   Toronto   Melbourne

Library of Congress Catalog Card Number: 77-24512
ISBN: 0-442-29205-8

Published by Van Nostrand Reinhold Company
450 West 33rd Street, New York, N.Y. 10001

Published simultaneously in Canada by Van Nostrand Reinhold Ltd.

15   14   13   12   11   10   9   8   6   5   4   3   2   1

Library of Congress Cataloging in Publication Data

Warner, G F
  The biology of crabs.

  Bibliography: p.
  Includes index.
  1. Crabs.   I. Title.
QL444.M33W37   595'.3842   77-24512
ISBN 0-442-29205-8

Contents

Figures

The frontispiece shows (above) the mangrove crab *Goniopsis cruentata* in a Jamaican mangrove swamp, about 50 mm carapace width, and (below) a large male spider crab *Maia squinado* on a sandy sea-bed in the English Channel, about 170 mm carapace width.

Tables

Acknowledgements

I have received considerable help and encouragement from colleagues here at Reading and elsewhere who have read, criticized and discussed sections of the manuscript. The book has ended up far better than it would have done without their attentions and I am very grateful to them. They include Drs R.S.K. Barnes, D.M. Broom, R. Goldring, A.R. Jones, S.M. Lobb, G. Thompson, G.J. Vermeij, and Professors E. Naylor and K. Simkiss. Needless to say any errors that remain are entirely my own.

I should also like to thank the following for giving permission to use copyright material in the preparation of the illustrations: E.J. Brill, Leiden (36B, C, 42C); Gauthier-Villars, Paris (9); Macmillan Journals, Ltd. (21); Pergamon Press, Ltd. (8, 17, 19C, 37); The American Society of Zoologists (16); The Carnegie Institute of Washington, DC (26D, E, F); The Company of Biologists, Ltd. (18A); The Geological Society of America and University of Kansas (*Treatise on Invertebrate Paleontology*) (2, 41A, B, C); The Marine Biological Association of the United Kingdom (35A, 36A); The Rosenstiel School of Marine and Atmospheric Science of the University of Miami (34C, 35C, 41D, 42B); The Royal Society, London (19A, B); The Zoological Society of London (34A, B, D, 35B, D, 42A); Williams and Norgate, London (7, 11). The authors of the relevant articles are acknowledged in the captions to the figures.

Preface

Complexity, convenient size and ready availability make a good recipe for an experimental animal. Crabs have been investigated over a very wide range of biological fields and one of the factors which stimulated me to write this book was the feeling that the mass of accumulating literature should be pulled together into a single volume before it became too vast. Of course, I soon discovered that it already was too vast, but by then I had gone too far to turn back. The result will, I hope, be useful to interested observers at all levels and also to those who seek to add to our knowledge of crabs, not by instructing them in their own chosen fields — this would be an immoderate ambition — but by showing that crabs are complete animals: complete, complex and diverse. This lesson is important since the results gained within a limited field of investigation often have a meaning which overlaps this field and may not be correctly interpreted without a deeper knowledge of the experimental material. Fruitful zoological study can take two directions: towards topics which span the groups, in which one learns that all animals (populations, ecosystems) face similar situations and survive by operating in similar ways; or towards groups which span the topics in which one learns that single species (families, phyla) can do many things at once. Both directions are intellectually satisfying but I believe that they are not exclusive. It is my impression that in recent years zoological study has tended to accentuate the topic approach at the expense of the groups. These are left to organize themselves into whole animals in the mind of the student. This book seeks to redress the balance with respect to crabs. Here is a group in which one can study, all at once, most of the topics at present dealt with in zoological teaching and research, and hence grasp at the concept of a whole animal.

There is, however, no typical crab that one can take as a model of a whole animal; indeed, the diversity of crabs is a microcosm of the diversity of all animals and is, therefore, like all other aspects of biology, part of the whole animal concept. A result of the multiplicity of parts of a whole animal is that there can be no typical 'biology of crabs'. Any book on such a subject must fail in the eyes of some readers by leaving out, or by treating too lightly, some important point or area of study. I will not expose my ignorance by listing the topics that I have left out, nor will I presume to justify any omissions. The book is a personal approach to the biology of crabs, and I can only hope that this approach of mine is not too uncommon.

G.F. Warner,
Reading, 1977.

Introduction

When one considers the Crustacea one may be surprised by two things: First, the multiplicity of groups; second, that most of the species are in rather few of these groups. In the class Crustacea there are eight sub-classes and thirty Recent orders. The class contains about 26 000 species but the only sub-classes which contain more than 10 per cent of this total are the Copepoda (4500) and the Malacostraca (18 000). Thus the Malacostraca contains some 70 per cent of all crustacean species. But within the Malacostraca the position is the same: a multiplicity of groups with most of the species contained within three orders — the Amphipoda (sandhoppers — 3600), the Isopoda (woodlice — 4000) and the Decapoda (8500). The Decapoda is the group that contains the crabs, and it also contains other such familiar crustaceans as lobsters and shrimps. But most decapods are crabs, 4500 of them. Thus crabs, despite being of lowly taxonomic rank (an infra-order of a sub-order) are, in terms of numbers of species, one of the biggest groups of the Crustacea. In this sense when one studies crabs one studies Crustacea and, indeed, because of their easy availability and convenient size, more is known about crabs than about any other single group of crustaceans.

However, crustacean groups which are relatively poor in species are often important in terms of numbers of individuals. One might single out the Cladocera (water fleas), the Cirripedia (barnacles), and the Euphausiacea (krill, whale-food). The crabs, indeed the whole of the Malacostraca, are relatively conservative in their anatomy and to grasp the diversity of crustaceans one must look at these smaller groups. But the organization of crabs is crustacean enough and, since it is relatively conservative, its study is a good starting place in the study of Crustacea. Such a study provides a firm basis which the smaller groups, for all their apparent simplicity, do not. This may seem like working backwards from a peak of evolution (which crabs are certainly at) back to more primitive forms, and so it is. And so, in my view, it should be in the case of the Crustacea, since the phylogeny of the group is poorly understood and is a bad thread on which to hang one's knowledge.

Why else should one study crabs? Man's interest in crabs goes back a very long way: there are only two invertebrates in the Zodiac and one of them is Cancer the crab. Both Cancer and Scorpio have chelae and it is possible that this may have helped man to identify with these two invertebrates sufficiently closely to see them in the stars. Chelae, after all, are more like hands than are the limbs of most animals. Backing up the chelae, Scorpio has his sting, a considerable inducement to take notice of him. Crabs, despite their pinch, are less deadly, but they do have character. This arises in part from the arrangement of their eyes, mouth and chelae giving them an expression that is less alien to man than are the expressions of most invertebrates. Add to this the complex and opportunistic behaviour of crabs, and the fact that you can eat them, and one has an animal that captures the attention of an interested observer in a way that a worm, ant or sea urchin might fail to do. Let me hasten to say, as a zoologist, that these last three animals are also fascinating; but they do not appear in the Zodiac and they do not fasten themselves in grim delight to the toe of the fat lady in the seaside postcard.

Another reason for studying crabs is their position in the Arthropoda. There in a case for regarding crabs as the most advanced members of this, the largest of the phyla. I do not propose to argue the case, nor to try to define 'advancement', but on any sensible definition of the word I believe that one would have great difficulty proving that crabs were less advanced than any other group of advanced arthropods, for instance than the social insects. One pinnacle, however, that is not open to question is that of size: the biggest arthropods are crabs. The giant Japanese spider crab grows to a chela-spread of 3·6 m. This is mostly spindly legs, the body being about 40 cm across. Large compact crabs, however, are not uncommon. One of the largest, *Pseudocarcinus gigas* from south Australia, grows to some 43 cm across the body and has a chela of about the same size; it can weigh about 14 kg. The largest lobsters weigh about 20 kg but cannot approach the giant spider crab in overall dimensions.

This book, therefore, is about crabs as engaging creatures, as important arthropods and as model crustaceans. But for all their conservatism compared with other crustaceans they are, nevertheless, very diverse. In the first place there are two broad groups of crustaceans called crabs: true crabs belong to the infra-order Brachyura but hermit crabs and their allies belong to the infra-order Anomura. In discussing crabs I have found it impossible to leave out these crab-like anomurans and they crop up from time to time. Even within true crabs, however, there is considerable diversity, but it is not a baffling diversity since it rests on the standard organization. This organization is the subject of the first four chapters which describe properties which almost all crabs possess. Of course there is no such thing as a typical crab and it is impossible to exclude diversity completely. Chapters 5 and 6 are directly concerned with diversity, of life-style and feeding, and complete the picture of the crab 'as it stands'. Population continuity, through social organization, growth and reproduction, is introduced in Chapters 7 and 8. Chapter 9, on physiological adaptations to diverse environments, completes the survey of the biology of living crabs. In Chapter 10 the systematics and evolution of crabs are briefly reviewed and those readers who, like me, like to hang names on a taxonomical tree so that they know where they are, may like to read this chapter first. It contains a classification (Table 4) on page 165 in which all genera mentioned in the text are listed as examples of their families. Lastly, Chapter 11 reviews the economic importance of crabs to man.

1 Anatomy and life-support systems

A crab dissection is one of the few zoological exercises that may be handed to one on a plate. The whole animal is present and although the gourmet may only be interested in the brown meat and the white meat and how to get at them, there is every reason why a zoologist should look further. The functional serial arrangement of the appendages is clearly seen. The elegant jointing of the legs and the arrangement of the muscles inside may be examined. The complicated musculature at the leg bases inside the endophragmal skeleton must be investigated. The heart and stomach may have to be removed to get at the oily and strong-tasting brown meat or hepatopancreas which, with the gonad, fills much of the space inside the body. I am not suggesting that the best way to prepare a crab for dissection is to boil for 20 minutes with salt and bay leaves! However, the exercise is instructive as well as being nutritious and since there are very few poisonous crabs (Holthuis, 1968) it can be applied to almost any species of sufficient size.

BODY FORM AND APPENDAGES

Despite the wide range of form it is generally not difficult to recognize a crab (Fig. 1). This is because the variation is superimposed upon a basic morphology which is quite distinct from the morphology of their nearest relatives, the other decapod crustaceans. The body of a typical crab is squat, broad and compact with the abdomen reduced and tucked away underneath. At the front there is a pair of claws or chelipeds and four pairs of walking legs radiate out from the sides. The transverse axis of the body is generally the longest and this fits with the well known fact that crabs usually walk sideways. In other decapods, for instance lobsters and shrimps, the body is quite a different shape being long and domed with a well developed abdomen. This difference in form has far-reaching consequences on the life-styles of the animals in that the compact crab-like form is at once stronger and allows greater mobility to the individual than the long lobster-like form. These advantages have lead to the present wealth of crab species all over the world, the result of an explosive adaptive radiation which started with the attainment of the crab-like

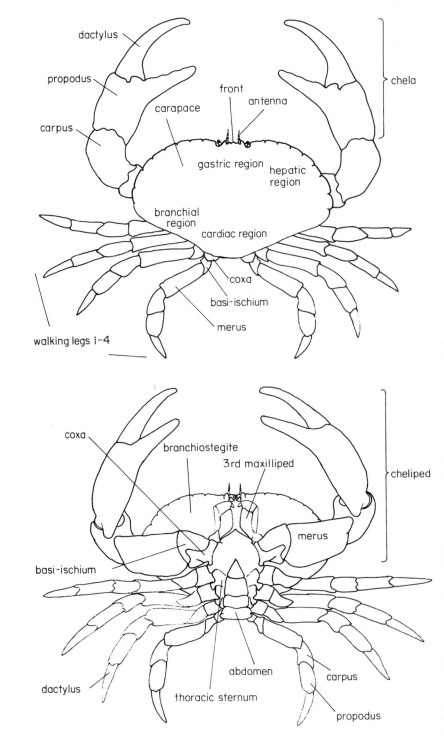

Fig. 1   The external parts of the European edible crab *Cancer pagurus* (♂) A, dorsal view; B, ventral view.

form in the Jurassic (Chapter 10). Apart from this important difference in body shape, however, there is little difference between crabs and other decapods in what one might call body plan. Like other decapods, crabs are segmentally organized with six head segments all fused together, eight thoracic segments and six abdominal segments. The typical decapod has a pair of appendages on every segment except the first. These, with the exception of the 1st antennae, are similar morphologically and can all be derived from an appendage such as that shown in Fig. 2. This uniformity of structure allows standard names to be used for the segments (podomeres) of the appendages. Another decapod feature is the carapace; this is a shelf of cuticle which extends back from the head to cover the thorax dorsally and laterally. It is fused to the thorax dorsally but is free laterally where it encloses the branchial chambers in which lie the gills arising from the bases of the thoracic appendages (Fig. 2). The fusion of the carapace with the thorax and, on the ventral side, fusion of the thoracic sternites, results in the formation of a strong and compact cephalothorax to the back of which is attached the jointed abdomen.

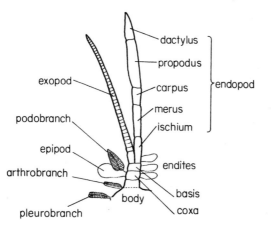

Fig. 2 A possible basic decapod appendage from which the appendages of crabs can be derived. After Hothuis, in Glaessner, 1969.

Although the appendages of a decapod can be derived from a basic appendage they are nevertheless very varied and are all specialized for particular functions. The usual pattern for the head appendages is as follows (Figs. 1, 3). Starting anteriorly there are two pairs of sensory antennae, a pair of mandibles on either side of the mouth and two pairs of maxillae. The 1st antennae are biramous but in crabs the 2nd antennae have lost their lateral branches or exopods. The base of each mandible is enlarged and bears a strong biting edge, but there is not much left of the rest of the appendage: the exopod has been lost and the inner branch or endopod is reduced to a palp. The maxillae are flattened leaf-like appendages which lack proper joints; various lobes or endites developed along their medial edges are used for holding and manipulating food in front of the mouth. The 1st maxillae have lost their exopods and each one consists of little more than a group of endites bearing spines. The 2nd maxillae, however, are of wider significance since they each have a lateral flap called a scaphognathite. These are important in respiration as they pump water through the branchial chambers. Lateral flaps developed on an appendage are called epipods (Fig. 2) and the scaphognathite may be the result of fusion between an epipod and the exopod of the 2nd maxilla.

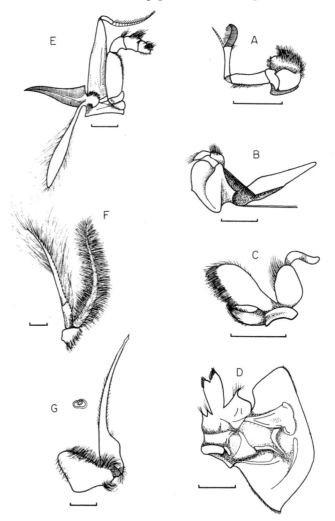

Fig. 3 Crab appendages taken from large specimens of the edible crab *Cancer pagurus*. A, 1st antenna; B, mandible; C. 1st maxilla; D, 2nd maxilla; E, 2nd maxilliped (arthrobranch omitted); F, female pleopod; G, male 1st pleopod and TS showing sperm duct. A, B, C and D are appendages of the righthand side; E is of the lefthand side. They are all drawn as seen from the mid-line. F and G are the anterior aspects of righthand side appendages. Scale = 10 mm.

The thoracic appendages of a decapod are modified for three different functions: feeding, grasping and walking. The first three pairs are called maxillipeds and are deflected forwards over the mouth where, together with the other mouthparts (mandibles and maxillae), they are used for manipulating food. The maxillipeds are all biramous and in addition all three bear epipods which extend back into the branchial chambers where they serve to clean the gills. Posterior to the maxillipeds are the chelipeds with claws or chelae adapted for grasping. The remaining four pairs of thoracic appendages are long pointed walking legs. Both the chelipeds and the walking legs are uniramous having lost their exopods. The abdomen is articulated to the back of the cephalothorax and is a jointed structure showing external evidence of segmentation. In decapods other than crabs the abdominal appendages are used in swimming and comprise five pairs of biramous pleopods and a single pair of biramous uropods. The anus is at the end of the abdomen on the post-segmental telson.

The appendages of true or brachyuran crabs only depart from the decapod pattern at the front and back ends of the body. At the front the antennae are much reduced when compared with the long sensory flagellae of lobsters and shrimps, and the mouthparts are more flattened. The 3rd maxillipeds, instead of being limb-like, resemble double doors hinged at the base which close over the buccal region hiding all the other mouthparts. At the back end the differences are much greater; the abdomen, reduced and tucked away under the body, has lost all locomotory functions and has instead become specialized for reproduction. In both sexes the uropods have been lost but the female retains a fairly broad abdomen with four pairs of biramous pleopods which are used for holding the developing eggs. The abdomen of the male is narrower than that of the female and some of the segments may be fused together, only the first two pairs of pleopods are retained. These are uniramous and form intromittent structures; the second pair work as pistons inside channels in the first pair to pump sperm into the female during copulation.

Anomuran crabs

The hermit crabs of the infra-order Anomura are quite different from true crabs in their morphology (Fig. 4). Indeed, with their long domed carapaces and well developed abdomens they more closely resemble lobsters and shrimps in general form. Hermit crabs inhabit old gastropod mollusc shells and they are adapted to this way of life in several characteristic ways. The large abdomen is not protected by a calcified exoskeleton and is soft to the touch. It is asymmetrically coiled such that it fits into a gastropod shell and the uropods are adapted to cling to the shell deep within the coils. The pleopods are reduced, particularly on the inside of the coiled abdomen, and the posterior two pairs of walking legs are also reduced and modified to support the shell. When danger threatens, the hermit crab retreats into its shell leaving the tips of its legs and chelae projecting. It is probable that these animals are called hermit crabs rather than 'hermit lobsters' because living in a gastropod shell has given them protection and the added mobility of a compact shape. Their way of life is thus crab-like rather than lobster-like and they range freely over the sea bed scavenging with their strong claws.

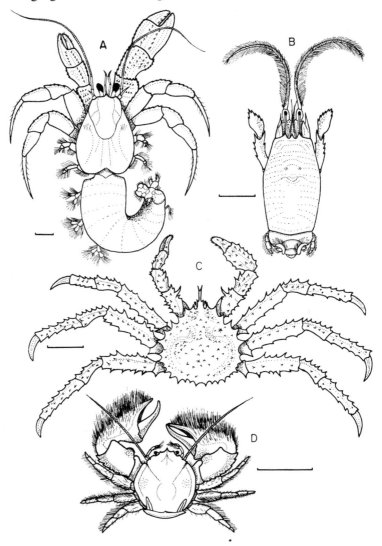

Fig. 4 Anomuran crabs. A, a European hermit crab *Pagurus bernhardus*; B, mole crab *Emerita*; C, stone crab *Lithodes maia*; D, a European porcelain crab *Porcellana platycheles*. Scale for A, B and D = 10 mm; for C = 50 mm.

Certain other anomuran crustaceans are more truly crab-like in their morphology being squat and compact with the abdomen reduced and tucked under the body (Fig. 4). Uropods, however, are generally retained and the abdomen as a whole is less strongly reduced than in brachyuran crabs. Some crab-like anomurans (the stone crab *Lithodes* and the robber crab *Birgus*) have asymmetrical abdomens indicating a hermit crab ancestry and in most forms the last pair of walking legs is reduced and tucked up under the posterior margin of the carapace.

THE EXOSKELETON

The entire surface of the body of a crab, including most of the lining of the gut, is covered by a tough cuticle which constitutes the exoskeleton. This cuticle, even in small crabs, is very heavily calcified over most of the outside of the body giving protection from predators and aiding the freedom which crabs enjoy on the sea bed.

Typically the cuticle is composed of four layers: epicuticle, exocuticle, endocuticle and membranous layer (Fig. 5). The epicuticle is distinct from the other three layers in not containing chitin. It is a thin, light brown, translucent layer composed of lipo-protein and is very tough as a result of tanning in which the protein molecules are bound together by quinone cross-links. It is not so heavily calcified as the deep layers of the cuticle and retains some flexibility. This makes it ideal for resisting abrasion and a thick epicuticle is often found in areas liable to wear and tear such as the tips of the walking legs, the teeth of the gastric mill and the bearing

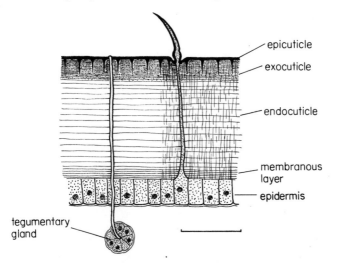

Fig. 5   Transverse section of crab cuticle. Pore canals are indicated on the right of the figure only. Based on Dennell (1960) and Krishnan (1951) for the cuticle of the merus of the walking leg of the north Atlantic shore crab *Carcinus maenas*. Scale = 1 mm.

surfaces of the leg joints. There is some evidence that the epicuticle is the chief layer responsible for limiting the permeability of the cuticle as a whole; no doubt the lipid material which is concentrated in the outer layers is important in this context. Green and Neff (1972), who studied the cuticle of the fiddler crab *Uca* under the electron microscope, found that in these crabs the epicuticle is composed of six layers. The outer five are orientated parallel to the surface while the much thicker sixth layer is orientated perpendicular to the surface and tails off into the underlying exocuticle.

The exocuticle and endocuticle are similar in that they are both built up of layers of chitin–protein microfibrils. These microfibrils form monolayers or lamellae parallel to the surface of the cuticle and within a lamella all the microfibrils are parallel to each other. However, with respect to microfibrils in successive lamellae, the orientation changes in a regular fashion; in *Uca* the average change in microfibrillar orientation between lamellae is about 5° (Green and Neff, 1972). The crab cuticle is built up of many hundreds of these lamellae and thus the microfibrillar orientation spirals through the thickness of the cuticle making many complete 360° turns. This fine structure clearly adds to the strength of the cuticle as a whole. It is only fair to say here that this model for the structure of arthropod cuticles, the Bouligand model, apparently confirmed for *Uca* by Green and Neff, may not hold for all crabs. There is disagreement on the applicability of the model to thicker shelled crabs such as *Carcinus* (see Bouligand, 1971, and Dennell, 1974, for opposing views).

Apart from the above similarities in composition and structure, the differences between the exocuticle and endocuticle are sufficient to make them clearly distinct in microscope sections (Fig. 5). First of all the outer exocuticle is laid down in the form of hexagonal pillars orientated perpendicular to the surface; each pillar probably represents the secretion of an individual epidermal cell. Tanned protein tails down from the epicuticle into the spaces between the pillars while within the pillars the chitin–protein lamellae are discontinuous and irregular. In the inner exocuticle the pillars coalesce and the lamellae become continuous. Deposits of melanin occur throughout the exocuticle and this layer has sometimes been called the pigmented layer to distinguish it from the endocuticle which is unpigmented. A further difference revealed in the fine structure is that in the exocuticle the lamellae are fine and tightly packed whereas in the endocuticle they are larger and loosely stacked. The two layers are also distinct from a developmental point of view in that the epicuticle and exocuticle are secreted before moulting while the endocuticle is laid down after the moult (Chapter 8). Both the exocuticle and the endocuticle are strengthened by heavy calcification within the chitin–protein matrix and in the exocuticle tanning of proteins also takes place. The innermost layer of the cuticle is called the membranous layer, it is similar to the endocuticle in construction but is uncalcified.

Penetrating through the cuticle are pore canals and the ducts of the tegumentary glands. The former are very fine branching canals containing cytoplasmic extensions of the epidermal cells, they are very numerous (about 4 million per mm^2) and penetrate to the inner edge of the epicuticle. They probably aid in the transport of material during cuticle growth. The tegumentary glands are situated below the epidermis and their ducts, which are far larger and less numerous than the pore canals, extend through the cuticle to open on the surface. Tegumentary glands are commonest in areas liable to abrasion where there is a thick epicuticle and it is likely that their chief function may be to repair damage by the secretion of epicuticle-like material. Other cellular extensions penetrating the cuticle are pores leading to bristles on the surface. Many of these bristles are sensory (Chapter 3) and contain nerve endings.

The typical cuticle depicted diagrammatically in Fig. 5 is found over much of the body surface but local variations in structure are common. The thickness, for instance, varies considerably from place to place, being particularly thick on the fingers of the chelae and usually relatively thin on the branchiostegites. The cuticle over the gills is extremely thin to allow for gaseous exchange, and the cuticle over chemosensory bristles is also very thin to allow diffusion through to the nerve endings. In some places the cuticle is flexible instead of being rigid, an obvious example being the arthrodial membrances which permit movement between podomeres at the joints of the appendages.

Although the cuticle is generally thought of as an external protective covering its function as a skeleton is no less important. This function is dealt with in Chapter 2 and involves the translation of muscular activity into organized movement; muscles are attached to the inside of the skeleton such that their contractions are transmitted by the skeleton to produce particular movements. In the limbs of a crab tendon-like invaginations (apodemes) are developed to provide for the muscle insertions, and at the bases of the limbs plate-like invaginations of the body wall (arthrophragms) provide skeletal attachments for muscles located within the body which move the limbs from their bases. Both apodemes and arthrophragms are cuticular invaginations and often form rigid calcified plates; apodemes, however, always have flexible insertions to allow for relative movement. Around the bases of the thoracic appendages, particularly the legs with large powerful basal muscles, the arthrophragms arise as a series of plates to form a composite cage-like structure of considerable strength termed the endophragmal skeleton (Fig. 7B). The development of this internal skeleton adds greatly to the strength of the body as a whole and also provides useful attachments and supports for the various internal organs.

BRANCHIAL CHAMBERS, GILLS, AND VENTILATION

The branchial chambers are contained beneath the branchiostegites (Figs. 6, 7). Each chamber is roofed by a thin cuticular membrane which separates it from the hepatopancreas anteriorly and from the inside of the carapace posteriorly. Ventrally it is bounded by the branchiostegite on the outside and by the body wall on the inside. At the front end each branchial cavity narrows down to a constriction beyond which a small pump chamber houses the scaphogathite. The roof of the pump chamber is formed from the cuticular membrane stiffened by skeletal struts; it is floored posteriorly by the expanded base of the epipod of the 1st maxilliped and anteriorly by the exopods of the 1st and 2nd maxillipeds. The gills are associated with the bases of the thoracic limbs as shown diagrammatically in Fig. 2. There are three different positions from which gills may arise leading to three different names for the gills: podobranchs arising from the epipods, arthrobranchs from the junction of the limb with the body, and pleurobranchs from the body wall. In most crabs nine gills are present in each branchial chamber: the 2nd maxillipeds each bear a podobranch (orientated horizontally as opposed to the near vertical orientation of the rest of the gills) and an arthrobranch; the 3rd maxillipeds bear a short truncated podobranch and two arthrobranchs;

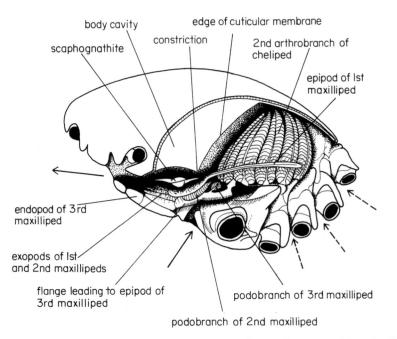

Fig. 6   The branchial chamber of a Caribbean xanthid *Carpilius corallinus*, exposed from the side by removing the branchiostegite and overlying carapace. Arrows show the normal direction of the respiratory stream.

the chelipeds bear two arthrobranchs; and the 1st and 2nd walking legs each bear a single pleurobranch. Also lying in the branchial chambers are the epipods of the maxillipeds; those of the 2nd and 3rd maxillipeds clean the ventral surfaces of the gills while the long epipod of the 1st maxilliped sweeps the dorsal surfaces.

The inhalant respiratory stream enters the branchial chambers through various gaps guarded by hairs between the bases of the legs and under the lower edges of the branchiostegites (Fig. 6). The largest of these openings are the 'Milne-Edwards openings' above the bases of the chelipeds. Having entered, water passes between the gill bases into the hypobranchial space below the gills. Each gill is made up of a series of plates or lamellae arranged on both sides of a flattened central axis and the respiratory stream passes up between the lamellae into the epibranchial space above the gills. It is during the passage between the lamellae that gaseous exchange takes place; this is facilitated by a counter current system in which the blood flow within the lamellae is in the opposite direction to the water flow between the lamellae (Hughes et al., 1969). In each epibranchial space the exhalant current flows forwards into the pump chamber from which the scaphognathite expels it through the exhalant opening. Each scaphognathite performs undulating movements achieved by a crossed muscle system operating on springy pieces of cuticle; about two waves per second travel from posterior to anterior along the scaphognathite propelling water forwards through the pump chamber. This activity, in the case of the shore crab Carcinus maenas, results in a standing pressure in the epibranchial space about 1 cm H_2O lower than outside (Hughes et al., 1969). The exhalant openings lie on either side of the epistome just above the mouth, and the current issuing from them can be quite powerful and helps to disperse the depleted water.

The amount of water normally pumped through the branchial chambers by the scaphognathite varies from 1–2 ml/g/min (Arudpragasam and Naylor, 1964, 1966). However, this volume may vary considerably with the physiological state of the crab; for instance, a tidal rhythm has been demonstrated in Carcinus in which ventilation reaches a peak just after high tide (Arudpragasam and Naylor, 1964). Variations also occur under conditions of respiratory stress: ventilation is usually increased at low oxygen tensions while high carbon dioxide tensions may lead to a reduction in pumping rate. The quantity of oxygen extracted from the respiratory stream by Carcinus is normally about 20 per cent of that available. Under normal conditions this percentage extraction varies inversely with ventilation volume but under respiratory stress both ventilation and extraction may be increased (Chapter 9).

Alterations in ventilation rate may be brought about by a variety of mechanisms. First, the rate of pumping by the scaphognathites may be altered. A large amount of variation is possible in this way since the

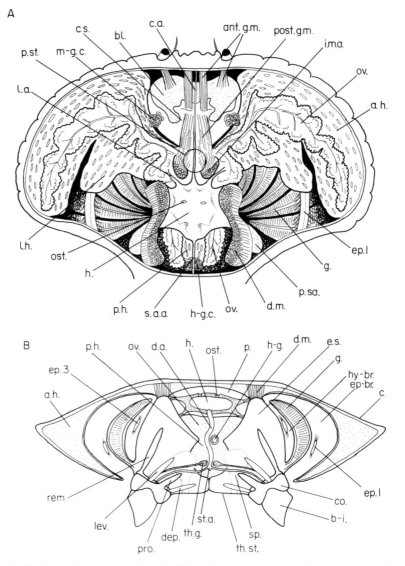

Fig. 7 The internal anatomy of a female edible crab *Cancer pagurus*. A, the arrangement of tissues and organs directly under the carapace; B, a diagrammatic TS through the cardiac region, anterior view. Both after Pearson, 1908. *a. h.*, anterior lobe of the hepatopancreas; *ant. g. m.*, anterior gastric muscles; *b.-i.*, basi-ischium; *bl.*, bladder; *br.*, branchiostegite; *c.*, carapace; *c. a.*, cephalic artery; *co.*, coxa; *c. s.*, cardiac stomach; *d. a.*, descending artery; *dep.*, apodeme of the depressor muscle of the basi-ischium; *d. m.*, dorsal muscle; *ep. 1*, epipod of the 1st maxilliped; *ep. 3*, epipod of the 3rd maxilliped; *ep.-br.*, epibranchial space; *e. s.*, endophragmal skeleton; *g.*, gill; *h.*, heart; *h.-g.*, hind-gut; *h.-g. c.*, hind-gut caecum; *hy.-br.*, hypobranchial space; *i. m. a.*, internal adductor muscle of the mandible; *l. a.*, lateral artery; *lev.*, apodeme of the levator muscle of the basi-ischium; *l. h.*, lateral lobe of the hepatopancreas; *m.-g. c.*, mid-gut caecum; *ost.*, ostium; *ov.*, ovary; *p.*, pericardium; *p. h.*, posterior lobe of the hepatopancreas; *p. sa.*, pericardial sac; *p. st.*, position of pyloric stomach; *post. g. m.*, posterior gastric muscles; *pro.*, apodeme of the promotor muscle of the coxa; *rem.*, apodeme of the remotor muscle of the coxa; *s. a. a.*, superior abdominal artery; *sp.*, spermatheca; *st. a.*, sternal artery; *th. g.*, thoracic ganglion; *th. st.*, thoracic sternum.

scaphognathites appear to be under independent control and can operate at different rates on the two sides of the crab at the same time; indeed they can even pump in different directions simultaneously. Second, variations in ventilation volume may be brought about by altering the inhalant and exhalant openings. A flange on the coxa and epipod of the 3rd maxilliped (Fig. 6) can alter the dimensions of the Milne-Edwards opening and thus alter the volume of the inhalant stream. Indeed, this flange appears to be able to control the direction of the inhalant stream as well as its volume and can divert water to bathe either the anterior or the posterior gills (Hughes *et al.*, 1969). Inhalant apertures posterior to the Milne-Edwards openings can also be altered by raising or lowering the carapace. This may occur in the edible crab *Cancer pagurus* in which 50 per cent of the respiratory stream normally enters posteriorly (Arudpragasam and Naylor, 1966). A further way in which the ventilation rate may be altered is to change the flow pattern at the exhalant openings. Lashing with the exopods of the maxillipeds and lowering the 3rd maxillipeds, often seen in crabs under respiratory stress, may augment the through-flow of water.

Regular short duration (5-second) reversals of the normal pumping direction of the scaphognathites are a common feature of decapod crustacean respiratory patterns. In crabs there is considerable variation between different species in the frequency of these reversals, about one per minute is normal in *Carcinus*, whereas half that rate is found in *Cancer* (Arudpragasam and Naylor, 1966). Within a species the frequency of reversal may vary depending both on the ventilation volume, to which it is usually directly proportional, and on the environmental situation. Thus in *Cancer* reversal frequency is increased by the addition of particles to the water (Arudpragasam and Naylor, 1966), an observation which indicates that one function of the reversals may be to remove detritus from the ventral sides of the gills. Without a current reversal any particles dislodged by the brushing action of the epipods of the 2nd and 3rd maxillipeds would simply be sucked back onto the gills and would tend to clog them (Hughes *et al.*, 1969). However in other species (*Macropius*, *Carcinus*) the evidence for a primary cleaning function of the reversals is not so clear and it is possible that in crabs in which most of the inhalant water enters anteriorly at the Milne-Edwards openings the reversals may aid circulation around the posterior gills (Arudpragasam and Naylor, 1966). Another possibility is that the sudden increase in pressure in the branchial cavity (a change of about $2 \cdot 0 \, cm \, H_2O$) which occurs at reversal may help to flush blood from the gills and thus increase respiratory efficiency (Blatchford, 1971).

BLOOD CIRCULATION AND FUNCTION

The circulatory system in crabs is generally described as 'open' or haemocoelic. This implies direct contact between blood and tissue and is contrasted with the more familiar vertebrate system in which the blood circulates entirely through 'closed' vessels. The open nature of the blood system in crustaceans has led to the obliteration of the coelom as a body cavity since extensive blood sinuses fill the gaps between tissues and organs to form a blood-filled body cavity, the haemocoel. The coelom itself is restricted to the cavities of the excretory and reproductive organs. However, although much of the blood volume is contained in haemocoelic spaces there is in addition a well defined system of blood vessels, particularly on the arterial side, through which blood is pumped from the heart and by which a constant circulatory pathway is maintained. This circulatory pathway is shown diagrammatically in Fig. 8 and some details of the system are shown in Fig. 7.

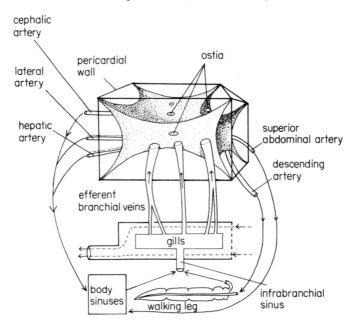

Fig. 8   Schematic representation of the blood circulatory system. After Blatchford, 1971.

The heart lies in the blood-filled pericardial cavity situated directly beneath the cardiac region of the carapace. It is suspended within the cavity by eleven elastic ligaments which originate on the pericardial wall and which serve to re-expand the heart after contraction (systole). The heart is supplied with blood from the pericardium through slit-like holes or ostia in the heart wall. There are three pairs of ostia, two dorsal and one lateral, and they are valved to ensure that blood only passes into the heart. During systole the heart contracts forcing blood out along the seven arteries which emerge from it and stretching the eleven elastic ligaments which attach it to the pericardium. Contraction of the heart also reduces the pressure in the pericardial cavity causing blood to flow into it from the venous system. Each artery is valved to prevent blood flow back into the heart so that during re-expansion (diastole) pressure is reduced within the heart causing it to be refilled by blood flowing in through the ostia from the pericardial cavity.

The seven arteries which emerge from the heart supply all parts of the body and vessels penetrate out even to the tips of the legs. Anteriorly five arteries emerge: a single medial cephalic artery running forwards to the eyes; a pair of lateral arteries which send branches forwards to the antennae and also down to the viscera; and a pair of hepatic arteries which originate ventrally and supply the hepatopancreas. Posteriorly two arteries emerge, the superior abdominal artery which supplies blood to parts of the posterior viscera and to the abdomen, and the descending artery which emerges ventrally, runs directly downwards to the right of the gut and passes through the middle of the thoracic ganglion. This large artery branches below the ganglion to form the longitudinally-running sternal artery which sends branches to the thoracic appendages. As the arteries penetrate the tissues they branch and the individual vessels become increasingly smaller. Ultimately capillary-sized vessels open within the tissues and the blood is no longer confined but flows amongst the tissues bathing them directly. From the tissues the blood collects into the extensive and interconnecting system of sinuses which form the haemocoel. Blood flow within the haemocoel is towards the infra-branchial sinuses which lie on each side of the thorax at the base of the gills. Afferent branchial sinuses take the blood up along the outer margin of each gill from which it flows through the lamellae (in the opposite direction to the respiratory stream) and is collected into efferent branchial veins running down the inner side of each gill. On each side the efferent branchial veins give rise to branchio-pericardial veins which convey the oxygenated blood to the pericardial cavity.

Pressures within the circulatory system of *Carcinus* have been measured by Blatchford (1971) who found that the entire system was heart driven. During systole the pressure in the heart rose to about 14 cm H_2O and dropped to about 0 cm at diastole. Sinus pressures were in the region of 4 cm H_2O but were lower still, about 1 cm, in the infrabranchial sinuses. A very slight pressure drop occurred over the gills and finally a drop to about 0 cm H_2O in the lateral parts of the pericardial cavity. The dorsal part of the pericardial cavity, however, was maintained at a relatively high pressure, between 9 and 13 cm H_2O, and probably acts as an accessory heart chamber from which the heart is filled during diastole. These pressures are much lower than those found in closed circulatory systems. In man, for instance, arterial blood pressure is about 160 cm H_2O at systole and 100 cm during diastole.

Crab hearts are neurogenic, that is, they respond to a neural pace-maker rather than a muscular one as is the case in vertebrate hearts. The regular bursts of neural activity which result in the heartbeat originate in the cardiac ganglion which is closely associated with the heart muscle. This ganglion fires in response to the stretching of the muscle as the heart refills during diastole. However, the system is not independent of outside influence and the heart rate can be modified by a variety of factors. The central nervous system sends both accelerator and inhibitor fibres to the heart and the neurosecretory pericardial glands, situated in the pericardium near the openings of the branchio-pericardial veins, contain a substance which speeds up the heart. External conditions which affect the heart rate include temperature, oxygen tension and carbon dioxide tension: the heart rate increases with temperature but decreases under respiratory stress. Heart rate is also related to size and activity: small crabs' hearts beat faster than those of large crabs and the rate increases with activity. Variation in heartbeat rate can, therefore, be quite considerable: in *Carcinus* the range is from 40–200 beats per minute. The output rate of the heart per gram body weight is similar to that of mammals but overall circulation is more sluggish because of the relatively much greater blood volume, a consequence of the open nature of the system.

The functions of crab's blood are similar to those of the bloods of other animals. Transport of respiratory gases is perhaps the most important, while transport of metabolites, hormones, etc. also occurs. The blood forms clots when exposed to air and thus functions as a primary wound sealing tissue. Somewhat less normal was the discovery by Johnston *et al.* (1971) that crab blood carries large quantities of glycogen stored in the blood cells (haemocytes); more glycogen in fact than in the main storage organ, the hepatopancreas. It seems likely, therefore, that crab blood has a subsidiary storage function; possibly a relatively short-term store concerned with day to day needs while the hepatopancreas with its largely lipid reserves functions as a longer term store. Crab haemocytes are far less numerous than vertebrate red cells, 33 000 haemocytes/mm³ (Evans, 1972) as compared with 4–5 million red cells/mm³, but are somewhat commoner than vertebrate white cells, about 10 000/mm³.

The pigment responsible for the transport of respiratory gases in crabs is a copper-containing protein called haemocyanin which is blue when oxygenated and colourless when deoxygenated. Haemocyanin occurs in solution in the blood in large aggregates of molecular weight 600–800 thousand. These molecules are sufficiently large to avoid being filtered out by the excretory organs but, being in solution, they increase the viscosity of the blood and thus place a limit on the amount of pigment which can be carried. This results in a low oxygen-carrying capacity (1–2 ml O_2/100 ml) compared with mammalian blood (15–20 ml

O$_2$/100 ml) in which a far greater load of respiratory pigment is contained within the red cells.

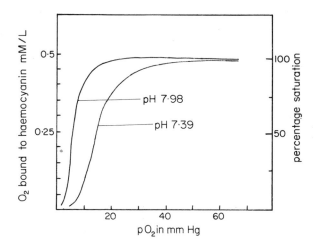

Fig. 9 Oxygen dissociation curves for the blood of the shore crab *Carcinus maenas* at two different pHs. After Truchot, 1971a. The oxygen affinity of *Carcinus* blood is higher than that of typical marine crabs (see Table 3, p. 161).

Respiratory pigments combine reversibly with oxygen and the percentage saturation depends on the oxygen tension (pO$_2$). Thus oxygen is taken up at the respiratory surface where pO$_2$ is high and is released at the tissues where pO$_2$ is lower. In most animals, including crabs, this process is enhanced by the Bohr effect in which the affinity of the pigment for oxygen is decreased under conditions of low pH such as are likely to occur in respiring tissues. Fig. 9 shows two oxygen dissociation curves for a crab haemocyanin and illustrates the percentage saturation of the pigment over a range of pO$_2$'s at two different pH values. The general shape of the curve is similar for most animals, the important point being the location of the steep part of the curve on the pO$_2$ scale since this is the functional zone over which most oxygen is released for a unit drop in pO$_2$. Generally lying in the middle of this steep part of the curve is the point at which the pigment is half saturated and the pO$_2$ at which this occurs, the P$_{50}$, is a convenient measure by which to compare the respiratory pigments of different animals. The P$_{50}$ is a measure of oxygen affinity, a low P$_{50}$ indicating a pigment with a high affinity for oxygen. The effect of lowering the pH is shown in Fig. 9 to shift the curve to the right, decreasing the oxygen affinity of the pigment. In functional terms this serves to further steepen the curve around the P$_{50}$ point and makes oxygen available to respiring tissues at a higher pO$_2$ than would otherwise be the case. The oxygen affinity of crab haemocyanin varies in different species according to the environment (Chapter 9) but a common P_{50} in a marine species would be about 20 mm Hg. In the Dungeness crab *Cancer magister* from the Pacific coast of North America, arterial pO_2 is about 91 mm Hg, the pigment being almost 100 per cent saturated; venous pO_2 is about 21 mm Hg with the pigment about 50 per cent saturated (Johansen *et al.*, 1970). Physiologically, the respiratory systems of crabs are not unlike those of other active marine animals such as cephalopods and fish.

THE DIGESTIVE SYSTEM

The main features of the gut are shown in Fig. 7. Both the foregut and hind-gut (oesophagus, stomach and rectum) are ectodermal in origin and are lined with cuticle. The short mid-gut, however, is endodermal and lacks a cuticle; it is in this region alone that assimilation takes place.

The mouth lies between and behind the mandibles which bite across its opening. It is surrounded by fleshy lips supplied with gland cells which help to lubricate the passage of food. The oesophagus is a short muscular tube also supplied with gland cells; it runs upwards into the large sack-like stomach which lies just beneath the gastric region of the carapace. The stomach is divided into two parts, a large anterior cardiac stomach and a smaller posterior pyloric stomach; it is well supplied with muscles and its cuticular lining is thickened in places to form a complex, articulating series of ossicles which are used to grind up and sort the food. The anatomy of the stomach was described in detail by Pearson (1908) and the major features are shown in Fig. 10. Food is stored in the anterior sack-like part of the cardiac stomach and digestive juices secreted within the hepatopancreas can be passed forwards to the stomach between meals to effect preliminary digestion. One of the main functions of the cardiac stomach, however, is the process of chewing and grinding the food into sufficiently small particles to be passed back to the mid-gut. Chewing does not occur during eating, the mandibles only cut and crush the food. This is probably advantageous since it saves time to eat now and chew later.

The structures concerned with chewing make up the gastric mill which lies at the posterior end of the cardiac stomach. Its mode of operation can be roughly demonstrated by dissection and manipulation. Chewing is brought about by contraction of the anterior gastric muscles which pull the urocardiac ossicle, bearing the dorsal tooth, forwards. Fig. 10A shows that the urocardiac ossicle is articulated to the propyloric ossicle such that, provided the upper end of this ossicle is anchored by the posterior gastric muscles, the dorsal tooth should be pulled through an arc, downwards and forwards between the two lateral teeth borne on either side on the zygocardiac ossicles. The lateral teeth meet the dorsal tooth by

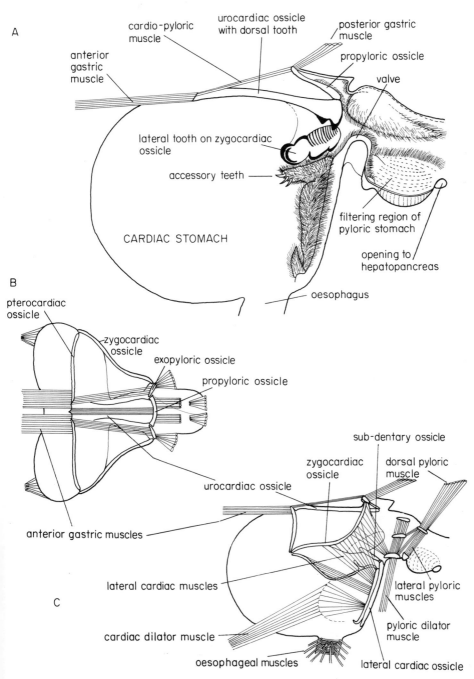

Fig. 10 The stomach and gastric mill. A, the gastric mill seen by looking into the stomach from the side, the near half of the stomach has been removed. B, dorsal view and C, side view of an entire stomach.

moving inwards from the sides and rotating upwards. These movements are accomplished partly by the anterior gastric muscles since the anterior ends of the urocardiac and zygocardiac ossicles are joined by the pterocardiac ossicles (Fig. 10B, C). As the urocardiac ossicle is pulled forwards the anterior ends of the zygocardiac ossicles are drawn inwards moving the lateral teeth towards the mid-line. Upward rotation of the lateral teeth can be achieved by contractions of the lateral cardiac muscles which pull the lateral edges of the zygocardiac ossicles downwards (Fig. 10C). During this movement the sub-dentary ossicles act as props preventing the lateral teeth from moving down and ensuring their rotation into the mid-line to meet the descending dorsal tooth. The exopyloric ossicles (Fig. 10B), anchored by posterior gastric muscles, articulate with the propyloric ossicle at their inner edges and with the zygocardiac ossicles at their outer edges; they form secure pivots allowing independent relative movements on both sides. Following the chewing action the teeth return to their resting positions partly through the elasticity of the cuticle but also through the contraction of the cardio-pyloric muscles (Fig. 10A, B).

Food can be moved about within the stomach by muscular contraction. Intrinsic muscles (those with both origin and insertion on the stomach) can squeeze food from one place to another while extrinsic muscles (origins on some point external to the stomach) can dilate the stomach and suck food from place to place. The gastric mill may also function as a sucking device since the dorsal tooth, as it moves forwards, is rather like a piston being withdrawn from its barrel. The space left behind by the dorsal tooth can be filled from the ventral side or by sucking material out of the pyloric stomach. As shown in Fig. 10A, food sucked up from the ventral side must pass through a fence of filtering hairs to reach the space behind the dorsal tooth. This filtered fluid could be pushed into the pyloric stomach on the return of the dorsal tooth or could be sucked into the pyloric stomach by contraction of its extrinsic muscles. The accessory teeth (Fig. 10A) probably help to gather material between the lateral teeth prior to chewing. The anatomical complexity of the stomach is considerable and it is likely that, as in our own mouths, a great variety of chewing, manipulating, sucking and swallowing movements can be performed.

The pyloric region of the stomach, separated from the cardiac region by a valve, is concerned with filtering and sorting the food which has been ground up in the gastric mill. In the narrow ventral part of the pyloric stomach the cuticular lining is thrown into longitudinal ridges from which project large numbers of fine hairs. These hairs only allow the passage of liquid and small particles of food, larger particles and indigestible material pass through the wider dorsal region. The mid-gut opens directly behind this filtering and sorting region; it is a very short section being only about 1 cm long in a full-grown edible crab *Cancer pagurus*, a species which may reach more than 20 cm across the carapace. Arising ventrally on either side of the mid-gut are the main ducts to the hepatopancreas. This large gland is a lobate mass of blind-ending tubules taking up more space within the cephalothorax than any other single organ. Three main lobes arise on either side, the anterior lobes lie just behind the anterior margins of the carapace, the lateral lobes extend out to lie over the anterior parts of the branchial chambers and the posterior lobes lie underneath the heart between the muscles of the leg bases. The hepatopancreas has three different functions: it secretes the digestive enzymes (protease, amylase and lipase are generally present); it is the main site of assimilation; and it is the main storage organ for metabolic reserves. Food material from the ventral pyloric filter enters the ducts of the hepatopancreas but the coarser material bypasses the mid-gut completely by means of a valve system projecting from the back of the dorsal region of the pyloric stomach. The coarse material, together with such waste as may be produced by the hepatopancreas, is transported by peristalsis down the long hind-gut to the anus where it is ejected in compact cylindrical faeces.

Three long coiled caeca open from the guts of crabs. A pair of mid-gut caeca emerge just anterior to the hepatopancreatic ducts and a hind-gut caecum emerges just anterior to the abdomen. These caeca all ascend almost to the dorsal body wall where they form tightly coiled knots of white tubes (Fig. 7).

THE EXCRETORY SYSTEM

The excretory organs or green glands are a pair of ducts which lie just behind the eyes and open at the bases of the 2nd antennae. Functionally each organ is divided into four parts: the end sac, the labyrinth, the bladder and the ureter. The end sac and the labyrinth are closely applied to each other and form a small compact greenish spongy mass situated just behind the orbit. The bladder is an extensive lobate sac lying partially over the stomach (Fig. 7) and the ureter connects the bladder with the excretory pore which is guarded by a small operculum.

The chief function of these glands is not the elimination of nitrogenous waste since the main nitrogenous excretory product, ammonia, is readily lost by diffusion over the gills. The function that falls to the green glands is that of ionic regulation for, although most crabs are roughly iso-osmotic with sea water, the differences in ionic composition between blood and sea ensure that unwanted ions are constantly diffusing in down their concentration gradients. The largest difference involves the magnesium ion which is generally 2–3 times more concentrated in the sea than inside crabs. Other differences involve the sulphate ion concentration which may be reduced within crabs while calcium and potassium concentrations are often increased (Lockwood, 1968). The movements of the two commonest ions, sodium and chloride, during osmotic regulation are mainly effected by specialized cells on the gills (see Chapter 9) but this route of excretion does not appear to be open to magnesium and sulphate and the concentrations of these ions seem to be controlled almost entirely by the excretory organs. Subsidiary functions include the excretion of waste materials which are too large to be lost by diffusion, and also the elimination of water during osmotic regulation in dilute media (Chapter 9).

The green glands probably work by ultrafiltration of the blood at the end sacs followed by selective absorption and secretion within the labyrinths. Each end sac is held expanded by attachments to the surrounding tissues and the blood supply from a branch of the lateral artery is thought to be at a sufficiently high pressure to force fluid through into the lumen of the end sac (Mangum and Johansen, 1975). A basement membrane separates the blood from the end sac lumen and allows the passage of molecules up to a molecular weight of about 100 000. The fluid which passes through into the end sac is therefore identical to the blood except for the absence of haemocytes and large molecules such as haemocyanin.

Modification to the primary urine as it passes through the labyrinth involves the reabsorption of useful blood constituents such as glucose and amino acids (Binns, 1969b, c) and the concentration of waste substances such as magnesium (Lockwood and Riegel, 1969). This concentration may be achieved by selective absorption of ions other than those which are to be concentrated (water being absorbed along with the ions and the urine remaining iso-osmotic to the blood) or waste substances may be secreted into the urine during its passage through the tubules. Absorption and secretion is often studied by injecting a foreign substance such as inulin into the blood; this substance enters the excretory organs but is neither secreted nor absorbed during its passage through to the outside. The subsequent ratio of concentrations in the urine and in the blood (U/B inulin) is compared with the ratios for other substances to determine the extent of their absorption or secretion. Experiments with *Carcinus* have shown that under normal conditions U/B inulin varies between 1 and 1·5 indicating a small reduction in fluid volume during urine formations; U/B magnesium, however, averages about 7 (Lockwood and Riegel, 1969) indicating active secretion of this ion into the urine.

The volume of urine released is generally about 3–10 per cent body weight per day. In dilute media, however, the elimination of excess water via the green glands can lead to a marked increase in urine production (Chapter 9).

THE REPRODUCTIVE SYSTEM

The gonads in both sexes are paired organs situated just under the carapace and lying above the anterior and lateral lobes of the hepatopancreas (Fig. 7). They are connected to each other by a bridge of gonad tissue just behind the stomach and in the female the gonads extend back below the pericardium to join up posteriorly. The state of development of the gonads depends both on the age of the individual and on the time of year (Chapter 8). They are very small in immature crabs but may be enormous in females which are just about to lay eggs (the extra space required for these ripe swollen ovaries is provided for in the female by the shape of the carapace which is generally rather domed compared with that of a male). The gonads of the male are altogether smaller than those of the female but are still conspicuous in mature crabs in the mating season. Most noticeable at this time are the vasa deferentia which emerge from the testes on either side of the stomach as a pair of thin white coiled tubes. Further back where they run beneath the pericardium the coils become swollen with stored sperm and are readily seen in dissections. The vasa deferentia lead into ejaculatory ducts which open on the ventral sides of the coxal segments of the last pair of legs (8th thoracic segment). The openings are borne on tiny papillae which extend into the bases of the tube-like first pleopods.

In females the paired genital openings are situated on the sternite of the 6th thoracic segment. Each opening leads up via a short duct into a sac-like spermatheca lying amongst the basal muscles of the 2nd walking leg. (Fig. 7B). Short oviducts on either side connect the posterior lobes of the ovaries to the spermathecae. Sperm is stored in the spermathecae following copulation and the eggs are fertilized as they are laid during their passage through to the outside.

THE NERVOUS SYSTEM

The anatomy of the central nervous system (Fig. 11) reflects the attainment of the crab-like body form in that it too is compact and centralized when compared with the long ganglionated nerve cord typical of most arthropods. It consists of a pre-oral brain supplying the eyes and antennae and a post-oral ganglionic mass (thoracic ganglion) which is derived from the fusion of the post-oral segmental ganglia and supplies the rest of the appendages. These two parts of the system are joined by circum-oesophageal commissures which are quite long since the brain is located between the eyes at the extreme front end of the body while the thoracic ganglion lies deep between the muscles of the leg bases (Fig. 7B). On the circum-oesophageal commissures are the para-oesophageal ganglia which give rise to the stomatogastric nerve supplying the gut.

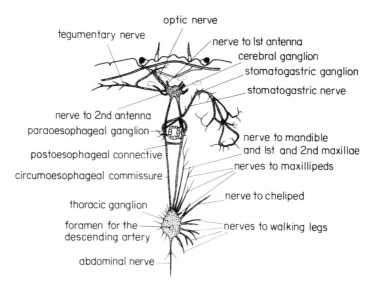

optic nerve
tegumentary nerve
nerve to 1st antenna
cerebral ganglion
stomatogastric ganglion
stomatogastric nerve
nerve to 2nd antenna
paraoesophageal ganglion
postoesophageal connective
circumoesophageal commissure
nerve to mandible and 1st and 2nd maxillae
nerves to maxillipeds
nerve to cheliped
thoracic ganglion
foramen for the descending artery
nerves to walking legs
abdominal nerve

Fig. 11   The crab nervous system. After Pearson, 1908.

The function of the central nervous system is to integrate the behaviour of the whole animal. This occurs by simple reflexes and by more complex chains of integration in which information from a variety of sources may combine with centrally programmed activity patterns to determine behaviour (Chapter 2). Peripheral ganglia concerned with local integration occur on the heart (cardiac ganglion) and stomach (stomatogastric ganglion) but both are subject to central control. The optic ganglia are accumulations of neurones which analyse information from the eyes and pass it on to the central nervous system.

Longer term control is achieved by means of neurosecretory cells which are scattered throughout the nervous system. Particularly important locations are in the optic ganglia, the brain, the post-oesophageal connective and the thoracic ganglion. The hormones secreted by these cells control many of the rhythms in the lives of crabs, such as colour change and activity which often operate by tidal and diurnal cycles (Chapter 4); the longer term rhythm of the moult cycle is also controlled by neurosecretion (Chapter 8).

The peripheral and some central functions of the nervous system are described in the next two chapters. In Chapter 2 the nervous control of muscular activity is covered while in Chapter 3 the sensory end of the nervous system is described.

2 Movement

The main moving parts of a crab are the appendages: the long legs by means of which different species can run, swim, jump, climb or burrow (Chapter 5); the mouthparts which manipulate the many different types of food (Chapter 6); the chelipeds which are used for catching prey, impressing rivals and attracting mates (Chapters 6 and 7). Each appendage consists of a chain of segments articulated by firm joints and moved by muscles which insert on tendon-like apodemes. Movement of any part of an appendage is achieved by the operation of a lever system such as that shown in Fig. 12A. Contraction of the closer muscle results in a force at a which is transmitted through the PD joint to the limb-tip b. Both a and b rotate about the joint as shown by the arrows. The opener muscle works antagonistically to the closer by pulling at the other side of the joint. Each crab appendage is a series of such lever systems and flexibility of movement is achieved by alternating the planes of operation of the joints as shown diagrammatically in Fig. 12C. This gives the limb-tip a very wide range of possible positions, painfully apparent to anyone who picks up a live crab without due care and attention.

The mode of operation of a lever system depends on three main factors: (1) the lengths of the levers; (2) the strength and smooth operation of the pivot; (3) the magnitude of the applied force. In crabs the applied force is that produced by contraction of the striped skeletal muscles and therefore the properties of these muscles and of the nerves which control them are important in determining the nature of the movements. Crab movement is discussed below under these headings and also under the heading of coordination, an essential part of the movement of any animal.

LEVERS

A lever system is a mechanism for transmitting forces via a pivot (Fig. 12B); f_1, the force applied to the system at a, results in a force, f_2, applied by the system at b. f_2 is not the same as f_1: it differs both in magnitude and direction due to the different lengths (l_1 and l_2) and relative positions of the levers. Fig. 12B represents the closer system in Fig. 12A and shows

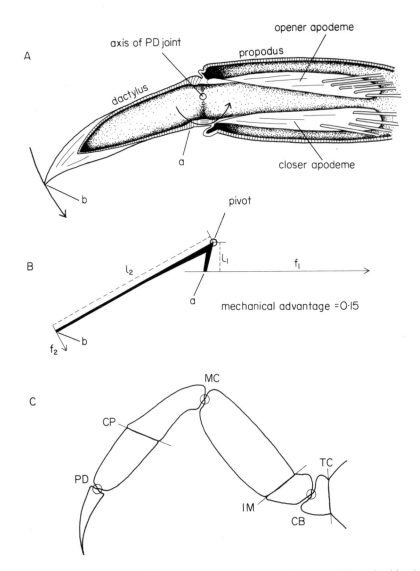

Fig. 12 The lever system of a crab's leg. A, the dactylus and propodus dissected from the side with all but a few muscle fibres removed; the arrows show the movements of the dactylus at *a* and *b* which would result from closer muscle contraction. B, the lever system of the closer muscle in A above; force (f_1) is applied to the system at *a* and by the system (f_2) at *b*, the arrows indicate directions and relative magnitudes of the forces, dashed lines indicate lever lengths (l_1 and l_2). C, a whole leg showing alternating planes of movement at successive joints; circles and lines represent the axes of joints: circles indicate axes perpendicular to the paper, lines indicate axes in the plane of the paper; joints are named according to the podomeres that they connect (Figs. 1, 2).

that each lever length is measured as the shortest distance between the pivot and the line of action of the force. As the joint bends l_1 will increase slightly and then decrease, and f_2 will change its direction. The relationship between the forces and the lever lengths in a system with a frictionless pivot is $f_1 l_1 = f_2 l_2$, thus for a given f_1 the magnitude of f_2 is increased either by an increase in l_1 or a decrease in l_2. The factor by which the magnitude of the force is altered (the mechanical advantage) is $\frac{f_2}{f_1}$ and is equal to the ratio of the lever lengths, $\frac{l_1}{l_2}$. These simple leverage principles are in everyday use in such mechanisms as doorhandles and pliers in which large forces are produced by applying smaller forces further away from the pivot.

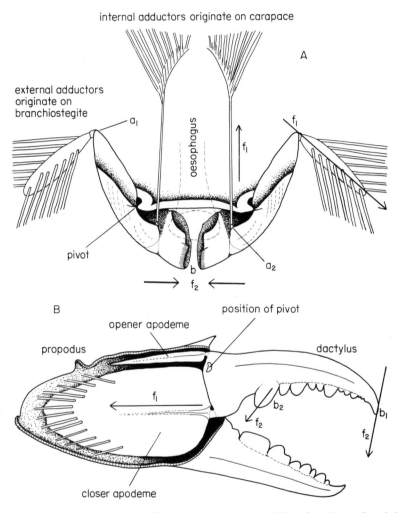

Fig. 13   The lever systems of the mandibles and chela. A, the mandibles of a crab seen from behind, from within the body cavity, some fibres are shown to indicate the lie of the muscles; the forces (f_1) produced by contraction of the external and internal adductors are applied to the mandibles at a_1 and a_2 respectively, the resultant forces (f_2) are applied by the mandibles at b. B, a chela dissected from the side with all but a few of the muscle fibres removed; the force produced by contraction of the closer muscle (f_1) results in a force (f_2) applied at any point chosen by the crab (b_1, b_2) along the biting edge of the dactylus.

In the lever system in Fig. 12B the forces would produce the rotation of a and b about the pivot. b would travel further and faster than a during any movement and thus the relationship between lever lengths and velocity, $\frac{v_1}{l_1} = \frac{v_2}{l_2}$, is the opposite of the force relationship; the smaller the mechanical advantage, the greater the speed at b. Lever systems can therefore be adapted either for strength or for speed, but not for both.

In a crab appendage each lever has a mechanical advantage suited to its particular function; interesting and contrasting examples are seen in the mandibles and chelae which have high and relatively low mechanical advantages respectively. The lever systems which close the mandibles are shown in Fig. 13A. On each side the large external adductor muscle originates on the branchiostegite and inserts on an apodeme which is attached at a_1 on the end of the mandibular apophysis (a rigid internal extension of the base of the mandible). The smaller internal adductor muscles originate on the carapace roof and insert on a pair of long thin apodemes which lie one on either side of the stomach and attach to the mandibles at a_2. If the mandibles bite at b then the mechanical advantage of each external adductor system is about $1\cdot3$ while that of each internal adductor is about $0\cdot4$ (*Cancer pagurus*). Since there is more need for strength than for speed when biting food, the external adductors which exploit a high mechanical advantage appear to be the more important of the two sets of muscles. This conclusion is reinforced by their size which is much greater than that of the internal adductors. Thus, as far as closing the mandibles is concerned, the internal adductors appear to be redundant. What, then, is their function? Fig. 13A shows that when a hard object is bitten at b this point becomes the pivot of a lever system in which each external adductor applies a force at its original pivot with a mechanical advantage of about $2\cdot0$. These forces will tend to dislocate the mandibles. The internal adductors, however, pulling on each side between b and the pivot, will tend to counteract these forces by pulling the mandibles towards their pivots. It is possible, therefore, that one function of the internal adductor muscle system is to lessen the forces at the pivots due to biting on solid objects.

Large objects are never bitten by the mandibles but are first crushed or cut up by the chelae. The closer system of a chela is shown in Fig. 13B and in this case the crab can control the mechanical advantage by choosing the position (b) along the biting edge of the dactylus at which to apply the force (f_2). If an object is pinched at b_1 the mechanical advantage is $0\cdot28$, but closer to the pivot at b_2 it is $0\cdot75$, almost three times greater. Although this gives the crab some control over the force that it can apply, it is still limited by the size of objects: only small objects can be crushed at b_2. A partial way round this problem is to increase the mechanical advantage at b_1 (where larger objects can be accommodated) by increasing the separation between the pivot and the insertion of the closer muscle apodeme (l_1). This adaptation has occurred in a number of crab species, an example is *Cancer pagurus* in which the mechanical advantage at b_1 is 0·33.

If strength were the only important factor in chela function, one might expect all crabs to have chelae rather like those of *Cancer* with a relatively long l_1 and a fairly high mechanical advantage at b_1. This is not the case and it is probable that, in those forms which have low mechanical advantage chelae (0·20), such as swimming crabs, the extra speed is useful in catching fast-moving prey such as fish and shrimps. This conclusion is backed up by the overall morphology of the chelae in which heavy blunt teeth suitable for crushing are associated with a high mechanical advantage, while chelae with a low mechanical advantage tend to be lightly built with sharp pointed teeth suitable for cutting (Warner and Jones, 1976; and see Chapter 6).

Many swimming crabs achieve great flexibility by having one chela apparently adapted for speed while the other, with a higher mechanical advantage, appears to be adapted for strength. This is an advantage to a fast-moving crab, since it confers the ability to deal with a wider range of food objects. In slow-moving crabs, the capture of fast-moving prey is out of the question and chela dimorphism, where it occurs, usually serves to separate the actions of crushing and picking. One chela, the major, is large and strong and is used to crush or crack open the prey, the other, the minor chela, is used to pick out morsels and pass them to the mouthparts.

Comparison of the chelae and the mandibles reveals that the latter exploit higher mechanical advantages. As has been suggested, high mechanical advantages are not suitable for the chelae since they must be able to deal with large objects. However, another way of increasing f_2 is simply to increase f_1 and, as anyone who has eaten a crab or been pinched by one will know, the chela closer is almost always the crab's biggest single muscle.

JOINTS

Each joint in a crab's leg permits movement in one plane only (Fig. 12C). This is achieved by two types of articulation: external condylic and internal cuticular (Fig. 14). Externally, on either side along the axis of the pivot, joints of a ball and socket type are formed between the two podomeres. The articulating faces of these joints are lined with a thick layer of epicuticle which gives very smooth operation. Internal to these condylic articulations paired bars of rigid cuticle project into the lumen of the limb from either side along the axis of the pivot. These bars of cuticle are joined by very tough but flexible cuticular articulations, extensions of the sheath of arthrodial membrane which surrounds the joint.

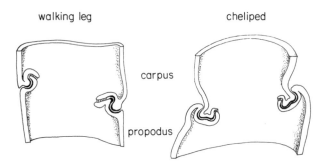

walking leg   cheliped

carpus

propodus

Fig. 14   Anterior view of the carpus/propodus joint of a walking leg and of a cheliped, sliced through the axis of the pivot.

Fig. 14 shows longitundian sections of the joint between the carpus and the propodus (CP joint) of a walking leg and of a cheliped. The two types of articulation vary in relative importance. The rigid condylic articulations provide low friction pivots which ensure movement in one plane and counteract any tendency for the podomeres to telescope. The cuticular articulations on the other hand help to hold the podomeres together. Where the condylic articulations are elaborate, as in the cheliped, the need for cuticular articulations is less and they are therefore less extensive. The walking leg, however, with its relatively poorly developed condylic articulations, has a much more extensive cuticular articulation system.

MUSCLES

Arrangement

The muscles of a crab's limb originate on the internal cuticular walls and insert on apodemes which extend back from distal podomeres. The apodemes are generally flat sheets of cuticle and the muscles insert on both sides resulting in a pinnate arrangement (Figs. 12, 13, 15). Such an arrangement has been shown by Alexander (1968) to be advantageous from two points of view. First, it is ideally suited to working in a confined space such as the lumen of a podomere because pinnate muscles, when they contract, do not swell in the same way as do parallel fibred muscles, all that happens is that the angle of pinnation increases (Fig. 15). In the chela closer muscle a common angle of pinnation is 21° with the chela open and 39° when closed (*Carcinus maenas*). The second advantage is that a pinnate muscle such as the chela closer develops about twice as much force on contraction as does a parallel fibred muscle of the same shape and volume. This difference is largely due to the much greater number of individual fibres in a pinnate muscle. Unfortunately, however, the amount of work (force × distance) that a muscle can perform during contraction depends on its mass and since muscles contract through a fixed percentage of their length an attendant disadvantage of pinnate muscles is that the large number of short fibres produces a smaller movement of the muscle insertion than a small number of long fibres would do. Where considerable movement is required this difficulty can be surmounted either by arranging for relatively small mechanical advantages or by decreasing the angle of pinnation and lengthening the muscle fibres. This latter state occurs in the muscles which operate the merus/carpus (MC) joint of the walking legs. The angle of pinnation of the carpus extensor muscle when stretched is about 10° and when fully contracted is about 22° (*Carcinus maenas*). This gives the carpus an arc of movement of about 140°, comparable to the arc of movement of the human forearm. In contrast, in the chela closer system with its higher mechanical advantage and larger angle of pinnation, the arc of movement of the dactylus is only about 75°.

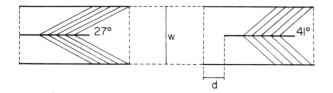

Fig. 15 Schematic representation of the operation of a pinnate muscle. The muscle is extended on the left and contracted on the right. During contraction the angle of pinnation increases from 27° to 41° and the apodeme moves through a distance *d*. Although each muscle fibre becomes shorter and thicker the width of the whole muscle, *w*, does not change.

Performance

So far the assumption has been that different muscles are similar in their physiological properties. This is, of course, quite untrue and was implied only to clarify the issues of leverage and fibre arrangement. The true picture is that crab muscle fibres vary considerably in both microscopic structure and performance and the different whole muscles vary in turn depending on their fibre populations (Atwood, 1973). The main variation is in the speed of contraction and relaxation and, taking the two extremes, one can define two fibre types: fast and slow. Fast fibres generally require a fairly large depolarizing potential to be built up at the neuromuscular junction before they will contract (high threshold); contractions in response to single stimuli of sufficient strength take the form of rapid twitches followed by rapid relaxation while during fast movement bursts of excitatory impulses result in short duration tetanic contractions. In contrast, slow fibres have a relatively low threshold but hardly respond at all to single stimuli. A suitable train of stimuli, however, results in a slow smooth contraction; the rate of contraction is proportional to the stimulation frequency. Relaxation between stimuli hardly occurs and relaxation following the cessation of stimulation may take several seconds. Maximum tension developed by slow muscle is generally much greater than that developed by fast muscle. This was illustrated by Jahromi and Atwood (1969) with measurements on two lobster muscles; the tensions developed were equivalent to 838 and 4511 g/cm² for the fast and slow muscles respectively.

Correlated with differences in fibre performance are differences in fine structure. The most consistent of these involves the sarcomere length (distance between the stripes) which varies between about 3 μm for fast muscle to about 13 μm for slow muscle. Another common difference is that in slow muscle there are more thin (actin) filaments to every thick (myosin) filament; for instance, Jahromi and Atwood (1969) found thin/thick filament ratios of 3:1 in fast muscle and 6:1 in slow muscle. Other differences occur as a result of these main differences, thus in slow muscle the higher thin/thick filament ratio leads to a less organized appearance in transverse section; also, because of the long sarcomeres, there are fewer excitation–contraction coupling points (diads) per unit length of slow fibre.

The above descriptions of fast and slow muscle represent the two extremes and only rarely are whole muscles so specialized as to be dominated by just one type of fibre. More usually, as is the case in the walking legs of crabs, each muscle is made up of a population of fibres of which some are slow and some are fast but the majority are of intermediate nature. Sometimes the different fibre types are grouped separately with the faster fibres at one end of the muscle and the slower fibres at the other, alternatively the fibre populations may be mixed with no particular specialized groups. This lack of specialization correlates with function in crab walking legs which are required to perform a wide variety of movements. Specialized muscles do, however, occur and a familiar example is the chela closer system (see p.29). In specialized claws the muscle type tends to be correlated with the mechanical advantage; crabs such as *Cancer pagurus* with heavy crushing claws have mainly slow fibres in the chela closer muscle while the fast cutting claws of swimming crabs contain a relatively high proportion of faster fibres (Warner and Jones, 1976).

NERVOUS CONTROL

The excitatory system

The nerve supply to crustacean muscles is quite different from that in vertebrates. In the latter case each muscle is supplied by a large number of excitatory axons and each axon innervates a small group of fibres. Graded contractions are usually achieved by recruiting a variable number of these groups of fibres. In contrast, crustacean muscles are supplied by very few excitatory axons, sometimes only one for the whole muscle, making the achievement of graded contractions rather more complicated. The simplest case is that of the closer, bender and extensor muscles, each of which is supplied by two excitatory axons (Fig. 16). Where there is dual excitatory innervations there is generally specialization of function in that one axon, the 'fast' axon, preferentially innervates the faster fibres while the other, the 'slow' axon, innervates the slower fibres (Atwood, 1967). Thus the slow axon can produce slow contractions by stimulating the slow fibres while faster contractions are produced by fast axon stimulation of the fast fibres.

The intermediate fibres, which often make up the bulk of the muscle, are supplied by both axons and contract appropriately according to whichever axon is active at the time. This situation was shown up by Lang *et al.* (1970) in the closer muscle of the Alaskan king crab *Paralithodes camtschatica*. They found a fairly uniform fibre population in which the proximal and distal fibres were preferentially innervated by the fast and slow axons respectively while the central fibres were apparently equally innervated by both axons. Individual central fibres were found to develop tension more rapidly in response to stimulation via the fast axon than via the slow axon and this difference correlated with the extent of depolarization of the fibre membrane produced by stimulation (see below). Fast axon stimulation at low frequencies resulted in larger depolarizations and therefore faster contractions than was the case with the slow axon which required much higher frequencies of stimulation to build up large depolarizations. In these dual innervated fibres with intermediate properties, therefore, it seems likely that muscle performance is determined by the nature of the neuromuscular connections or synapses.

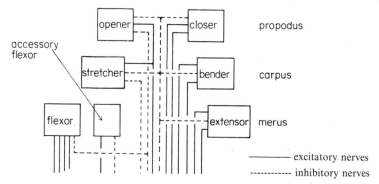

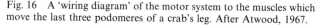

Fig. 16   A 'wiring diagram' of the motor system to the muscles which move the last three podomeres of a crab's leg. After Atwood, 1967.

Each axon in a crab muscle makes a vast number of synaptic connections and, since the individual muscle fibres are generally rather thick (1 mm in diameter is not unusual in a large crab), these synapses often occur deep within the fibre, branches of the axon penetrating into clefts in the fibre membrane. Nerve impulses are transmitted across synapses by the release, at the synapse, of a chemical transmitter substance from the axon termination in response to the arrival of the nerve action potential. The effect of this transmitter substance is to produce a temporary depolarization of the muscle fibre membrane called a post synaptic potential (psp) which, if it reaches the threshold for the particular fibre, will spread over the fibre membrane and produce contraction. The size of the psp in a given fibre is controlled by the amount of transmitter released and this, in turn, probably depends on two factors, the area of the synapse (larger areas permitting the release of more transmitter per stimulus) and the extent of facilitation. At a facilitating synapse the amount of transmitter released per stimulus depends on the proximity in time of the preceding stimulus. At higher frequencies of stimulation the amount of transmitter released increases from one stimulus to the next leading to a rapid increase in size of the psp's; at lower frequencies, however, the psp's remain relatively small. Specialization of synapses both in area and in extent of facilitation occurs in crab muscles and appears to correlate with function (Lang and Atwood, 1973; Atwood, 1973).

Synapses of fast and slow axons have been investigated in the crayfish abdominal extensor muscle (slow) and in the fast fibres of the closer muscle of the American north Pacific coast lined shore crab *Pachygrapsus crassipes* (Jahromi and Atwood, 1967; Atwood and Johnson, 1968). The terminals of the slow axon were found to have rather small areas but were packed with synaptic vesicles (containing the transmitter substance). The fast axon terminals, however, had larger areas and were less densely packed with synaptic vesicles. These differences suggest first, that the slow axon terminals release less transmitter per stimulus than the fast axon terminals, and second, that the fast axon terminals are more vulnerable to fatigue through exhaustion of synaptic vesicles than are the slow axon terminals. If differences such as these are of general occurrence at fast and slow axon terminals they would explain the observed differences in contraction speeds of identical muscle fibres when stimulated via the two different axons. They would also explain the fact that fast contractions generally fatigue more quickly than slow contractions.

The situation in muscles with single excitatory innervation requires further specialization since in this case both slow and fast contractions must be produced by stimulation via the same axon. A muscle of this type, the stretcher of the north Atlantic spider crab *Hyas araneus*, has been studied by Sherman and Atwood (1972) who found that the speed of contraction increased with stimulation frequency. This occurred through the joint operation of moderately specialized fibres and synapses specialized both in terms of area and in extent of facilitation. The slower fibres were activated by relatively large-area non-facilitating synapses whereas the faster fibres were supplied with smaller-area facilitating synapses. The model for the operation of this system is that at low frequencies of stimulation the larger-area synapses are able to function independently to produce contraction in the slower fibres while the smaller-area synapses, across which less transmitter per stimulus can pass, only operate to produce faster contractions when the frequency of stimulation rises sufficiently high for facilitation to occur.

The inhibitory system

The wide spectrum of specialization in both the excitatory system and in the muscle fibres provides mechanisms by which fast, slow and graded contractions may be achieved with the minimum of innervation. The inhibitory system (Fig. 16) probably acts largely as a fine control over the gross features of these mechanisms.

Inhibitory axons make synaptic contact with the muscle fibre membrane but the effect of the inhibitory transmitter substance, released at the synapse on stimulation of the axon, is to temporarily hyperpolarize the membrane—the opposite of the effect of the excitatory transmitter. This makes the muscle more reluctant to contract since it effectively increases the size of the excitatory psp required to reach a threshold depolarization. If the muscle is already in a state of contraction, however, the inhibitory activity serves to reduce or abolish the tension that has been developed. During graded contractions in crab muscle it is often the case that both the excitatory and the inhibitory axons are active simultaneously and the contraction achieved is probably the result of a delicate balance between the two (Atwood, 1968). This use of the inhibitory system fits with the observed distribution of inhibitory innervation in which the highly specialized fast fibres are generally free from inhibitory control (Atwood, 1967). Such fibres tend to respond with all-or-nothing twitches and inhibitory innervation, if it were present, instead of controlling the extent of contraction would simply prevent the fibres from contracting at all.

Another function of the inhibitory system which fits with the observed distribution of inhibitory innervation is to increase the rate of relaxation of slow contractions. It will be remembered that specialized slow fibres relax very slowly, clearly a disadvantage during an activity, such as walking, in which reciprocal contraction of antagonists is constantly recurring. An interesting but extreme example of this function was described by Hoyle (1968) who found certain specialized slow postural fibres in a wide range of crab muscles – from the levator of the eyestalk to the paddles of swimming crabs. These fibres were found to develop a fairly low 'resting tension' in the absence of excitatory stimulation which could only be relaxed via the inhibitory axon. Resting tension of this nature is clearly advantageous in situations in which a particular posture, such as raised eyestalks, needs to be maintained for a long time.

Fig. 16 shows that most of the muscles in the crab leg are innervated by a common inhibitor; this even applies to some of the antagonistic pairs. In the latter case there is generally a second, more specific inhibitor which helps to make the antagonists independent. This occurs in the opener–closer and stretcher–bender pairs in which the opener and the stretcher each have a relatively specific inhibitor while the closer and the bender are supplied by the common inhibitor. In the case of the opener and the stretcher their specific inhibitors are also important in making these two muscles independent since the entire excitatory innervation for both muscles comes from the same axon. The function of the common inhibitor is rather more obscure; where there is also a specific inhibitor the common inhibitor appears to be redundant, and, indeed, generally produces less inhibition on equivalent stimulation, yet when it is the only inhibitor to a particular muscle it still cannot act independently. Possibly the common inhibitor functions mainly in the background having little influence over the effect of excitatory stimulation but speeding up the relaxation of slow contractions once the excitatory stimulation has ceased.

COORDINATION

In the last few pages models for peripheral coordination have constantly been implied. Each muscle has been shown to possess the necessary mechanism to act independently of the other muscles and in a variety of different ways. All that is required for overall coordination is that the right signals should arrive at the various muscles at the right times. These signals, in the form of excitatory and inhibitory impulses, are sent out from the central nervous system (CNS) in response to external or internal (spontaneous, hormonal, etc.) stimulation. One approach to the study of overall coordination in crabs has been to describe relatively simple reflexes in the hope that these can be built into a model for the description of more complex activities.

A typical study involves recording the activity in the motor nerves to a localized part of a limb during the stimulation of a particular sense organ. Thus Bush (1962) stroked the inside of the chela of *Carcinus* and found that this caused the chela to close and also caused reflex inhibition of the opener muscle via the specific inhibitor axon. Another simple and much studied reflex, the resistance reflex, is that evoked by passive or imposed movement of a joint (Bush, 1963; Spirito *et al.*, 1972). In the case of the propodus/dactylus (PD) joint passive opening results in reflex excitation of the closer muscle and inhibition of the opener, the imposed movement being resisted by the crab. Resistance reflexes have been found to operate at all crab leg joints and the sense organs involved are stretch receptors which monitor position and movement at each joint (Chapter 3). In both of the specific reflexes detailed above the same action pattern results from the stimulation of different receptor organs.

One of the interesting features of resistance reflexes is that active stimulation of the stretch receptors occurs constantly during normal activity. This led Barnes *et al.* (1972) to investigate the possibility of the involvement of these reflexes in the normal activity pattern for walking. They found, however, that resistance reflexes do not play a part in normal locomotion and they therefore concluded that the pathways leading from the stretch receptors to the resistance reflexes were centrally inhibited during walking. This conclusion poses two questions: first, what is the normal function of the resistance reflex? Second, does stretch receptor input play any part in normal locomotion? The answer generally given to the first question is that resistance reflexes may come into play during locomotion over uneven ground when alterations of load on particular joints are likely to occur. Thus the reflexes are seen as compensatory mechanisms by which the animal adjusts the tension in its muscles to achieve the desired joint angles irrespective of alterations of load.

This answer to resistance reflex function suggests a possible function of stretch receptor input during normal locomotion since it follows that the crab can distinguish 'expected' input, which occurs as a result of its own walking movements, from 'unexpected' input due to alterations in load. During unexpected input the activity pattern is altered (Evoy and Fourtner, 1973; Spirito *et al.*, 1973) but during expected input the pattern is maintained. It does not seem unlikely that this very maintenance is partly the result of the expected input not just from the stretch receptors but from the whole battery of sense organs likely to be stimulated during walking (Chapter 3). Expected sensory input, therefore, probably increases the likelihood that the current dominant activity pattern will be maintained while new or unexpected input tends to lead to compensatory alterations or to major changes in behaviour.

The activity patterns referred to above are reasonably discrete sequences of coordinated actions such as occur during walking or swimming. These activities, together with the various possible modifications such as resistance reflexes etc., are probably centrally programmed —built into the CNS in the form of integrated pathways made up of interneurones. Little work on such central pathways has been attempted in crabs, probably because of the difficulty of getting at the CNS, but it is likely that the situation is similar to that in crayfish in which the ventral nerve cord in the abdomen is more readily accessible. In crayfish the CNS contains so-called command interneurones, the activity of which leads to coordinated activity in large numbers of efferent axons. Central programming, therefore, can be visualized as occurring by means of appropriate connections between such command interneurones (for reviews see Wiersma, 1961, and Evoy and Cohen, 1971). From the observed behaviour certain deductions can be made about the connections which go to make up these central programmes. First, they must be such that different activities, such as walking and feeding, can proceed at the same time. Second, individual, minor movements must be sufficiently independent to form part of different 'whole animal' activities. Third, there must be a range of built-in modifications or switches such that the current activity pattern can be altered as a result of new sensory information. And lastly, the sensory input which impinges on this network of interneurones must be sufficiently catholic in its connections to ensure that particular motor patterns can be evoked by a variety of sensory stimuli, for instance, chela closure either by stimulation of touch receptors or by passive opening. Behavioural complexity, therefore, is seen as reflecting the complexity of the central programmes with their multiplicity of interconnections and behaviour itself as the observable outcome of the activation of these programmes.

3 Sense organs

To the casual observer it is at once apparent that crabs can see, and little additional experimentation is required to prove that they can also touch, smell and taste. Their sense of balance is slightly less obvious and their sense of hearing very difficult to demonstrate. Least obvious of all but relatively easy to demonstrate is their ability to monitor the positions and activities of their own appendages: the so-called proprioceptive sense, essential for the coordination of movement. The bald statement of the existence of these senses, however, gives only a general picture of crab sensory equipment. For instance, one might want to know about colour vision or about the threshold concentration for the detection of smells. One would like to know what is included under 'touch': can crabs detect water movement and vibrations? When does a vibration become a sound? In fact, as one might expect of an advanced animal, crab sensory equipment is quite sophisticated and almost all the secondary divisions of the major senses are served by specialized sense organs.

Sense organs function at the cellular level by converting the stimulus into a change in the electrical potential across the receptor cell membrane. This receptor potential, if sufficiently large, results in the initiation of nerve impulses (action potentials) which are transmitted along nerves to the CNS. Their frequency is a measure of the strength of the stimulus (for review see Mellon, 1968). Each receptor cell is specialized to convert a particular type of stimulus (light, mechanical deformation, etc.) and each has a particular threshold below which the stimulus is insufficient to trigger nerve impulses. Maintained stimulation generally results in the threshold of a receptor being raised (i.e. the receptor becomes less sensitive). Thus many receptor cells, described as rapidly adapting, respond with a short burst of impulses only at the initiation of stimulation. Others which respond over longer periods of maintained stimulation are referred to as slowly adapting or, in extreme cases, non-adapting. Single sense organs may be composed of several receptor cells each with a different rate of adaptation.

Sense organs can be primarily classified according to the type of stimulus to which they are sensitive, and secondly according to their function in the entire animal. Broadly speaking there are three types of stimulus affecting crab sense organs: mechanical deformation, chemical and light. The functions of chemoreceptors and photoreceptors are sufficiently distinct for there to be no further need for subdivision, but the mechanoreceptors serve such a wide variety of functions that several secondary divisions are necessary. First there are the sensory bristles and hairs concerned with touch and related functions; second, the statocysts, also supplied with sensory hairs and serving the sense of balance; third, the large group of proprioceptors concerned with position, movement and stress along the appendages; and finally, a secondary but important function of certain proprioceptors, the sense of hearing.

TOUCH

Bristles or hairs which project from the surface of the cuticle contain cellular extension and thus form convenient sites for the location of sensory endings close to the outside environment. Hairs containing mechanoreceptive endings serve the function of touch and may also be sensitive to currents and low frequency vibrations in the water.

The simplest type of touch receptor is a straight bristle (Figs. 17A, B) which, when bent by contact with a solid object, signals this information to the CNS. These bristles possess directional sensitivity since they are usually innervated by a pair of bipolar sensory neurones and differential stimulation of the two sensory endings which extend from the neurones into the bristle takes place according to the direction of bend. Touch receptor bristles occur singly or in groups all over the body but are most frequent on the walking legs, particularly at the ends where they occur in rows along the dactyli. An interesting ability which crayfish, and probably also crabs, possess and which is served by bristles of this type situated close to the biting edge of the chelae is the ability to distinguish hardness and softness in the object being pinched (Muramoto and Tamasige, 1971).

The hairs which are sensitive to currents and low frequency vibrations are called hair-peg organs and hair-fan organs respectively (Figs. 17B, D, E). They are very short branched hairs situated in shallow pits in the cuticle and are sufficiently flexible to be bent by water movements. They have a similar distribution to that of the touch receptor bristles but generally occur singly and are quite common on the outer faces of the chelae. Laverack (1962a, b) who studied these receptors in the lobster, found that the hair-peg organs bear up to 100 branches all in one plane and have a flattened appearance. They are hinged at the base such that a water current against the flat face bends the hair over. Dual innervation ensures sensitivity to current direction and responses are shown to currents as slight as 3 mm/s. Rapidly adapting bursts of impulses give 'on'

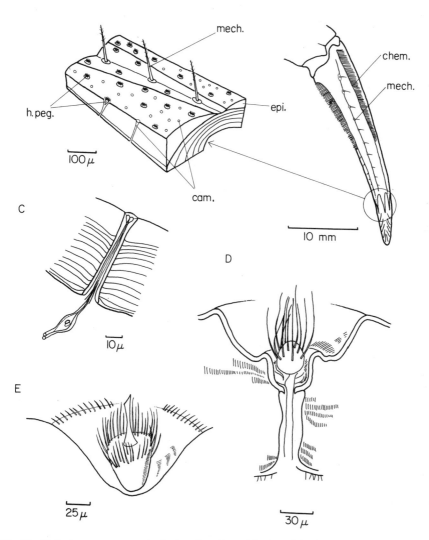

Fig. 17 Cuticular sense organs. A, the dactylus of a walking leg of the shore crab *Carcinus maenas* showing rows of chemoreceptor hairs (*chem.*) and rows of mechanoreceptor hairs (*mech.*). B, stereogram including part of the epicuticular tip (*epi.*) of the dactylus and showing campaniform organs (*cam.*), hair-peg organs (*h. peg.*) and mechanoreceptor hairs (*mech.*). C, a campaniform organ; D, a hair-fan organ; E, a hair-peg organ. A, B and C after Shelton and Laverack, 1968; D after Laverack, 1962b; E after Laverack, 1962a.

and 'off' responses while a non-adapting component provides continuous information on current strength.

Hair-fan organs are not flattened and have longer branches than hair-peg organs. Laverack (1962b) found that they were sensitive to low frequency vibrations (analogous to the lateral line of fishes) and responded intermittently to agitation of the water nearby; unlike the hair-peg organs, a non-adapting component was not found. The disturbance caused by a drop of water dropped from half an inch above the surface could be detected by a hair-fan organ beneath it 2·5 cm below the surface.

BALANCE

The sense of balance in crabs resides in the hairs lining the cavities of the two statocysts. Each statocyst is a complex fluid-filled cuticular invagination contained within the swollen base of the 1st antenna and sealed off from the outside. It consists of a more or less horizontally orientated circular canal which is continuous along its medial side with the upper part of a more or less vertically orientated circular canal. The horizontal canal is tubular while the vertical canal is formed from a disc-shaped space with the medial side pushed in forming the 'sensory cushion', so that, in functional terms, it also forms a circular canal (Fig. 18A). Several types of hair project into the lumen of the statocyst and three of these hair types (thread hairs, free hook hairs and statolith hairs) have been assigned a sensory function (Dikgraaf, 1956; Sandeman and Okajima, 1972). Rotation of the statocyst about the vertical axis causes fluid to swirl round the horizontal canal in the opposite direction and also causes some fluid movement in the vertical canal (Fig. 18A). This fluid movement deflects the sensory hairs, particularly the dorsal group of thread hairs which project across the horizontal canal at its junction with the vertical canal. Rotation about a horizontal axis causes fluid flow in the vertical canal stimulating the ventral group of thread hairs. Turning movements about the various possible horizontal axes (transverse, longitudinal, diagonal) can be distinguished by comparing the sensory input from the left and right statocysts, the vertical canals of which are at right angles to each other (Fig. 18B).

By blowing fluid through the statocyst canals of the large Indo-Pacific swimming crab *Scylla serrata*, Sandeman and Okajima (1972), found that the thread hairs (300 μm long) were the most sensitive of the hair types and could detect a rotation about the vertical axis of 6° per sec (1 revolution per min). The shorter (50 μm) free hook hairs were less sensitive to fluid movement while the short statolith hairs (3–4 μm) were the least sensitive. These sensitivity differences, related to the different lengths and stiffnesses of the hair types, are of functional significance since they provide the statocyst with a much greater total sensitivity range than would be possible with a single hair type. Another functional difference related to the lengths of the hairs is that the shorter stiffer hairs take less time to regain their normal positions when stimulation ends. The thread hairs continue to fire after stimulation has ceased (because they are

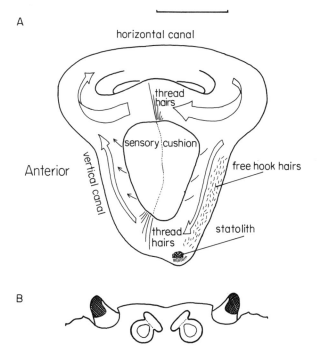

A

horizontal canal

thread
hairs

sensory cushion

Anterior

vertical canal

free hook hairs

thread
hairs

statolith

B

Fig. 18 The statocyst. A, view from the mid-line of the righthand statocyst showing water movements during anticlockwise rotation about the vertical axis. Scale = 1 mm. After Sandeman and Okajima, 1972. B, diagrammatic view from above to show the orientation of the statocysts (their size is exaggerated).

still bent), but the free hook hairs and the statolith hairs return rapidly to their normal positions and stop firing. This provides a mechanism for signalling 'off' which might be important to combat giddiness.

The function of the thread hairs and free hook hairs is probably primarily the detection of rotational movements. The statolith hairs, however, are too short to show much response to normal rotational movements and since these hairs support the statoliths, it seems likely that their function is the detection of gravity. The statoliths of a Mediterranean spider crab *Maia verrucosa* were described by Dikgraaf (1956) as a 'cluster of numerous miniscule stone particles . . . apparently identical to volcanic particles on the surrounding sea floor'. It seems probable that, like the statoliths of prawns and crayfish, crab statoliths are of external origin and are inserted by the crab just after moulting while the cuticle is still soft and before the statocysts are sealed off from the outside. The statoliths lie on top of the statolith hairs at the bottom of the posterior arm of the vertical canal (Fig. 18A) and any movement of the statoliths due to gravity should be transmitted to the hairs.

The responses of the statocyst hair types to maintained stimulation suit their suggested functions. The thread hairs and free hook hairs have a rapidly adapting 'on' response and a more slowly adapting response to maintained stimulation. The response of the statolith hairs to maintained stimulation, however, is non-adapting.

PROPRIOCEPTION

As was stressed in Chapter 2 sensory input concerning positions and activities of the appendages is of great importance in the coordination of behaviour. The information required can be grouped under four different headings: (1) rate of relative movement of any appendage or podomere, (2) relative position of any appendage or podomere, (3) stress applied to the apodeme of any muscle, and (4) stress applied to the exoskeleton. It may readily be seen that, for the crab to know what is going on in each appendage, all four pieces of information are essential and, for a complete picture, they need to be supplied from every joint. It is highly likely that this state of affairs obtains in all crab appendages, at least at the more important articulation points. The following discussion is limited to the legs since the vast majority of work on proprioceptors has concentrated on these appendages.

The best known of crab proprioceptors, the chordotonal organs, take the form of richly innervated elastic sheets or strands associated with the leg joints (Fig. 19). Chordotonal organs vary in length according to the position of the joint, the usual arrangement being that the proximal end of the organ is attached to an apodeme while the other end is attached to the inside of the exoskeleton nearby. When the muscle attached to the apodeme contracts the apodeme moves in a proximal direction relative to the surrounding exoskeleton and the chordotonal organ is stretched. Embedded in each chordotonal organ are large numbers (40–80) of bipolar sensory neurones the dendrites of which are sensitive to the mechanical stimulation provided by such length changes (Mill and Lowe, 1973).

Chordotonal organs are named according to the joint at which they are located; the PD organ is situated at the propodus/dactylus joint while the CB organ is a thin elastic strand running from the coxa to the basi-ischium. Both the PD and CB organs are single but often there is more than one chordotonal organ at a joint. This occurs at the carpus/propodus, merus/carpus and basi-ischium/merus joints where the organs are referred to as CP_1 and CP_2, MC_1 and MC_2, and IM_1, IM_2 and IM_3 (the 'I' refers to the fact that the joint with the merus is at the ischium end of the basi-ischium; this terminology follows Alexandrowicz, 1972). CP_1, MC_1 and IM_1 appear to be homologous since all three are elastic

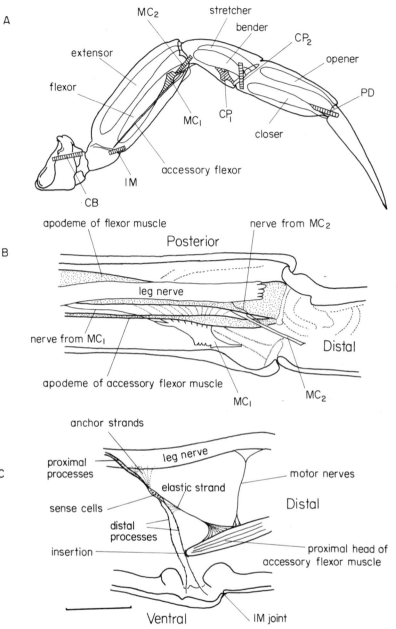

Fig. 19 Proprioceptors. A, view from the front of a walking leg of *Carcinus* showing the positions of the chordotonal organs (their sizes are exaggerated, *cf.* B); apodemes are labelled according to the muscles which insert upon them; the three IM organs at the basi-ischium/merus joint are not distinguished. B, the merus/carpus joint of *Carcinus* dissected from above to show the two MC organs. C, the basi-ischium/merus joint of *Cancer magister* dissected from the front to show the association of the IM₃ organ with the accessory flexor muscle. Scale = 5 mm. A and B redrawn from Whitear, 1962; C simplified from Cohen, 1963.

sheets situated on the proximal sides of their joints. CP_2 and MC_2, on the other hand are elastic strands which span their joints; they originate on an apodeme in the proximal segment and insert on the exoskeleton of the distal segment of the joint. The PD and CB organs also span their joints. The percentage length change during movement of an organ which spans the joint is often much less than in an organ which runs from an apodeme straight to the adjacent cuticle. Bush (1965) cited possible length changes of 15–40 per cent for organs which span the joint and 60–80 per cent for those which do not.

IM_2 and IM_3 are an interesting pair of chordotonal organs since they are associated with the accessory flexor muscle to form the so-called myochordotonal organ. The small proximal head of the accessory flexor muscle originates at the proximal end of the merus very close to the IM joint. It inserts on the thin accessory flexor apodeme which runs the entire length of the merus to insert, in turn, on the main flexor apodeme close to the MC joint. IM_2 is associated with the origin of this muscle, while IM_3, a strand running across the basi-ischium, is attached to the muscle by an elastic strand so that a pull on this strand due to extension of the muscle stretches the IM_3 strand by pulling it sideways (Fig. 19C). The myochordotonal organ, therefore, although situated near the IM joint, is actually concerned with MC joint movement.

The mode of action of chordotonal organs has received considerable physiological study (Wiersma, 1959; Cohen, 1963; Bush, 1965; Hartman and Boettiger, 1967; Clarac, 1968; Mill and Lowe, 1972; and many others) and the conclusion is that they are sensitive to movement and position, but not to stress. Movement receptors are unidirectional; an individual unit (sensory neurone) is sensitive either to stretching or to release of the elastic strand, but not to both. Increasing speed of movement leads to some increase in firing rate but also to recruitment of other units which have higher thresholds. Such overlapping sensitivity ranges lead to an increase in the total sensitivity range of the organ. Where there is just one chordotonal organ at a joint, as is the case at the PD joint, receptors for both directions of movement are present. Where there is a pair of organs, however, some specialization occurs and here one finds that sensitivity to release of the strand is commoner than sensitivity to stretch. At the CP joint, CP_1 is attached to the bender apodeme and CP_2 to the stretcher. Both organs are sensitive mainly to release, but since they are attached to antagonistic apodemes both possible directions of movement are adequately monitored. At the MC joint, however, the position is somewhat more complicated since both MC_1 and MC_2 are attached to the flexor apodemes (Fig. 19B) and as both organs are mainly sensitive to release of the elastic tissue both fire most strongly during extension of the leg. Sensitivity to flexion appears to be under-represented at this very important leg joint. It is here that one function of the myochordotonal organ becomes apparent. During flexion of the MC joint the accessory flexor muscle shortens and thus releases both IM_2 and IM_3. As in the cases detailed above, units sensitive to release of tension are commonest in these organs and the myochordotonal organ, as a whole, is most sensitive to flexion of the MC joint. This makes up for the relative lack of flexion sensitivity in the MC_1 and MC_2 organs and indeed, makes sure that, with four chordotonal organs, the crab is very well supplied with proprioceptive information from this important joint.

Position sensitivity in chordotonal organs is achieved mainly by slowly adapting or non-adapting sensory neurones whose rate of firing is dependent upon static joint position. Such receptors have been found in all chordotonal organs and, as in the case of the movement receptors, they can be divided into two types according to which direction of joint movement stimulates an increase in their rate of firing. For instance, at the MC joint, one type of position receptor will increase its rate of firing as the position approaches full flexion while the other type will increase its firing rate as the joint is extended. Also like movement receptors, each unit only signals position within a limited arc of movement and the total sensitivity range is achieved by overlapping these individual ranges. This gives a wide total range while retaining sensitivity to small position changes. Both types of position receptor are found in single organs such as the PD organ but where more than one organ occurs at a joint some specialization occurs and generally follows the trend set by the movement receptors.

Apart from the MC joint, the other highly important articulation point in the crab leg is the 'universal' joint at the base. This is composed of two joints very close together; the joint between the thorax and the coxa (TC) which allows forward and backward movement of the leg (promotor and remotor muscles) and the joint between the coxa and the basi-ischium (CB) which allows up and down movements (levator and depressor muscles). The only chordotonal organ here is the CB organ but three other non-chordotonal proprioceptors are also present (Whitear, 1965). These are: (1) a muscle receptor originating in the thorax and inserting on the promotor muscle apodeme in the coxa (this receptor is a specialized part of the promotor); (2) an elastic strand running from the thorax to insert on the levator muscle apodeme in the basi-ischium; and (3) another elastic strand running from the thorax to the depressor muscle apodeme in the basi-ischium. All three receptors differ from chordotonal organs in their innervation which is from cell bodies located in the thoracic ganglion rather than from neurones embedded within the organ itself.

The muscle receptor has been investigated by Ripley et al. (1968) who found it sensitive to both movement and position. Its method of signalling this information, however, is unusual. Instead of responding to stimulation with a train of nerve impulses this receptor responds with a maintained depolarization the extent of which is dependent on the severity of the stimulation. This depolarization along the receptor nerve is presumably coded into impulses within the CNS. The muscle receptor is composed of an inner strand of muscle and an outer sheath of connective tissue and these two components are separately innervated. Both directions of movement of the TC joint are thought to be monitored by comparing the input from the two components. The two elastic strand receptors which run to the depressor and levator apodemes are clearly able to signal information on both directions of movement of the CB joint and are, in any case, supplemented by the CB chordotonal organ.

The existence of proprioceptive input from the crab leg on position and movement has been known for some time. Stress detection, however, has only relatively recently been demonstrated. Stress detection can be divided into two compartments: first, direct stress on an apodeme produced by muscle contraction and second, resultant stress on the exoskeleton. It should of course be possible for the crab to compute the stress on an apodeme from the known motor output to the muscle. It is much better, however, to measure this stress directly and sense organs which fulfil this function are present on the apodemes of the leg muscles (Macmillan and Dando, 1972). Each sense organ consists of a number of bipolar sensory neurones whose endings innervate the insertions of the muscle fibres on the apodeme. These so-called apodeme organs have been found to occur on the apodemes of a number of different leg muscles and are quite probably present on all. The sensory units are non-adapting and their rate of firing is dependent on the stress developed by the muscle at its insertion irrespective of movement and position of the joint. They clearly serve a quite different sensory input channel from those served by the various elastic organs discussed above.

When considering stress detection in the cuticle one is faced with the anatomical consideration that such detection is not equally important at all points along the limb. The most important points are clearly the two ends: the tip, on which the crab stands, and the base, where the leg joins the body. These two places have been found to be well supplied with cuticular stress detectors. At the base of the limb within the basi-ischium two groups of sensory neurones are associated with certain relatively soft areas of the exoskeleton and respond to deformation of the cuticle in this region (Clarac et al., 1971). These receptor groups are close to the pre-formed autotomy plane: the point halfway along the basi-ischium at which the crab can voluntarily break off its limb when this limb is seized by an attacker or otherwise becomes a liability to its owner (p.123). The cuticular stress receptors play a part at the sensory end of such autotomy behaviour and are also well situated to monitor the load at the proximal end of the whole leg. At the other end of the leg a rather different type of cuticular stress detector occurs; this is a large group of so-called crustacean campaniform organs embedded within the epicuticular tip of the limb (Figs. 17A, B, C). Each campaniform organ consists of two concentric tubes embedded in the cuticle and sealed off on the outside by a delicate cap. The inner tube, which probably represents a sunken hair, is innervated by a pair of sensory neurones and terminates just below the surface of the cuticle as a small peg which rises to meet the cap. These organs are sensitive to distortion of the cuticle in which they are embedded and, since the epicuticular limb tip is slightly flexible and bends under stress, this group of campaniform organs monitors the load on the whole limb from the distal end.

HEARING

It has long been known that sound production forms part of the behavioural repertoire of many crab species. Perhaps the best known example is the semiterrestrial ghost crab of tropical sandy beaches (*Ocypode*, Fig. 22) which can stridulate with its larger cheliped by rubbing a row of tubercles on the chela over a ridge on the basi-ischium. It was assumed that crabs could hear the sounds they were producing. More compelling evidence for the existence of a sense of hearing was revealed by the finding that sound production is important in social behaviour (see Chapter 7). Male fiddler crabs (*Uca*, Fig. 30) produce a variety of sounds during courtship: banging on the ground with their chelae, vibrating their walking legs. Each species produces its own characteristic sounds or patterns of sounds. These sounds are composed of broad bands of frequencies mostly below 2000 cycles per second (Hz). They are small sounds but, transmitted through the substratum, they appear to attract females and to affect the behaviour of other males (Salmon and Atsaides, 1968).

Experimental evidence for the existence of hearing in fiddler crabs has been obtained both by observing reactions of crabs to substratum borne sounds and by recording electrical responses to such sounds with an electrode implanted in the merus of a walking leg. The sense organs concerned are presumably the various proprioceptors which a number of workers have shown to be sensitive to vibration. Likely candidates are the movement receptors in the chordotonal organs and the campaniform stress receptors at the tips of the legs. Greatest sensitivity in most fiddler crab species is to relatively low frequency sounds (below 1000 Hz), but slight differences between species occur in the location of peak sensitivity on the frequency spectrum. Salmon (1971) showed that in each of two species peak sensitivity occurred over the frequency range which was most characteristic of the produced sound. In other words each species was preferentially sensitive to its own sounds. This is important from a behavioural point of view since different species of fiddler crab often occur in the same area and without such differential sensitivity there might be a danger of females being attracted to males of the wrong species. Although fiddler crab sounds are very small, the crabs are sufficiently sensitive to be able to hear one another at distances up to 75 cm (Salmon and Horch, 1972).

Ghost crabs produce much louder sounds than fiddler crabs both by rapping on the sand and by stridulating. Maximum sound energy in both cases occurs below 3000 Hz (Salmon and Horch, 1972). Recording the rapping sound in the field, Horch and Salmon (1972) came to the conclusion that the crabs were calling to each other, the calls presumably serving a territorial function. Transmitted through the substratum, such calls can probably be heard by crabs up to 10 m away. Laboratory work on sound detection in ghost crabs (Horch, 1971) showed that they could hear both air borne and substratum borne sounds. The greatest sensitivity in both cases was to frequencies between 1000 and 2000 Hz, somewhat higher than the frequencies to which fiddler crabs are most sensitive. In this work the IM_2 (part of the myochordotonal organ) was identified as being the organ mainly responsible for hearing. Removal of the IM_2 (leaving the accessory flexor muscle and IM_3 intact) abolished responses to air borne sound and to the higher frequencies of substratum borne vibrations. Air borne sound is probably picked up by the cuticle of the merus, the anterior and posterior faces of which form two vertically orientated flat sheets. These sheets of cuticle may act as a sort of ear drum, their vibrations being passed on to the sensory elements of the IM_2 which are intimately associated with the cuticle at the accessory flexor muscle insertion.

TASTE AND SMELL

Chemoreception, like the sense of touch, is essentially concerned with stimulation from the external environment and as a result is served by sensory hairs. Such hairs are thin walled at their distal ends to allow the diffusion of chemicals through to the sensory endings. The difference between the senses of taste and smell is partly a matter of threshold, smell receptors generally being more sensitive, and partly that taste is really a combination of chemoreception and touch. Of the two main types of chemoreceptor hair in crabs, the long unbranched aesthetascs which occur in a tuft at the end of the 1st antenna are concerned with the sense of smell while the chemical side of the sense of taste is detected by various types of branched hair occurring on the mouthparts, on the dactyli of the walking legs (Fig. 17A) and along the biting edges of the chelae. Investigation of the function of these chemoreceptor hairs has been largely restricted to their use in the detection of food. Hazlett (1968d) showed that food searching behaviour in hermit crabs (increased locomotion and grasping) was stimulated by the presence of fish juice in the water and that crabs were able to locate food by chemical means alone. Both these responses were abolished by the removal of the 1st antennae, indicating the aesthetascs as the smell detectors involved. Extending his study Hazlett (1971) showed that the threshold concentration of fishy smell for the stimulation of food searching behaviour was about 2·5 parts per million (refers to the weight of fish, 2·5 g, before masceration and filtration).

The grasping phase of food searching behaviour brings into play the chemoreceptors on the ends of the walking legs. When these receptors come into contact with a piece of food, this food is rapidly grasped and passed to the mouthparts. Hazlett (1971) was able to stimulate grasping behaviour by squirting fish juice onto the dactyli but the threshold concentration of mascerated fish in this case was 100 times greater than that required to stimulate food searching behaviour via the aesthetascs. Grasping could be stimulated by a much lower concentration of fish juice if this stimulation was combined with touching the dactyli with a glass rod. Clearly in this latter case the full sense of taste is stimulated.

The chemical stimulation used by Hazlett, mascerated and filtered fish, is a mixture of many different organic compounds. Much study has been directed towards finding out which, if any, of the substances commonly present in crab food is the most important attractant and stimulant of feeding behaviour. Kay (1971) found that the amino acid isoleucine was particularly effective in stimulating feeding behaviour and several species of crab were induced to eat pieces of clean filter paper when immersed in a roughly $1·5 \times 10^{-6}$ M solution of this compound. The feeding response was not stimulated by other amino acids or by mixtures lacking isoleucine. In apparent contradication, Shelton and Mackie (1971), working with *Carcinus*, found that the attractiveness of a synthetic mixture of chemicals based on the composition of clam meat was much greater than the attractiveness of any one of its major constituents. The same situation has been found in lobsters. The indication here is that each receptor unit is sensitive to a specific compound and that food searching is not stimulated unless there is sensory input from a variety of such units. An idea of the specificity involved may be judged from the fact that substitution of D amino acids for the natural L forms greatly decreases the attractiveness of a mixture. It is difficult to reconcile Kay's findings on isoleucine with the results of Shelton and Mackie, but Kay was dealing with feeding behaviour involving taste, the tactile stimulation being provided by the piece of filter paper, whilst Shelton and Mackie were looking at food searching behaviour elicited by chemical stimulation alone. Possibly the mouthpart receptors are mainly sensitive to isoleucine while the aesthetascs contain a more diverse mixture of receptor units.

Physiological work on both aesthetascs and dactylus chemoreceptors supports the conclusion that, as a group, these hairs are sensitive to a wide range of different compounds but that individual units are sensitive to specific chemicals. One difficulty has been to isolate the responses from single receptors since each hair may be innervated by a large number of cells (about 130 sensory neurones to a single aesthetasc—Snow, 1973). Thus considerable variation in the responses of preparations to different chemicals has been found. Laverack (1963) obtained good responses to trimethylamines from the dactylus receptors, but found little response to amino acids. Case (1964), on the other hand, showed that these receptors were sensitive to a wide range of amino acids, more sensitive to amino acids in fact than to other possible stimulants. Sensitivity to amino acids has also been shown in lobsters. Where specific responses are found the receptors are generally slowly or non-adapting with thresholds in the region of 10^{-6} M.

From the evidence, therefore, the sequence of stimulation and behaviour during feeding on a piece of fish is as follows: chemical stimulation of a variety of specific receptor units in the aesthetascs leads to orientated searching behaviour until the food is touched by a leg tip. Here again the stimulation of diverse chemoreceptor units occurs and this is combined with tactile stimulation due to touching the food. This sensory input results in the food being grasped and passed to the mouthparts where a further combination of chemical and tactile stimulation leads to it being torn up and eaten.

SIGHT

Crab eyes, like those of insects, are compound eyes. They are made up of several thousand optical units or ommatidia each of which consists of a cuticular facet or cornea on the outside, a crystalline light gathering device or cone, and internal to this, a group of six to eight long sensory cells or retinulae. Running down the axis of the group of retinulae is the light sensitive rhabdome which contains the photosensitive pigment (Fig. 20). Each ommatidium has a relatively small field of view and the visual picture built up by the whole eye is thought to be a mosaic, each piece representing the input from a single ommatidium. The focusing of an image is not important since the picture is built up in the same way as a picture in a newspaper: from large numbers of dots of different intensities. Crabs appear to see quite well with these eyes and fiddler crabs when feeding on mud flats exposed at low tide react to a moving figure 20 or 30 metres away. *Ocypode* is even more sensitive and can perceive a large moving object more than 100 m away (Hughes, 1966). Unlike insects, crab eyes are on stalks and may be lowered into sockets on the carapace for protection. Sometimes the eyestalks are very long and these often occur in species which live on level substrata (e.g. fiddler crabs). Long eyestalks may be of use in increasing the range of vision on such flat plains (Barnes, 1968a). On irregular substrata where the majority of species live, however, such an adaptation would be of little value since, to increase significantly the range of vision, ridiculously long eyestalks would be required!

Two different types of eye based on the structure of the constituent ommatidia, have been recognized in arthropods. In apposition eyes, characteristic of species which are active in bright light, the retinulae are situated directly below the crystalline cones. Dark pigment contained in distal pigment cells surrounds each crystalline cone while dark proximal pigment in the retinulae shields the rhabdome from all extraneous light (Fig. 20A). This structure seems well adapted to the building up of a picture by a mosaic of inputs since visual acuity clearly depends on the separate identity of each ommatidium and this is ensured by the complete shield of pigment around the light path.

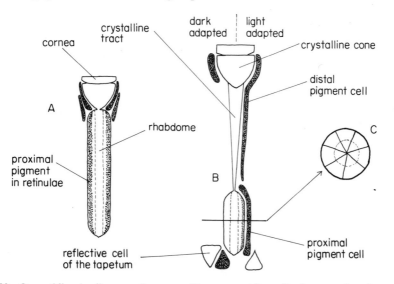

Fig. 20 Ommatidia. A, diagram of an apposition ommatidium. B, diagram of a clear-zone ommatidium showing dark (left) and light (right) adaptation. C, diagrammatic TS of the retinulae of an ommatidium to show the organization of the rhabdome.

In superposition or clear zone eyes, found in nocturnal species and those active in dim light (includes most crab species), the retinulae of each ommatidium are situated some distance below the crystalline cone, to which they are attached by a crystalline tract (Fig. 20B). As in the apposition eye, pigment to shield the light path is present, but this pigment is mobile and moves to adapt the eye to different light intensities.

In the light adapted state the distal pigment is dispersed around both the crystalline cone and crystalline tract while the proximal pigment shields the rhabdome. Such light adapted ommatidia, therefore, only differ from apposition ommatidia in that the light path is longer. In the dark adapted state, however, the distal pigment concentrates at the side of the crystalline cone leaving the crystalline tract free of pigment and creating a clear zone between the tips of the cones and the outer ends of the retinulae. The proximal pigment withdraws from around the rhabdome and a white reflective pigment or tapetum emerges from beneath the basement membrane at the inner ends of the retinula cells. Distal pigment migration is a slow process, hormonally controlled according to an endogenous rhythm (Chapter 4), but movement of the pigment within the retinulae occurs more rapidly and can be used for short-term adjustment to changing light intensity.

The clear zone eye is an adaptation to dim light; however, although its structure is well known, the way that it works is not completely understood. There are two main theories. The first, expounded by Kuiper (1962), is that the crystalline tract in the dark adapted state is a high refractive index thread embedded in a relatively low refractive index matrix and thus acts as a light guide conducting the light gathered by the cornea and crystalline cone down to the rhabdome. The rhabdome is also a light guide, but one in which the light, as it travels down, is progressively absorbed by photosensitive pigment. In the light adapted state the pigment which sheaths both the crystalline tract and rhabdome increases the refractive index of the matrix and allows non-axial light to escape from the light guide and to be absorbed thus reducing the intensity at the rhabdome. Clear zone eyes, therefore, are seen as extremely sensitive photoreceptors; the long crystalline tract and migrating pigment cut down high intensity light rather than being in themselves, adaptations to seeing in dim light.

The second theory (Horridge et al., 1972) maintains, on the contrary, that the clear zone in dark adapted eyes is, in its own right, an adaptation to seeing in the dark. According to this theory, in the dark adapted state light gathered by each cornea is scattered from the tip of the crystalline cone across the clear zone such that it stimulates a number of different rhabdomes. All the light entering a single ommatidium gets through to the retinula cells whereas in the light adapted state any light not entering along the axis of the ommatidium is absorbed by the pigment. Thus light from a single source enters more ommatidia in the dark adapted eye and, since it scatters across the clear zone, stimulates many more receptors than it would in the light adapted state where each ommatidium is isolated by its pigment. Lastly, and perhaps most important, light from a single source can impinge on a single rhabdome via many different crystalline cones leading to a greater stimulation of that rhabdome than would otherwise have been the case. The net result is a great increase in sensitivity, but since the ommatidia lose their isolation, there is a corresponding loss of visual acuity.

These two theories are not, perhaps, as different as they seem. In both cases the dark adapted eye receives all possible light while in the light adapted state excess light is absorbed by the masking pigment. In both cases it is non-axial light which is absorbed and the best visual acuity is achieved in the light adapted state in which the field of view of each ommatidium is at a minimum. Thus, according to both theories, dark adaptation results in a loss of visual acuity. The main difference in the dark adapted state is that in Kuiper's model the ommatidia retain their isolation whereas in Horridge's they do not. It is difficult to say which model gives the greatest sensitivity with the least loss of visual acuity since in Horridge's model, these factors depend on the exact optical properties of the crystalline cone. The tapetum at the basement membrane is of interest here since it must function to reflect light which has escaped from the axial light paths back onto the rhabdomes. Such light is much more likely to be present in the light scattering model (Horridge) than in the light guide model (Kuiper).

The other problem in crab vision is the sort of light that they actually see. Two variables which they might detect are wavelength, to give colour vision, and the plane of polarization of sunlight. The ability to detect colour requires the presence either of different photosensitive pigments, each one being maximally sensitive to a different wavelength, or of some arrangement involving coloured filters. Two different photosensitive pigments, bluish sensitive and reddish sensitive, occur in crayfish eyes but the spectral capabilities of crab eyes are by no means clear. It has been found that the eyes of a variety of species (*Carcinus, Callinectes, Libinia, Sesarma, Uca*) are sensitive to light within the normal visible spectrum but the majority of workers have found only one sensitivity peak, to greenish light, indicating the presence of only one pigment and hence the absence of colour vision (see Scott and Mote, 1974). Other workers, however, have found evidence for the presence of two pigments, bluish sensitive and reddish sensitive, in the eyes of *Carcinus* and *Uca* (Wald, 1968; Hyatt, 1975) and Hyatt has shown that female *Uca* in a choice chamber choose blue rather than red or white over a wide range of relative intensities. These findings indicate the presence of colour vision. In addition to this there is good circumstantial evidence for colour vision from the social behaviour of many semiterrestrial species in which bright colours are employed in agonistic and courtship displays (p. 108)— colourful displays are known to be associated with colour vision in insects. Thus it seems likely that, despite the inability of most workers to demonstrate more than one pigment, crabs may nevertheless be able to distinguish colours.

They can also detect the plane of polarization of light. This is a very useful ability since light from the sky is polarized, the plane of polarization depending on the position of the sun. If the plane of polarization of light from different parts of the sky is known, the position of the sun can be computed and can be used for navigation. This is possible even when the sun is obscured by clouds. This system of navigation has been demonstrated by Herrnkind (1966) in fiddler crabs which, he found, tend to run landwards when escaping from danger and are able to find their way back landwards when placed in shallow water offshore. These responses can be reorientated by the judicious use of a polaroid filter. Herrnkind (1967) showed that navigation by the plane of polarization of the sky is a skill which takes some time to perfect and is not fully developed until the young fiddler is about ten months old.

In insects the structural basis for the detection of the plane of polarization lies in the rhabdome which is built up from six to eight long wedge-shaped segments or rhabdomeres each contributed by and, indeed, forming the light sensitive part of, one of the retinulae (Fig. 20C). Each rhabdomere consists of a tightly packed stack of parallel microtubules containing photosensitive pigment. The parallel arrangement results in each rhabdomere being particularly sensitive to that place of polarization which 'fits' the orientation of its microtubules. Since this orientation differs from one rhabdomere to the next, the plane of polarization can be detected by comparing the inputs from the different retinulae of an ommatidium (Snyder et al., 1973).

4 Rhythms

The important activities of life—eating, competing with one's neighbours and reproducing—are, in most animals, organized on a rhythmic basis in which regular bursts of activity alternate with periods of relative inactivity or rest. A familiar example is our own activity and rest rhythm; we feel sleepy at bed time irrespective of the fact that on the other side of the world people are just getting up. The advantage of an organization in which temporary activities recur in a rhythmic or predictable fashion can be viewed from two angles. First, if an activity can be predicted, the whole organism can be 'geared up' to serve that activity. Such gearing up might take the form of appropriate hormone levels; individual hormones are probably most economically deployed by being secreted according to a rhythmical pattern. Second, all animals are adapted to a particular way of life within an environment which changes rhythmically. It follows that at certain times animals are better adapted to their immediate environment than at others. An obvious example is that nocturnal animals are at a disadvantage out in the open by day; a daily rhythm enables them to predict the dawn and take refuge before it occurs. Similarly, shore crabs active at high tide can, by the use of a tidal rhythm, predict the ebb and take refuge before they are stranded. Rhythms are also useful in controlling activities which take place over longer time-scales. Reproduction is often best carried out at a particular time of year, according to an annual rhythm. Rhythmicity, therefore, is first an efficient way of organizing temporary but recurrent activities; second, a necessity for survival in a rhythmic environment; and lastly, the rhythms themselves are, perforce, phased to natural environmental cycles.

As far as crabs are concerned, the important environmental rhythms, to which their own rhythms are synchronized, are as follows in order of increasing cycle length (for reviews see Barnwell, 1968; Allen, 1972; Palmer, 1973; Naylor, 1976). (1) The tidal cycle; roughly 12·4 hours elapses between consecutive high tides. (2) The 24-hour daily cycle of light and dark. (3) The 14·8-day semilunar cycle from one spring tide to the next. (4) The 29·5-day lunar cycle between consecutive full moons. (5) The annual cycle in which the chief environmental variables are temperature and day-length in the higher latitudes and the alternations between rainy and dry seasons in the tropics.

To return to the human activity/rest rhythm, it is well known that if we travel rapidly to the other side of the world it may take us more than a week to adjust to the apparent time change. We feel sleepy during the day and very much awake at night; also we feel hungry at the wrong times. Clearly the 'gearing up' takes place to some extent irrespective of the immediate environment which, once the rhythm has become established, ceases to be directly causative and acts simply to maintain synchronization. Rhythms such as these, which are sufficiently stable to persist in the absence of appropriate environmental stimulation, are known as endogenous rhythms implying the existence of a 'biological clock'. Such rhythms are found in a wide variety of animals including crabs. In the laboratory under constant conditions they may persist for several weeks, usually gradually drifting out of phase with the environment. Under a new environmental rhythm however, a new endogenous rhythm which is in synchrony with the new situation relatively rapidly appears; this process is known as entrainment.

The crab rhythms most commonly studied under constant conditions in the laboratory are activity rhythms and pigment migration rhythms. In the former case one of the main methods of study has been to confine individual crabs in pivoted boxes called actographs which tilt one way or the other as the crab moves about inside. The movement of the box on its pivot is recorded on a slowly turning drum and the activity expressed as the number of tilts per hour. A rather different method of study which allows a more natural environment is to shine narrow beams of dim light across various parts of the experimental container. These beams of light are focused on to sensitive photocells. As the crab moves about it interrupts the light beams and the number of interruptions per hour gives a measure of activity. In the case of pigment migration rhythms the experimental animals are examined under the microscope at regular intervals to judge the extent of dispersion of the pigment in their chromatophores. Longer term rhythms of social behaviour, reproduction, and growth are less suitable for laboratory analysis. Their existence has been demonstrated mainly by field observation. They are clearly of great importance in the lives of crabs and there is no reason to doubt that they are paced by a similar type of biological clock to that which helps to synchronize the short-term rhythms.

ACTIVITY

When diving in the sea at night one is at once struck by the high level of activity shown by crustaceans in general. By day most crabs and lobsters hide away under boulders or in rocky crevices while others conceal themselves by burrowing into the substratum. At night, however, they are out and about: swimming crabs dart past in the torchlight, the more heavily built crabs and lobsters are found walking in the open, and small long-legged spider crabs climb tall seaweeds to fish for plankton. Apart from the hermit crabs which are frequently active by day (no doubt this behaviour is connected with the fact that each crab carries its own personal hiding place) marine crabs living below low water mark are predominantly nocturnal. The activity rhythms of these sublittoral crabs have received rather little laboratory study. In one case, however, that of the European mud-burrowing crab *Goneplax*, an endogenous rhythm of nocturnal activity was shown to persist under constant conditions for five weeks (Atkinson and Naylor, 1973).

Moving up onto the shore the position changes in that the alternation of high and low tide imposes further restrictions on activity. Here rhythms are phased to the tides and, depending on the way of life, the active period may occur at high tide or at low tide. The shore crab *Carcinus* is only active when submerged and is most active at night. This gives it both daily and tidal rhythms in which peaks of activity occur at high tide, roughly two per day, with the greatest activity during the night time peak (Naylor, 1958). These activity peaks follow the tides and occur 0·8 hours later each day. Under constant conditions this 12·4-hour rhythm persists for five to six days, after which time the crabs become randomly active or arhythmic. Such patterns of high tide activity are characteristic of many species of shore crab (Fig. 21). In some shore crabs, however, in particular the ocypodids, the position is reversed and low tide activity is the rule. These crabs are commonest on tropical and subtropical sandy or muddy beaches and construct burrows in the intertidal zone into which they retire over the flood tide. On the ebb they emerge to feed and to engage in social activity. Ghost crabs, *Ocypode*, are mainly active at night, but may also emerge by day on undisturbed beaches. Fiddler crabs, *Uca*, are mainly active by day in the tropics but temperate species are also active at night. North Australian soldier crabs *Mictyris longicarpus* and Indo-Pacific sentinal crabs *Macrophthalmus*, both of which feed, like *Uca*, by sifting sand or mud, are mainly active by day. In *Uca* these rhythms of low tide activity have been found to persist under constant conditions for up to five weeks.

Longer term rhythms of activity derive from three sources. First, tidal and daily rhythms in shore crabs interact to produce semilunar peaks of activity. *Carcinus*, for instance, is most active when high tide occurs at midnight; the two rhythms are in phase at such times. A week later, however, the tidal rhythm has advanced six hours with high tide occurring at 6.0 a.m. and 6.0 p.m. — the two rhythms are opposed and activity is at a minimum. Thus the tidal activity peaks reach maxima at roughly fortnightly intervals. The second source of longer term

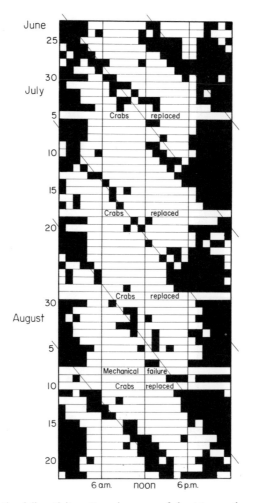

Fig. 21 Consecutive daily activity patterns in groups of about ten northwest Atlantic marsh crabs *Sesarma reticulatum* over a period of two months. Daily and tidal rhythms are shown: crabs are active at night and at high tide. Parallel oblique lines indicate the times of high tide in the environment from which the crabs were collected. Mean hourly activity was calculated and the black squares indicate hours in which observed activity equalled or exceeded the mean. Each crab was maintained in the dark at constant temperature in an individual actograph and the entire group was replaced with fresh crabs every 10–12 days. After Palmer, 1967.

rhythmicity is the semilunar tidal cycle between consecutive spring tides. This cycle is particularly important in low tide active forms since the length of time for which they are exposed varies according to the tidal range. Extreme cases are found on the upper and lower shores, which, during neap tides, may not be included within the tidal range at all: the upper shore may remain dry for several days while the lower shore may be continuously submerged. Von Hagen (1970), working in Trinidad, has shown that these factors have considerable influence on the ecology of upper and lower shore species of *Uca*. Both groups are most active during spring tides; on the upper shore it is too dry during neap tides and the crabs remain in their burrows. On the lower shore there is more time available for activity over the spring tides. Semilunar rhythms such as these may be controlled by mechanisms with semilunar periods and be quite distinct from those produced by the interaction of daily and tidal rhythms (Naylor, 1976). Lastly, the overall level of activity in temperate climates is greatest during the warmer months and this imposes a long-term annual rhythm on the activity of temperate species. *Carcinus*, indeed, moves offshore during the winter and also loses much of its short-term rhythmicity at this time of the year (Naylor *et al.*, 1971).

PIGMENT MIGRATION

Many species of crab show daily rhythms of colour change brought about by alterations in the degree of dispersion of pigment in their chromatophores (Fingerman, 1965). Pigments may be black, white, yellow, red or blue and individual chromatophores may contain one or more of these colours. In the latter case independent dispersal of each pigment is possible. When concentrated in the centre of the chromatophores the colour of the pigment is scarcely visible, but when dispersed throughout the root-like ramifications the colour shows through clearly. Pigment migration rhythms have mainly been studied in *Uca* and, like the activity rhythms, have been shown to possess both daily and tidal components. In this case, however, the daily component is the strongest. By day all pigment is dispersed and the crabs become dark (melanin is the commonest pigment), at night the pigment concentrates and the crabs are pale. The tidal rhythm manifests itself by producing increased pigment dispersion at times of low tide during the day. Interestingly enough the tidal rhythm is sufficiently accurately phased to show differences between crab populations at different levels on the same shore (Fingerman, 1960). Crabs living at the top of the beach darken earlier than those living lower down. These cycles coincide with the times at which the two populations would expect to emerge after being uncovered by the receding tide. Like the activity rhythms the pigment migration rhythms show a semilunar cycle resulting from the interaction of the daily and tidal components. Pigment migration rhythms in fiddler crabs persist in constant darkness for more than five weeks. Under constant illumination however, adaptive changes may obscure the rhythm.

The actual colour of a fiddler crab during the day depends on the relative amounts of its different pigments and on the extent of their dispersion. Local conditions can markedly affect pigment dispersion and the endogenous rhythm provides a backcloth against which environmentally induced changes can occur (Fingerman, 1965). The most important environmental variables are light, heat and the colour of the background. Increased illumination generally leads to increased dispersal of the black and white pigments. Increase in body temperature above 15°C, however, leads to concentration of black pigment and increase above 20°C to dispersal of white. These changes clearly serve protective and thermo-regulatory functions. The effect of background is best seen in the responses of the red pigment which concentrates on light backgrounds and disperses on dark. These changes presumably serve the functions of camouflage. The extent of dispersion or concentration of pigment in the chromatophores is controlled by hormones called chromatophorotropins which are produced by neurosecretion in the eyestalk and in the brain (Fingerman, 1966; Highnam and Hill, 1969). They are released into the blood stream at neurohaemal organs — small sinuses surrounded by the axon terminations of neurosecretory cells. Neurosecretions are stored in the swollen nerve endings and the neurohaemal organs are the release points for a wide variety of different hormones. The two main neurohaemal organs from which chromatophorotropins are released are the sinus glands in the eyestalks and the post commisural organs just behind the oesophagus. Extracts from these two sources and from various parts of the brain and eyestalk have been found to alter the state of dispersion of pigment in fairly specific ways. Each pigment appears to be under the specific, dual control of a dispersing hormone and a concentrating hormone, the state of dispersion reflecting a balance between the two. Rhythms of pigment migration must be produced by the rhythmic release of appropriate hormones from the neurohaemal organs. Removal of the eyestalks almost completely abolishes the rhythm (all pigment concentrates) while reimplantation of sinus glands can reinstate it.

OTHER RHYTHMS

Within the active periods of a crab's day are included all the various activities essential for life. Often these activities occur in a more or less regular sequence with particular activities occurring at particular times during the active period. In low tide active crabs the sequence generally starts with maintenance behaviour including both burrow repair and feeding, and leads, often via a period of wandering, to territorial behaviour and courtship. As the rising tide encroaches on the burrows more burrowing activity may occur after which the crabs retreat below ground sealing the burrow entrances behind them. A crab engaged in one of these activities is said to be in a particular phase: underground phase, maintenance phase, territorial phase, etc. (Crane, 1958). Although in a single active period an individual may pass through most of these phases there is often one phase which dominates its behaviour and such dominant phases may persist through several active periods. The commonest dominant phase is the maintenance phase, but sometimes social phases are dominant. The sequence of phases during a single active period follows a fairly short-term rhythm but the sequence of dominant phases follows a longer term semilunar cycle similar to those discussed above. The social display phase of male fiddler crabs (Chapter 7) is that which has received most attention and here it appears that particular species have preferred times of day for display. Primitive species, characterized by having narrow fronts, tend to be most active in display during the cooler parts of the day, often between 8.0a.m. and 10.0a.m. The broad-fronted advanced forms display later in the day. Since fiddler crab activity is restricted to low tide it follows that suitable low tides for display only occur at roughly fortnightly intervals and thus the dominant display phase occurs according to a semilunar rhythm (Crane, 1958). The magnitude of this effect increases lower down the shore since activity here may be severely restricted by the length of time for which the crabs are exposed. In such crabs sufficient time for display only occurs on spring tides thus placing further rhythmic restrictions on their activities (von Hagen, 1970).

The display phase in fiddler crabs and social phases in other crabs usually involve courtship and copulation. These activities lead naturally enough to egg laying and egg hatching and, in tropical crabs in which the time for egg development is relatively short (p. 132), the whole reproductive cycle may proceed according to a lunar rhythm. Egg hatching is often timed to occur during spring tides at which times the larvae receive the best send off into the plankton from the strong tidal currents. Such crabs may breed more or less continuously throughout the year and even species which are not restricted in their activity by the tidal cycles, such as the arboreal mangrove tree crab *Aratus pisoni* from the Caribbean and the tropical land crab *Cardisoma*, have reproductive cycles phased to lunar rhythms (Warner, 1967; Gifford, 1962). In these cases it may be suggested that lunar rhythmicity has been selected partly for the advantage of spring tide hatching and partly since these are the only environmental rhythms of suitable length by which to phase reproductive cycles. In *Aratus* which lives close to the sea, synchronized egg hatching occurs at both full and new moons. In *Cardisoma*, however, which may live a considerable distance from the sea, the full moon hatching peak is by far the most prominent. This difference may result from the signals available to the two species: *Aratus* has the semilunar tides by which to synchronize its rhythm, but *Cardisoma* has only the moon.

The breeding cycles of crabs inhabiting cooler waters tend to occur according to an annual rhythm. In larger species one batch of eggs may be laid per year, but smaller forms may lay two or more. Within each individual gonad maturation follows a cyclic pattern, but while there may be a general synchrony within a population, probably based on temperature, precise synchrony as occurs in the continuous-breeding tropical shore crabs is not found.

In the case of the moulting rhythm (Chapter 8) a distinction must be drawn between anecdysis, a period during which moulting is inhibited and the crab remains at stage C4 of the moult cycle, and diecydysis in which there is no apparent inhibition and moulting occurs as soon as the crab is ready. In temperate species, moults following periods of anecdysis are often synchronized to the annual cycle. Large male *Carcinus*, for instance, tend to moult in January and February while large females often moult in the autumn. These times fit in with the annual breeding rhythm. In the little estuarine crab *Rithropanopeus*, anecdysis in the winter gives way to diecdysis in the summer, the first moult occurs when the water temperature reaches 14°C (Turaboyski, 1973). In diecdysis moults occur according to a rhythm which is not phased to an environmental cycle and in which the period varies between individuals, being longer in larger animals. This rhythm is tied to the environment only in as much as the crab must complete the storage of food reserves before entering the moult-initiating phase of the cycle. Generally speaking diecdysis is found in young sexually immature crabs. Following sexual maturity periods of anecdysis allow the diversion of energy from growth into reproduction.

ENTRAINMENT AND CLOCK CONTROL

Two basic features of biological rhythms require explanation. The first is the period of the rhythm: the time interval between peaks, 12·4 hours and 24 hours in the tidal and daily rhythms respectively. The second is the phase of the rhythm: when, within a geophysical time framework, the peaks actually occur. It is at once apparent that whereas the period of a rhythm is more or less fixed, the phase of a rhythm can be radically altered. This, of course, is as it should be since although the periods of rhythms are adapted to unchanging geophysical periods, the environmental rhythms which occur as a result of these geophysical periods vary in their timing both with geographical location and with time of year. Tidal cycles for instance may be out of phase on the two sides of a peninsula while, on the same shore, we have already noted the difference in phase of pigment migration rhythms in fiddler crabs living at different levels. On an annual basis the changing photoperiod in the higher latitudes makes phase alternation necessary in daily rhythms. In the laboratory the phase of a rhythm can be readily altered simply by changing the environmental rhythm. If, for instance, one wants to arrange for the convenient observation of a nocturnal crab, one can simply leave its lights on all night and keep it relatively dark by day. The crab soon alters the phase of its rhythm such that it is active during the observer's day. Clearly the phasing of a rhythm is the result of environmental stimulation while the stable and persistent period is evidence of a biological clock.

Dealing with phasing first, a major question is which of the many possible rhythmic environmental signals do crabs actually use to phase their rhythms? The problem has been most fully investigated by Naylor and his co-workers using the tidal activity rhythm of *Carcinus* (summarized by Naylor *et al.*, 1971). The possible environmental signals by which this rhythm might be phased are as follows: (1) the cycle of immersion and exposure to air; (2) the temperature cycle—the sea is often cooler than the air; (3) the increase in pressure during high tide periods. Using arhythmic crabs Naylor found that a persistent tidal rhythm could be entrained by imposing for a few days an artificial rhythm of tidal period involving any one of these three variables. Curiously, the cycle of immersion and exposure in otherwise constant conditions was the least effective of the three. When this treatment was combined with a synchronized temperature cycle (immersion coinciding with low temperature), however, a rhythm could be entrained more easily than with temperature cycles alone. Clearly in the natural environment all three cycles are important and reinforce each other in maintaining synchronization.

The effect of temperature on biological rhythms is another problem which has attracted attention. One of the most interesting findings was that the rhythms are relatively independent of temperature change; most unusual in comparison with other biological processes (Chapter 9). In *Carcinus*, Naylor (1963) showed that phase and period of the tidal activity rhythm remained steady in crabs maintained at different constant temperatures from 10–25°C. The only effect was a transitory advance in the phase of the first peak following transfer to a lower temperature (the peak occurring sooner than expected), and conversely a temporary delay in phase following a rise in temperature. Such temperature independence is an adaptational necessity in these crabs since a rhythm in which the basic phase and period could be altered by temperature fluctuations such as might easily occur within the short-term environment would be a considerable disadvantage. Two exceptions have been found to the general principle of temperature independence. The first is the role as a phase setter of rhythmic temperature cycles, discussed above. The second is that periods of very low temperature (chilling) may completely reset the phase of the rhythm. Naylor (1963) found that in freshly collected rhythmic *Carcinus*, chilling to 4°C for more than six hours rephased the rhythm. The first activity peak occurred as the crab warmed up and subsequent peaks followed at 12·4 hour intervals. Chilling was also found to initiate a tidal rhythm in otherwise arhythmic crabs. This treatment, therefore, can not only set the 'clock', it can also wind it up.

Having remarked on the constancy of period and the flexibility of phase it must now be admitted that one of the interesting properties of biological rhythms is that, under constant conditions, a systematic change in period generally occurs: the interval between peaks becomes an hour or two longer or an hour or two shorter than when under natural conditions. Since the alteration in period is constant and persistent the rhythm gradually drifts out of synchrony with the environment. This property is referred to when naming rhythms by the prefix 'circa-' (about), i.e. circadian and circatidal for daily and tidal rhythms under constant conditions (Palmer, 1973). Alteration of period under constant conditions is thought to represent a slight inbalance between tendencies which act to delay or to advance the phase of the rhythm. A delay in phase represents an increase in period while an advance corresponds to a decrease. Both tendencies are thought to be present and under natural conditions may provide a mechanism by which the phase of the rhythm can be rapidly adapted to alterations in environmental phase. The mechanism has been called autophasing (Brown, 1972) and may be regarded as a constant readiness for minor phase alteration. It is clearly a useful adaptation since without some means of period alteration, rephasing would always involve the destruction of the old rhythm and its replacement by another, a process involving some delay and liable to be both traumatic and dangerous. The mechanism further requires the presence of both the tendencies to advance and to delay since changes in environmental phase may go either way. The inbalance between tendencies which expresses itself as the 'circa-' phenomenon may itself reflect an adaptation to the most important direction (for the way of life of the particular species) of environmental phase change.

We are left with the biological clock, many of the properties of which are apparent from the above discussion. There are two theories on the nature of the clock: either it is internal or it is external. An internal clock would involve some system, probably secretory or nervous, with a built-in cycle time independent of environmental fluctuations, the period of which was adapted to a geophysical rhythm. There could be one of these systems for each rhythm or there could be a single clock with various gears each providing the period for a different rhythm. The external clock on the other hand requires the animal to be sensitive to subtle geophysical variables and hence to be always aware of the time. Evidence has accumulated for both theories.

For the internal clock, hormonal control of pigment migration rhythms must involve cycles of hormone release, but whether the cycle time is a standard property of the secretory system or is dictated from elsewhere is an unsolved problem. That the particular cycle time is dictated from somewhere is clearly shown by the persistence of rhythms, and particularly well in *Carcinus* where the single period of chilling induced a precisely timed tidal activity rhythm in arhythmic crabs. Chilling has even been found to initiate a good tidal rhythm in laboratory raised *Carcinus* which had never experienced tides on the shore (Williams and Naylor, 1967). This suggests that in these crabs the 12·4 hour period is an inherited feature, particularly when one considers that in Mediterranean *Carcinus* (which do not experience significant tides and are mainly nocturnal) chilling does not initiate a tidal rhythm (Naylor, 1963). Activity rhythms in *Carcinus*, like the pigment migration rhythms of *Uca*, appear also to be controlled by rhythmic release of neurohormones. Once again the eyestalk is important: it has been found that a tidal rhythm of activity cannot be induced by chilling eyestalkless crabs, but that, in intact crabs, chilling the eyestalks alone is effective in inducing the rhythm (Naylor and Williams, 1968). Hormonal control appears to be inhibitory. Eyestalkless crabs are hyperactive but their activity can be reduced by injecting eyestalk extract from normal rest-period crabs. Aréchiga *et al.*, (1974) measured activity and reactivity in *Carcinus* by implanting electrodes and recording neural activity. They found that night-time peaks could be reduced to levels characteristic of the day-time by injecting nervous tissue extracts. Eyestalk extract was particularly effective but extracts of brain and thoracic ganglion also depressed neural activity. The active substance in these extracts appeared to be a peptide.

There is thus a fair body of evidence to suggest that rhythmic neurosecretion systems with inbuilt tendencies to particular periods provide control over endogenous rhythms. Such systems can clearly be subjected to phase alteration by environmental input via the CNS. Unfortunately, this does not solve the clock problem. Although the secretory systems may be adapted to particular inherited periods, the independence of environmental fluctuation, particularly temperature, remains to be explained. It is possible to imagine a physiological mechanism for achieving temperature independence through the agency of hormonal promotors and inhibitors (Naylor, 1976) and the existence of such a mechanism would make an external clock redundant. Such a mechanism, however, has not yet been demonstrated and in the meantime evidence for the sensitivity of a wide variety of animals to subtle geophysical variables has accumulated (Brown, 1972). There is little reason to doubt that such sensitivity could provide a time sense sufficient to insulate biological rhythms from short-term environmental fluctuations. In conclusion therefore, the biological clock remains something of an enigma but the phenomenon of rhythmicity is nothing less than a way of life.

5   Life-styles

This chapter is an attempt to make some sense of the diversity of crabs. Much of this diversity stems from differences in life-style and although there are almost as many life-styles as there are species, it is possible to recognize several broad ecological categories. Five such categories are described below, each one being characterized by a particular type of behaviour and, in some cases, by particular morphological adaptations. The first category is a mixed bag of species all of which, when moving about, do so by walking, running or climbing; the second includes crabs which swim; the third is comprised of those which burrow; the fourth contains species to which inconspicuousness is important; and the last category includes crabs which have developed commensal, symbiotic or parasitic relationships with other species. Anyone familiar with crabs will know that these five categories overlap broadly with one another. It is not the intention that they be exclusive (such a classification would be almost impossible) but simply that they should provide a framework within which adaptations to life-style can be discussed. A previous ecological classification of crabs was that of Schäfer (1954) who divided them into runners, climbers, swimmers and burrowers. Many of my conclusions are similar to those of Schäfer.

WALKING, RUNNING AND CLIMBING

As is pointed out in Chapter 2, speed and strength often involve opposite adaptations. As a result, specialization may lead either to rapid movement or to strong movement but not generally to both. This dichotomy occurs in crab life-styles and each branch carries characteristic adaptations. Strong slow-moving crabs (Fig. 22A) are protected from predators by their thick heavy exoskeletal armour and by their chelae which form dauntingly massive defensive weapons. Short legs enable them to cling tightly to the sea bed and to pull themselves along through seaweed or into deep rock crevices. Being incapable of rapid movement they are not constantly on the alert for flight or attack and consequently have rather small eyes. This way of life restricts their predatory activities

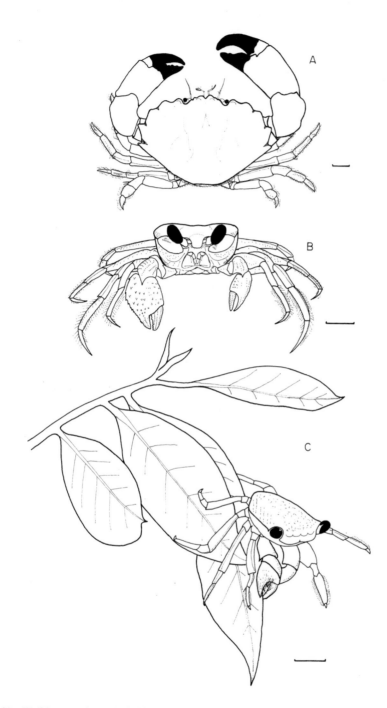

Fig. 22   Walking, running and climbing crabs. A, *Menippe nodifrons* (♂) a Caribbean xanthid. B, the west Atlantic and Caribbean ghost crab *Ocypode quadrata* (♀). C, the mangrove tree crab *Aratus pisoni* (♂) climbing on mangrove leaves (traced from photograph). Scale = 10 mm.

since they cannot catch fast-moving prey. They can, however, deal with heavily armoured prey such as molluscs and can dig for worms and other soft-bodied cryptic delicacies. Plants are also readily accessible and many crabs of this type are largely herbivorous. This life-style, the 'slow walker', is characteristic of xanthid crabs and of certain cancrids such as *Cancer pagurus*.

The other branch of the strength/speed dichotomy is represented in the sea by swimming crabs, discussed separately below. In semiterrestrial habitats and on land, however, there are several 'rapid runners' the best known of which are the ghost crabs, *Ocypode* (Fig. 22B); other ocypodids and certain grapsids, gecarcinids and potamids also fall into this group. Rapid runners share with swimming crabs a relatively thin light exoskeleton and large eyes. When active they are constantly alert and ready to race off after prey or to run for cover on the appearance of a predator. Ghost crabs have rather square carapaces and can run forwards and backwards as well as sideways at speeds of up to 2 m/s. It contrast to the slow walkers, the legs, and particularly the dactyli, of rapid runners are long and slender, employing relatively low mechanical advantages. Although most ghost crabs are predatory, the majority of semiterrestrial and land crabs have a mainly vegetarian diet and their speed is concerned more with flight than with attack.

Climbing is here defined as walking or running on vertical or near vertical surfaces. Under water, where weight is not a great problem, climbing is not a difficult activity and most slow walkers are able to clamber clumsily up underwater cliffs or boulders. More specialized, however, are some of the spider crabs which, with long legs radiating from small delicate bodies, are able to spread their light weight over a wide area (Fig. 26A). These crabs walk on vertical surfaces quite as readily as on the flat and are also able to climb flexible growths such as seaweeds. In some spider crabs the tips of the legs are adapted for clinging. In *Acanthonyx*, which climbs amongst seaweed, the walking legs are sub-chelate and each one is capable of gripping the seaweed as it sways to and fro with the waves (Fig. 23B). In *Mithrax*, which clambers amongst branching coral, the condylic articulations at the PD joints of the walking legs form catch mechanisms (Fig. 23A). Unless the dactylus is bent slightly forward prior to extension (a movement which occurs on contraction of the opener muscle) a hook on the dactylus catches on a flange on the propodus and grips it so tightly that, rather than the joint extending, the whole leg comes off! I have tied Trinidadian specimens of *Mithrax coryphe* to a spring balance and then allowed them to climb onto an irregular coral boulder. The pull on the spring balance required to detach a crab of about 15 mm carapace width from the boulder was usually 2–3 kg, and it was generally the coral which gave way rather than the crab! The forces resisted by these catch mechanisms are much greater than those expected of natural physical phenomena such as waves, and the adaptation is probably concerned with resisting the attempts of predators such as octopuses to pluck the crabs from amongst the coral.

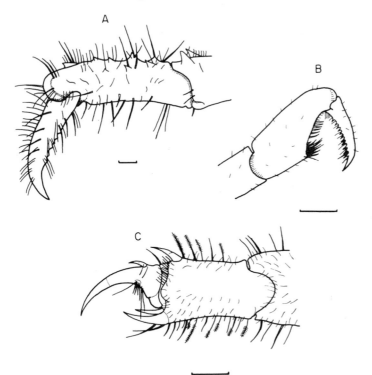

Fig. 23 Tips of walking legs of three Caribbean crabs adapted for clinging. A, *Mithrax forceps* (♂), 28 mm carapace width, 2nd leg). B, *Acanthonyx petiverii* (♀, 7 mm carapace width, 2nd leg). C, *Dromidia antillensis* (♀, 21 mm carapace width, 4th leg). Scale = 1 mm.

On land, as in the sea, slow and clumsy climbing is not uncommon. Some rapidly moving semiterrestrial crabs, however, have become exceedingly agile on vertical surfaces. Two such species are the tropical rocky-shore crab *Grapsus* and the mangrove tree crab *Aratus* (Fig. 22C). These crabs share with rapid runners light weight, large eyes and long legs, characteristic of quick movement. A striking difference, however, lies in the dactyli which, particularly in *Aratus*, are extremely short. This adaptation is concerned with the need to cling on tightly; short dactyli being analogous to a mountaineer's pitons. The shortness results in a high mechanical advantage at the tip, and ensures that the pull on the dactylus is close to the surface of the substratum. The ability of these crabs to cling on and to climb is quite remarkable. *Aratus*, when climbing up the branches of mangrove trees, can achieve speeds of about 1 m/s over short distances. At night they climb into the tops of the trees where they may be seen, 10 m or more above the ground, feeding on the leaves. *Grapsus*, which scrapes algal food from wave-washed rocks, is frequently submerged by breakers washing over it. When this occurs the crabs press their flattened bodies to the rock and cling on with limpet-like tenacity until the wave recedes. They then emerge from the boiling surf and go on feeding as if nothing had happened.

I cannot leave the subject of climbing without referring to the case of the robber crab *Birgo latro*. This animal is a huge shell-less hermit which lives on Pacific islands and is often cited as being able to climb coconut palms and eat the nuts. This crab was studied by Gibson-Hill on Christmas Island and, from his observations, it appears that it is actually a rather poor climber and quite incapable of opening coconuts. It can, however, climb sago palms and will eat the fruit. It also climbs to escape danger: 'fairly frequently, when disturbed, they climb some 4–5 feet up the trunk of a tree . . . but the manoeuvre seems to be one of doubtful utility as they often have the greatest difficulty in getting down again.' (Gibson-Hill, 1947). These robber crabs, which derive their name from their habit of walking off with things (Gibson-Hill mentioned sandals, cooking tins, knives, forks and a wrist watch), appear to be terrestrial slow walkers and, in comparison with *Grapsus* and *Aratus*, are rank amateurs when it comes to climbing.

SWIMMING

Many different types of crab are able to swim (Hartnoll, 1971) but in only one group, the Portunidae, does this ability dominate the life-style. Portunids are rapidly moving marine crabs. They have lightly built exoskeletons, slim legs and large eyes. The chelae may be quite large but are long and slim rather than bulky and are strengthened by longitudin-ally running ridges to economize on weight. Most portunid crabs are predators and their rapid swimming makes it possible for them to exploit fast-moving prey such as fish. They also depend upon speed to avoid the attentions of larger predators. When cornered, however, they will fight back by striking upwards at an aggressor with both of their long sharp chelae. This habit can be relied upon to produce a dramatic startle response in any person who pokes incautiously at a swimming crab such as the European velvet crab *Macropipus puber* or the west Atlantic blue crab *Callinectes sapidus* imprisoned in a bucket.

The propulsive force in swimming comes from the last pair of legs in which the last two podomeres are flattened into paddles (Fig. 24). At the base of each of these swimming legs the TC joint is aligned such that its axis is almost horizontal. This slight rotation from the position in non-swimming crabs allows the basal muscles of the leg to beat the paddle

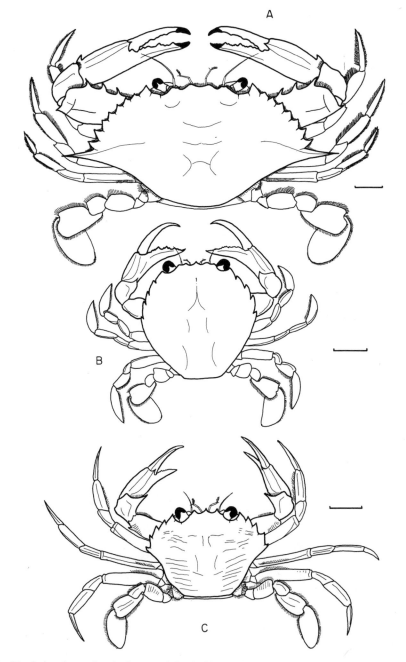

Fig. 24 Swimming crabs. A, the west Atlantic blue crab *Callinectes sapidus* (♀); B, a European swimming crab with pelagic habits *Polybius henslowi* (♂); C, a European swimming crab with benthic habits *Macropipus depurator* (♂). Scale = 10 mm.

forwards and backwards over the carapace. The arc through which the leg may beat is further increased by the MC joint which allows almost 180° of movement. The extra is mainly extension and permits the tip of the paddle to pass the mid-line on the forestroke. Swimming would still not be possible, however, were it not for the CP joint. This is aligned such that its axis is parallel to the long axis of the leg and it allows the paddle to be rotated through more than 90°. Thus the angle of attack can be altered on the forward and backward strokes to produce a sculling action (Spirito, 1972) which gives both propulsion and lift. The muscles involved on the forestroke during sculling are the levator and promotor at the base and the extensor at the MC joint; their antagonists are active on the backstroke. Most of the work is done by the levator and depressor muscles; the promotor and remotor control the attitude of the paddle (White and Spirito, 1973). The bender and stretcher muscles control the pitch of the paddle by adjusting the angle at the CP joint.

Sculling is used in both sideways and backwards swimming; the former is generally the most rapid. In backward swimming the paddles scull over the carapace, driving water forwards and downwards. In sideways swimming the trailing leg sculls sideways while the leading leg executes power and recovery strokes in which exaggerated forward sweeps alternate with back-strokes with the paddle feathered. These power strokes are produced largely by the contraction of the levator which is the largest of the swimming muscles (Hoyle and Burrows, 1973) and they drive water sideways over the carapace thrusting the crab along at speeds which may be well in excess of 1 m/s. Different degrees of lift can be achieved by altering the pitch of the paddles and some crabs, such as *Macropipus depurator* (Fig. 24C) can rise almost vertically upwards by backwards swimming modified in this way. Steering is possible by varying the effective direction of a stroke or the force that is applied to it. During sideways swimming the walking legs on the leading side perform irregular walking movements and these may also aid in steering. The rest of the appendages are held in streamlined positions with the chelipeds flexed and the trailing walking legs stretched out; the cheliped on the trailing side, however, may itself trail as a 'rear guard'.

In many swimming crabs the whole body is streamlined for sideways swimming and the carapace, in such forms as the blue crab *Callinectes sapidus*, is drawn out at each side into a long sharp spine (Fig. 24A). Other swimming crabs, however, lack these spines and in *Polybius henslowi*, which has sometimes been seen swarming on the surface in very deep water, the body is circular and lens-shaped in section, not unlike a flying saucer (Fig. 24B). Species of the genus *Macropipus* also tend towards the flying saucer shape rather than the fusiform. This shape is streamlined in all directions and probably aids backwards swimming and manoeuvrability. *Polybius*, indeed, is one of the most highly adapted swimming crabs, since its main paddles are supplemented by the other walking legs which are also flattened. Its pelagic habits testify to its swimming skill but the biological significance of its surface swarms unfortunately remains a mystery.

BURROWING

There are two main types of burrowing crab: back-burrowers and side-burrowers. Back-burrowers are usually found underwater on sandy substrata. They burrow by tilting backwards and digging down into the sand with their walking legs. Agitated in this way the sand becomes semi-fluid and the back-burrower works itself down until only the eyes or antennae are showing. Burrowing may be rapid in such forms as mole crabs (Fig. 4B) in which the body is elongated and the walking legs flattened for digging. Mole crabs live in the surf zone on tropical sandy beaches and need a fast burrowing mechanism to counteract the scouring action of the breakers. Elongated bodies are also found in the burrowing crabs *Corystes* (Fig. 25B) and *Ranina* (Fig. 41B). Some fast back-burrowers with flattened digging legs also use these legs for swimming. Examples include the little European portunid *Portumnus latipes* and the Indo-Pacific calappid *Matuta*. Indeed, it has been suggested that the ancestors of swimming crabs were back-burrowers and that swimming paddles may have evolved from flattened digging legs.

The majority of back-burrowers, however, do not have the legs noticeably adapted for digging and do not dig in particularly rapidly. They use burrowing chiefly for concealment during their inactive periods. *Carcinus* and *Macropipus depurator* provide good examples since they are frequently found during the day buried up to their carapaces with only their eyes protruding. The only adaptations which can be assigned to this behaviour concern respiration: it becomes more difficult when buried in sand to maintain a respiratory stream which enters ventrally. The problem is solved in back-burrowing portunids by the respiratory stream entering along the antero-lateral borders of the carapace, passing down to the Milne-Edwards openings between the inner faces of the folded chelae and the branchiostegites. The hair-fringed teeth so often found along the front edge of the carapace in such crabs (Figs. 24A, C) act as filters preventing the blockage of this respiratory route by sand. A similar adaptation is seen in the box crab *Calappa* (Fig. 25C) where the only part to project above the surface is the small hillock which bears the eyes at the front end of the domed carapace. The folded chelipeds fit perfectly around the branchiostegites and tall crests are developed on the chelae which reach up to the eye hillock. Hair fringed teeth at the tops of these crests guard the entrances of the respiratory stream on either side, while in the middle, guided by elongated 1st maxillipeds, the exhaled water spouts upwards in a powerful jet. Many leucosiid crabs also back-burrow to the level of their eye-hillocks (Fig. 25D). Here, however, the chelipeds are long and narrow and form no part of the inhalant passage. The inhalant stream flows from the surface of the substratum down channels running underneath the outer edges of the elongated 3rd maxillipeds and enters the branchial chambers at their bases. The Milne-Edwards openings have been eliminated and the carapace seals tightly around the bases of the

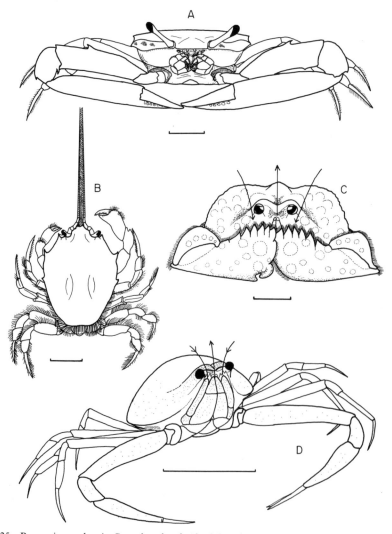

Fig. 25   Burrowing crabs. A, *Goneplax rhomboides* (♂) makes permanent burrows in the mud; B, *Corystes cassivelaunas* (♀), European, temporary burrowing in sand; C, *Calappa* sp. (♂), tropical temporary burrowing; D, *Persephona* sp. (♂), Caribbean, temporary burrowing. Arrows show inhalant and exhalant respiratory currents. Scale = 10 mm.

chelipeds. The exhalant flow spouts out from between the two inhalant points guided, as in *Calappa*, by elongated 1st maxillipeds.

The burrowing crab *Corystes* (Fig. 25B) has solved its respiratory problems in quite a different way. It digs more deeply into the substratum than any of the previous examples, becoming completely buried with only the tips of its antennae protruding. These are very remarkable antennae; they are long and stiff and, when opposed, form a breathing tube of interlocking hairs down which the crab sucks its respiratory water. To do this the direction of the respiratory stream is reversed. Elongated 3rd maxillipeds extend to the bases of the antennae and the stream flows behind them into the branchial chambers on either side. The exhalant flow gushes out at the leg bases and may be seen bubbling up through the surrounding sand.

The burrowing of a back-burrower results in the crab becoming temporarily embedded in the substratum. In contrast, side-burrowing results in the construction of a genuine burrow which may serve the individual as a shelter for several days or weeks. Most semiterrestrial and terrestrial crabs construct burrows of this type and a few sublittoral crabs, such as the mud crab *Goneplax*, construct burrows under water. Side-burrowing crabs are usually shaped such that they are almost circular in longitudinal section. With chelipeds folded the smaller ones in particular form a compact cylinder that fits neatly into the burrow (Fig. 25A). They use the legs, the dactyli of which may be slightly flattened dorso-ventrally, on one or other side to dig into the substratum and the excavated soil is formed into a ball which is carried up and deposited, or scattered around the burrow entrance. Sometimes the excavated soil is used to build a superstructure. Certain *Uca* species extend their burrows 1–2 cm above the surface of the substratum in the form of narrow mud funnels; other *Uca* and some sesarmines build mud porches over the burrow entrance. More spectacular are the pyramids built by several species of *Ocypode*. These may be 30 cm or more in height and probably serve social functions (p.112).

In *Uca* (Fig. 30) the burrow is usually excavated in mud or muddy sand and consists of a single, more or less vertical shaft. The depth varies with the size of the crab and with the substratum, being deeper in sand, but a tunnel 15 cm deep and 1·5 cm in diameter is not unusual. Many side-burrowers dig more complex burrows with several exits: in *Ocypode* the descending shaft may be spiral and near the top there is frequently a side branch leading to an 'escape hatch'. *Goneplax* burrows are usually in the form of a shallow 'U' with two main exits, but there are often one or more side tunnels leading to the surface. The large land crab *Cardisoma* digs burrows which may be a metre or so deep and 10 cm in diameter. These burrows descend to the water table where there is generally a small living chamber providing a damp cool retreat for the crab during the day.

Intertidal burrowers such as *Uca* take refuge in their burrows when the tide comes in, often sealing the entrances with plugs of mud or sand. When the tide is out the crabs forage on the surface but are constantly on the alert and ready to dart into a burrow at the least sign of danger. If they have wandered too far a neighbour's burrow may be used in an emergency.

Some intertidal burrowers construct temporary burrows which they only inhabit during the period of high tide: digging into the sand as the tide rises to cover their feeding grounds and emerging again to forage after the tide has fallen. *Ocypode* sometimes follows this habit and within a population there may be both permanent burrow owners and nomadic temporary burrowers. Some ocypodid sand-bubbling crabs (sub-family Scopimerinae from the Indo-Pacific) also construct temporary burrows and in *Dotilla mictyroides* a remarkable construction method which is neither side- nor back-burrowing has been described by Tweedie (1950). 'In wet, semi-liquid sand . . . a shallow depression is made in which the crab turns on its side and quickly runs round backwards, pushing pellets of sand upwards and outwards. The semi-liquid pellets coalesce at first to form a circular wall, then the top of this, as it increases in height, arches inwards so that a dome-shaped structure results' . . . in which . . . 'the crab is enclosed together with a quantity of air. . . . When the dome is completed the crab continues to push sand upwards and so achieves a downward progress, together with its trapped bubble of air.' This bubble of air apparently survives the high tide and may act as an oxygen store for the crab. *Dotilla* is also capable of digging conventional burrows which are used as temporary retreats or to stake territorial claims (p.107).

INCONSPICUOUSNESS

Rather few crabs are conspicuously coloured, most are cryptic and merge fairly well into their backgrounds. Exceptions include certain semi-terrestrial and land crabs such as the Pacific form of the rock crab *Grapsus* which is bright red (the Caribbean form of this species is mottled grey) and the adults of an eastern Pacific ghost crab *Ocypode guadachaudii*, also bright red. The juveniles, like other species of *Ocypode*, are sandy coloured. Conspicuous displays, however, are not uncommon and many crabs have brightly coloured patches around the mouth and on the insides of the chelipeds. These are visible in the common threat posture in which the chelae are spread wide and the body tilted backwards. Such warning flashes doubtless help to deter enemies but are also useful in social interactions where visual displays are used to establish rank and to attract mates.

Cryptic coloration may involve alteration in the state of dispersion of the chromatophore pigments according to the background. This is described for *Uca* above (p.62) and also occurs in *Ocypode* to adapt the crab to different shades of sand. In many crabs, however, the skeleton is too thick for the chromatophores to show through and the colour, contained in the pigmented layer of the cuticle, is more or less permanent during intermoult. Consequently cryptic coloration is often a compromise; greenish, brownish, purplish, sandy or off-white with irregular but symmetrical mottlings, it is adapted, like army camouflage, to fit a variety of backgrounds. Such camouflage colours are not always dull, juvenile *Carcinus* living amongst gravel are often very dandily attired with blotches of white, red and orange.

Other ways of achieving inconspicuousness include the development of thick growths of hair or irregular (but bilaterally symmetrical) sculpturing on the body surface. In *Pilumnus* large numbers of tufted hairs occur on the carapace and legs. Silt accumulates in the tufts to such an extent that the crab resembles little more than a small muddy excrescence. Disruptive surface sculpturing is common in xanthids; the intended resemblance both by colour and shape is to a small oval stone and admirably suits their 'slow walker' way of life. Similar camouflage is found in the parthenopid *Daldorfia horrida* which lives on Pacific coral reefs and looks exactly like a piece of coral rubble. Resemblance of the entire crab to a pebble is found in the genus *Ebalia*. These crabs live on gravel bottoms and their small rounded bodies with eyes on an eye hillock at the front are very difficult to distinguish from the surrounding gravel.

Despite this general tendency to inconspicuousness the masters of camouflage are undoubtedly to be found amongst the spider crabs. Here inconspicuousness is achieved by encouraging the settlement of sessile organisms on the exoskeleton. The main camouflaging agents in shallow water are algae but their growth varies from one species to another, probably controlled by the crab itself to achieve the best effect. Thus the long legged spider crab *Macropodia* (Fig. 26A), frequently found living out in the open on sandy or gravelly bottoms, goes in for a rather sparse growth of long trailing red or brown algae which disruptively exaggerates its normally etiolated appearance. The resemblance is to an unattached piece of alga such as is often encountered drifting about in such places. The shorter legged spider crab *Pisa* (Fig. 26B), however, is usually entirely covered with a dense growth of algae, blending in with the dense growth normally occurring on the rocks on which it lives. In deeper darker water the camouflage organisms are mainly sessile animals: sponges, hydroids, bryozoans and barnacles. The attachment of organisms to spider crabs is aided by the structure of their cuticles; a dense growth of hooked hairs is often present and surface irregularities which are likely to facilitate settlement are frequently found. Furthermore, the crabs themselves are known to 'plant' organisms (algae and sponges in particular) on their own

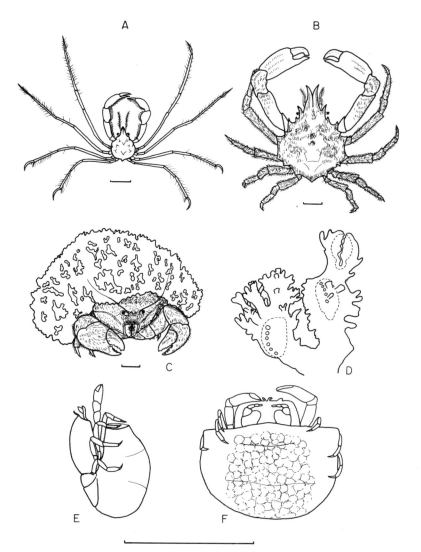

Fig. 26 Crabs which form associations with other organisms. A, long-legged European spider crab *Macropodia rostrata* (♂), camouflaging algae removed. B, shorter-legged European spider crab *Pisa tetradon* (♂), camouflaging algae removed. C, a Caribbean sponge crab *Dromidia antillensis* (♂). D, galls in the Indo-Pacific coral *Pocillopora* formed by the gall crab *Hapalocarcinus*, the topmost gall is the youngest—its edges have not yet closed. E and F, side and ventral views of adult female *Hapalocarcinus*. D, E and F after Potts. 1915. Scale = 10 mm.

backs and legs to restore camouflage after moulting (Wicksten, 1975).

Other crabs which use organisms or objects to camouflage themselves include members of the primitive Dromiacea. The sponge crab *Dromidia* (Fig. 26C) carries a sponge over its back while *Homola* (Fig. 41D) carries one half of a bivalve shell in the same way. In *Dromidia* the last two pairs of walking legs are sub-chelate (Fig. 23C) and are used to hold the sponge in place.

ASSOCIATIONS

Crabs associate themselves with other animals for protection, as commensals or parasites and as hosts to commensals and parasites. Associations for protection are often formed with anemones. Hartnoll (1970) described a casual relationship in which the spider crab *Inarchus* sits at the base of the snake-locks anemone *Anemonia* under a protective curtain of tentacles. Its presence does not elicit the anemone's normal feeding reactions. Closer associations are formed between anemones and hermit crabs. Here both partners benefit since the anemone, carried on the hermit crab's shell, gains both mobility and extra food in the form of animals disturbed by the crab's activities and scraps dropped while feeding. Several studies have shown the value to the crab of the anemone's protection; neither octopuses nor predatory crabs enjoy being stung while feeding and will discard such pernicious meals! Yet another advantage accrues to the European hermit *Pagurus prideauxi* in its association with the cloak anemone *Adamsia palliata*. This anemone envelopes the body of the crab in a deep fold of its column, its growth keeps pace with that of the crab and relieves the latter of the necessity of changing shells as it grows. In a mature specimen the original tiny shell can be found embedded deep inside the folds of the anemone. *Adamsia*, for its part, spreads its tentacles just below the hermit's mouth in an ideal position for catching scraps or for sweeping the sea bed as the hermit moves about.

These hermit crab–anemone associations are initiated by fascinating behaviour on both sides (Ross and Sutton, 1961a, b; Ross, 1974). Usually one partner plays the dominant role in initiating the association but, depending on the particular association, the most active partner may be either the anemone or the crab. The anemone genus *Calliactis* is a frequent associate of hermit crabs and in the association between *C. parasitica* and *Pagurus bernhardus* it is the anemone which is active. *C. parasitica* can recognize hermit crab shells and will transfer itself onto such shells from other substrata. To do this the anemone first attaches its oral disc to the shell by means of its nematocysts, it then detaches the basal disc, swings it across and reattaches it to the hermit crab shell. The crab cooperates only to the extent of keeping still while the anemone is transferring. In other associations, however, the crab may take the lead, all species of the hermit crab genus *Dardanus* are active partners in their associations with anemones. The crab stimulates the anemone to detach from a non-hermit crab substratum by prodding and stroking it with its chelae. When it detaches it is lifted up by the crab and placed in contact with the shell, whereupon it reattaches. The anemone clearly recognizes the stimulus of the crab since it does not contract and fire out stinging threads (which it does if poked by an enemy) but actively cooperates in the process of transference by relaxing, detaching and reattaching.

Some brachyuran crabs also carry anemones and their behaviour towards them is no less remarkable (Cutress *et al.*, 1970). *Calliactis tricolor* in the Caribbean is found in association with the spider crab *Stenocionops furcata*, up to 25 anemones being carried on the carapace and legs. The crab stimulates the anemone to detach from other substrata by poking and pinching it, and by pulling actively at it with chelae and walking legs. When the anemone is detached the crab manipulates it quite roughly and the anemone responds by relaxing completely. Finally, after apparently feeling over its carapace for a clear space, the crab grips the anemone firmly in one chela and hoists it up onto its back. The anemone adheres promptly and soon resumes its normal behaviour. *C. tricolor* is not specific to *Stenocionops* but is also found on two species of hermit crab and on the calappid *Hepatus*. Another brachyuran crab which carries anemones is *Lybia tessellata* which lives on Pacific coral reefs. This crab holds its anemones like fire-brands, one on each chela, ready to thrust into the face of an enemy.

Other interesting crab–coelenterate associations include those in which crabs live among the branches of coral colonies (Patton, 1974). Most species are small and possess catch mechanisms at the tips of their legs (Fig. 23A). One of the best known is the Pacific genus *Trapezia*: smooth-shelled shiny brightly coloured crabs, the adults of which often live in male–female pairs. Pairs are territorial and in any one species only one pair is normally found in a single coral colony. Different species, however, share colonies along with a variety of other commensals such as shrimps and fish. In hemispherical 30 cm-diameter colonies of the coral *Pocillopora* on the Great Barrier Reef, Patton (1974) found an average of about 10 crabs per colony.

These free-living commensals, however, are not the most specialized coral inhabiting crabs. This honour must go to the tiny Indo-Pacific coral gall crabs of the family Hapalocarcinidae (Potts, 1915). Female gall crabs (*Hapalocarcinus*) settle in the axils of young coral branches and their activities influence the growth of the coral such that, in each case, the two branches form flat sheets which grow up and around the crab entombing it in a purse-shaped gall. The edges of the flat coral sheets finally join leaving only a row of holes through which the crab can draw its respiratory stream (Fig. 26D). Before this happens, however, the female is fertilized by a much smaller wandering male. The related genus *Cryptochirus* lives in cylindrical or funnel-shaped pits in coral and has become lobster-like in body form. In some species of *Cryptochirus* the males and females live in pairs; the male is minute and clings on beneath the female's abdomen. In both *Hapalocarcinus* and *Cryptochirus* the abdomen of the female is greatly enlarged (Figs. 26E, F): not needing to fend for herself in the outside world she has become, like the females of many parasites, little more than an animated egg-bag.

The best known commensal or parasitic crabs are the pea crabs of the family Pinnotheridae. The habitats of these small round-bodied animals include the mantle cavities of bivalve molluscs, the tubes of the polychaete worm *Chaetopterus*, the burrows of callianassid shrimps and the atrial cavities of ascidians. Probably all pea crabs adversely affect their hosts since they feed by stealing its food. They either strain the inhalant feeding and respiratory currents of the host using their setose maxillipeds or they feed directly on mucus food strings which have been collected by the host's filtering activities. The latter is the case in most species of *Pinnotheres* which pick food from the gills of bivalve molluscs.

Within their comfortable protected habitats pea crabs have little need of armour or of rapid locomotion. Consequently they tend to be thin-shelled with rather poorly developed legs. There are times during the life cycle, however, when they must face the rigours of the outside world, in particular the stage at which initial 'infection' occurs and, later on at maturity, when they leave their homes to search for mates. Hard-shelled infective and mating instars, the former generally occurring immediately after the larval life, are found in many species and most are well developed for rapid locomotion by forward swimming. Propulsion is achieved by the serial beating of hair-fringed legs. The long swimming hairs stand up stiffly during the backward power stroke but fold flat on the recovery stroke (Hartnoll, 1971). After mating, pea crabs re-infect their hosts and the females moult to the soft-shelled form before producing eggs. Mature thin-shelled females, like female coral gall crabs, develop enormous abdomens. A similar way of life to that of the pea crabs has been adopted by some porcellanid crabs. Examples occur in the genus *Polyonyx*, often found in pairs in *Chaetopterus* tubes on the western shores of the Atlantic.

Crabs themselves provide a protected environment for many other animals. Apart from the camouflaging organisms discussed above, there are many filter feeders which, although usually free-living, may settle on crabs and use the latter's respiratory currents for feeding purposes. These casual associates include barnacles and spirorbid tube worms (which may encrust the mouthparts and branchiostegites), hydroids, bryozoans, tube-dwelling amphipods and ascidians. The branchial chambers are even more protected and, although infection here is relatively rare, barnacles, parasitic isopods and even small fish have been found within. In hermit crabs the cavity of the shell provides a similar protected environment and large individuals of *Pagurus bernhardus* frequently play what is probably rather reluctant host to the large worm *Nereis furcata* which lives alongside the crab within the shell. This worm feeds by seizing food from the crab's mouthparts and retreating with it into the shell.

The most frequently noticed parasite of crabs is the rhizocephalan barnacle *Sacculina*, the biology of which was reviewed by Hartnoll (1967). The infective stage is a cypris larva which settles on the cuticle at the base of a hair and enters the crab as a tiny cellular mass. Taking up its position at the base of the hind-gut caecum it gradually develops a mass of ramifying rootlets which serve a nutritive function and penetrate throughout the body of the crab, even to the tips of the legs. During this time *Sacculina* takes hormonal control of its host, gradually altering the structure, metabolism and behaviour towards that characteristic of the mature female crab. In male crabs this 'parasitic castration' (in fact the androgenic glands rather than the testes are destroyed) results in the atrophy or non-appearance of such secondary sexual characteristics as copulatory pleopods, a narrow abdomen and large chelae. All this happens over a number of moults but eventually the parasite calls a halt to the moulting of the host, probably by inhibiting the Y-organ (p.129). This occurs when the parasite, itself a hermaphrodite, is ready to reproduce. The developing eggs of *Sacculina* are contained in a sac-like 'externa' which erupts through the cuticle of the crab at the base of the abdomen. An externa looks not unlike the egg mass of a normal ovigerous crab but is smooth and shiny rather than granular and has an opening through which the nauplius larvae of the parasite escape. It remains for some time protected under the broad abdomen of the host (whether originally male or female) and may produce several batches of larvae. *Sacculina* is not only a large and easily noticed parasite of crabs, it may also be quite common. Hartnoll (1967) cited a population in which up to 70 per cent of crabs were infected; some individuals were carrying as many as five separate parasites!

6   Food and feeding

Primitively, crabs were probably opportunistic omnivores with a preference for animal food and with predatory tendencies. This feeding pattern is still followed by the majority of species and extreme specialization is relatively rare. Most species retain the ability to deal with a variety of foods and the only specialization shown is by tendencies towards particular types of diet. Thus grapsids tend to be mainly herbivorous, while portunids are mainly carnivorous. Within such groupings, however, diets are unspecialized with particular grapsids taking a variety of types of plant food and portunids catching many different types of prey. More strongly specialized are the deposit and suspension feeders, mainly ocypodids and anomurans respectively, but again it is the method rather than the diet which is specialized. The first five sub-headings in this chapter, therefore, are concerned more with methods and tendencies and should not be regarded as exclusive groupings. Lastly, it seems relevant to include a short account of the next link in the food chain: those animals which eat crabs.

OMNIVORES

Although one could include all crabs under this heading, there are some which are 'specialized generalists' and go in for a foraging existence. The little grapsid *Sesarma ricordi* living on the Caribbean strand line in tidal mangroves is one such crab. Feeding mostly on vegetation washed up by the tide this crab will also eat carrion and will seize and eat any small animal (insect, amphipod, worm) unfortunate enough to be spotted. Ghost crabs, *Ocypode*, on tropical sandy beaches, have similar habits and are said to walk along the strand line turning leaves over and seizing flies from underneath. They will also eat algae and will congregate around carrion (Hughes, 1966, mentioned dead birds, holothurians and a putrid giant clam); the substantial predatory skills of *Ocypode* are described below.

The Caribbean mangrove crab *Goniopsis* is another omnivore, feeding on mangrove mud, dead leaves, mangrove seedlings, sea grasses, carrion and any small animals that it can catch. These crabs are exceedingly exploratory and will investigate any unusual object. I have had them tugging at my shoe laces as I sat quietly on a mangrove root. On another occasion I watched them creep up on a brown rat which was foraging in the swamp and seize hold of its tail—much to the discomfort of the rat which ran off squealing! *Goniopsis* will also pounce on anything which lands suddenly beside it on the mangrove mud, a habit possibly concerned with predation on the tree crab *Aratus* which, when escaping from enemies, is inclined to leap from the tree tops onto the mud below.

Moving up onto land, one finds mainly omnivorous crabs with a tendency, probably because of greater availability, towards a plant diet. The red land crab *Gecarcoidea* on Christmas Island is a good example feeding on rotting leaves and some carrion. Its opportunistic tendencies are well illustrated by Gibson-Hill (1947) who described cannibalism occurring during the mass landward migration of baby crabs from the sea '. . . in hundreds of millions . . .' after a month of larval life in the plankton. 'The mortality is very high, and is further increased by some of the adults who take up their position in the line of a stream of young crabs and scoop them into their mouths with both claws.' Similar is the land hermit crab *Coenobita* which, on Aldabra, feeds mostly on giant tortoise faeces (Grubb, 1971). It will also take carrion but animal food is not essential since one individual is reported to have survived in captivity for eleven years on a vegetarian diet mainly of fresh lettuce. Fresh water crabs of the family Potamidae are often omnivorous, eating water plants, detritus, fish eggs and insect larvae. Some, however, must be quite skilful predators since they can catch and eat such active animals as fish and frogs. In the rain forests of South America the fresh water crab *Pseudotelphusa* feeds mainly on beetles.

Moving down to the sea again, one finds omnivores which probably gain animal food in the course of collecting algae. The diet of many spider crabs appears to consist largely of algae and amphipods (Hartnoll, 1963), the latter very likely disturbed from amongst the former. Similar diets to those of spider crabs are also frequently found in xanthids and the diet illustrates very well the foraging omnivorous habit—eating whatever is there, the high quality animal food being preferred if available.

Food collecting and processing organs (chelae, mouthparts and gastric mill) are relatively unspecialized in omnivores. Many spider crabs, however, have beak-like claws, possibly useful for plucking, for seizing small animals and for picking things out of crevices. Those species of semiterrestrial and land crabs which include vascular plants in their diets often have more and finer ridges than usual on the teeth of their gastric mills, but this adaptation is better developed in specialized herbivores and deposit feeders.

CARNIVORES

Carnivorous crabs are all predatory; although they may eat carrion, this forms a very small part of their diet — there is, after all, not much of it about except in special places such as along the strand line. The commonest form of predation is probably the eating of molluscs, both bivalves and gastropods. These are dug up or otherwise waylaid, cracked with the chelae and the meat is picked out of the shell and eaten. The abilities of different types of crab to perform this feat with variously armoured and sized molluscs differ according to the adaptations that the crabs possess. Thus *Cancer* and many xanthids which have heavily built chelae full of strong muscle (Fig. 27A) are well able to deal with a variety of sizes and shapes of mollusc. Portunids with their slim sharp-toothed chelae (Fig. 27B) are less able to crack large shells but can sometimes get at the prey by inserting the tips of their chelae into the aperture of a gastropod or between the valves of a bivalve. They may also be able to crack the shell by degrees; Muntz *et al.*, (1965) recorded that a *Macropipus puber*, by chipping away for 26 min at the aperture of a large topshell, was able to expose the snail and eat it. Progressive chipping is the process used by that voracious shell cracker, the box crab *Calappa* which feeds on gastropods, hermit crabs and bivalves. These crabs bear, on the largest of their two chelae, a large blunt tooth at the base of the dactylus which is deflected backwards and towards the outer face of the chela where it bites between two teeth developed on the propodus (Fig. 27C). The dactylus tooth exploits a high mechanical advantage and is used to chip shell margins which are positioned to span the propodus teeth (Shoup, 1968). In large gastropod shells a spiral incision may be chipped up the body whorl until the occupant is reached. With small hermit crabs the entire spire may be chipped off and the dactylus of a walking leg inserted to chase the hermit out. During the process of cracking, the shell is constantly manipulated by the walking legs to obtain the best grip for the chela. A basal tooth similar to that of *Calappa* but less well developed often occurs on the major chela of portunids and some xanthids and may be used in a similar way to chip shell margins.

The importance of crabs as predators of gastropod molluscs can be judged by a fascinating correlation shown by Vermeij (1975, 1976). A number of features of gastropod shells serve either to strengthen the shells or to limit the possibility of unwelcome intrusion through the aperture. Such features can be regarded as anti-predatory devices. They include strong, often ornate, external sculpturing, a lowering of the spire and a narrow aperture achieved by elongation or by development of teeth around the margin. Vermeij showed first that these anti-predatory features were better developed in tropical Indo-Pacific rocky shore gastropods than in ecologically equivalent gastropods from the tropical

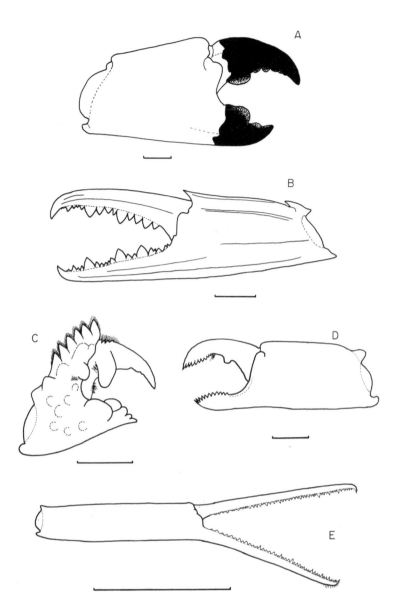

Fig. 27 Chelae adapted for different feeding methods. A, a strong crushing chela, *Menippe nodifrons*. B, a fast cutting chela, *Callinectes sapidus*. C, a chela with basal teeth adapted for chipping mollusc shells, *Calappa* sp. D, a serrated spoon-tipped chela for scraping algae from rocks, *Mithrax verrucosus*. E, a slender sharp-toothed chela for snatching at swimming prey, *Iliacanthus* sp. Scale = 10 mm.

Atlantic. Second, the efficacy of the anti-predatory devices was demonstrated by showing that tropical Pacific shell-cracking crabs such as *Carpilius*, *Eriphia* and *Daldorfia* could crack Atlantic gastropods more easily than they could crack ecologically equivalent gastropods from the

Pacific. In almost all cases the maximum crackable size of snail was greater for the Atlantic than for the Pacific demonstrating the extra strength of the shells of the latter. Third, Vermeij compared the chelae of Atlantic and Pacific species of the genera *Carpilius* and *Eriphia* and found that Pacific crabs had larger chelae than Atlantic crabs of the same size and genus. He concluded (1976): 'the arms race between Indo-West Pacific rocky shore gastropods and their crab predators has progressed further or remains in a more escalated state than in other tropical or temperate regions. Presumably this high degree of co-adaptation is related in part to the great age and stability of the tropical Pacific and Indian Oceans.'

Calappa and many other crabs such as *Carcinus*, *Cancer*, *Callinectes* and *Ocypode*, feed on burrowing lamellibranchs. A problem here, apart from cracking the shell, is locating and digging up the prey. *Calappa* and *Callinectes* probe the substratum with their walking legs and dig with these and with their chelae. *Cancer* may excavate great pits up to 20 cm deep. *Ocypode* feeding on the beach clam *Donax* apparently knows exactly where to dig, possibly picking up vibrations from the clam under the sand. With one scoop of its walking legs it unearths *Donax* and, if the shell is not too big, cracks it open and eats it (Hughes, 1966). A West Indian portunid crab *Arenaeus* also eats *Donax*, it cracks the clam using both chelae and can eat up to 24 in a night (Wade, 1967).

Other slow-moving prey frequently eaten by crabs include annelids (unearthed, dug out of crevices or cracked from their calcareous tubes) and such unlikely meals as starfish, sea urchins, sea cucumbers and brittle stars.

Faster moving prey can generally only be captured by portunids and, on land, by the rapidly moving semiterrestrial and terrestrial forms. The long slim sharp-toothed chelae of portunids contain a relatively high proportion of fast contracting muscle and are well adapted for the rapid snapping movements required to capture such creatures as fish. Equally, the thrust delivered by the swimming paddles is sufficiently great for them to be able to chase prey through the water or to dart from the bottom and seize it. I have watched *Callinectes* employing these tactics against tadpoles in a stream: darting up from the bottom into a swarm of these animals the crab was able to seize one in each chela. Some slow-moving crabs, however, are capable of lying in wait and grabbing suddenly. The small Trinidadian leucosiid crab *Iliacanthus* probably feeds in this way; buried in mud with only its eye-hillock showing, its long fine-toothed chelae (Fig. 27E) are ideally adapted for the rapid upward snatch required to catch a passing fish or shrimp. Similarly, spider crabs must perform quick and accurate movements when seizing amphipods. At night the spider crab *Macropodia* climbs seaweeds and catches passing crustaceans (Rasmussen, 1973); I have seen the rapidly moving portunid *Macropipus depurator* captured in this way.

Feeding on other crabs is not uncommon. *Ocypode* on tidal sand flats stalks and catches sentinel crabs, *Macrophthalmus*, which are carried off to the burrow to be eaten 'often struggling violently' (Hughes, 1966), and large *Ocypode* adults foraging in tide pools can apparently subdue and consume portunids and calappids almost as large as themselves. Here there is always a danger that the tables may be turned and that such large and ferocious prey may win the fight and themselves devour the relatively lightly built *Ocypode*. I have witnessed an analogous situation in a Jamaican mangrove swamp in which a large *Goniopsis* (not unlike *Ocypode* in body form and habits) foraging in shallow water was attacked and torn to pieces by an only slightly larger portunid, the aptly named *Callinectes exasperatus*.

The mouthparts and gastric mills of carnivorous crabs are adapted for tearing and crushing flesh. This is not a difficult operation and is served, on the mouthparts, by stout bristles to hold and tear pieces of food. The mandibles crush it as it enters the mouth and sever it into smaller pieces. Within the gastric mill, bathed in digestive juices, the food is crushed and torn by the knobbly dorsal tooth of the urocardiac ossicle rubbing between the lateral teeth of the two zygocardiac ossicles (Fig. 28B). The dorsal tooth and the anterior lateral teeth are large and blunt to crush and chew like the molars of a man or pig. The posterior lateral teeth, however, are fine and sharp arising in a comb-like row of spikes or transverse ridges on the dorsal and sometimes also on the ventral edges of the posterior ends of the zygocardiac ossicles. These teeth probably help to tear and strain the food. Since the effective stroke of the dorsal tooth is from posterior to anterior the series of events is a straining and tearing followed by a crushing and chewing.

HERBIVORES

Here a distinction must immediately be drawn between algivorous crabs and those which eat vascular plants. The former group includes many spider crabs, several xanthids and a few rocky shore-dwelling grapsids. The latter includes swamp-dwelling grapsids, some gecarcinids and some potamids. Many algivorous crabs are characterized by the possession of spoon-tipped chelae (Fig. 27D) with which they scrape algae from rocks; all algivorous grapsids possess this adaptation. The chelae scrape alternately and each delivers to the mouth a spoon-tip full of mixed algae, detritus and rocky fragments. Any solid surface may be scraped and the diet thus includes a greater or lesser proportion of detritus, sponge, hydroid and bryozoan. Small reef-dwelling spider crabs of the genus *Mithrax* sometimes scrape and ingest living coral. The mouthparts are generally well supplied with hairs which receive the finely divided food

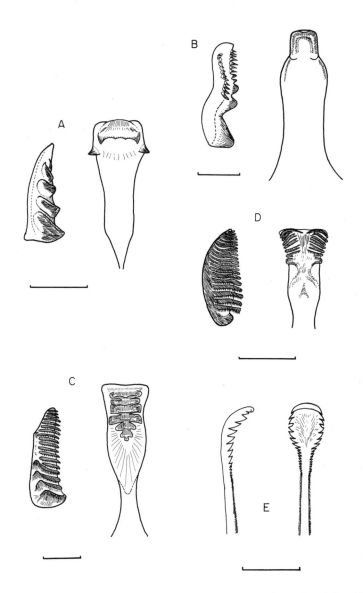

Fig. 28 Feeding adaptations: the opposing surfaces of the dorsal and lateral teeth from the gastric mills of crabs with different diets. A, an algivore, *Mithrax coryphe* (carapace width 19 mm). B, a predator, *Callinectes sapidus* (carapace width 48 mm). C, a vascular plant-eater, *Aratus pisoni* (carapace width 25 mm). D, a deposit-feeder, *Uca* sp. (carapace width 16 mm). Anterior is downwards, only left lateral teeth are shown. E. spoon-tipped hairs from the 2nd maxilliped of *Uca* sp. collected from a sandy-mud habitat. Scale for A, B, C and D = 1 mm; for E = 0·1 mm.

and press it into the mouth. Such hairs tend to be more numerous and finer than the grasping and tearing bristles of carnivores. Scraping algivores mainly gather fine filamentous green algae and diatoms but other algivores, such as the European wrinkled crab *Xantho incisus*, pluck and gather pieces of larger red and green seaweeds. Such food is probably pulled towards the mouth by the chelae (which are often of the heavy crushing type, not noticeably adapted to an herbivorous diet) and plucked by the maxillipeds. By the time the food reaches the stomach it has been neatly chopped into small pieces, presumably by the mandibles. The gastric mills of algivores are not unlike those of carnivores. Except in the grapsids there is little extra development of ridged teeth which, by analogy with mammals, one might expect in a herbivore. Spider crabs, in fact, often completely lack the fine posterior-dorsal ridges on the lateral teeth which are found in most carnivores (Fig. 28A). The reason for the lack of development of grinding surfaces must be the relative softness of algae when compared with vascular plants. The cell walls presumably split easily under the crushing action of the knobbly teeth and, since the particles are already small, there is little need of tearing and straining.

Semiterrestrial and terrestrial vascular plant eaters have a much tougher material to cope with. Chela tips tend to be sharp with a short cutting edge since they are used to tear off pieces of vegetation rather than simply to scrape. These pieces are cut into smaller fragments by the mandibles but the main job of breaking up the food falls to the gastric mill. Here the analogy with herbivorous mammals bears some fruit, since in specialized plant eaters like the hairy mangrove crab *Ucides cordatus* from the Caribbean and the mangrove tree crab *Aratus* one finds ridged rather than knobbly teeth on the ossicles of the gastric mill (Fig. 28C). These teeth are used to grind the food and to break up the tough fibres and cell walls.

DEPOSIT FEEDERS

The main deposit feeding crabs in the sea are hermit crabs. Although capable of scavenging, and even of minor predation, their most frequent method of feeding consists of scooping up muddy or sandy deposits with the slightly spooned minor chela and sorting it with the mouthparts. This process is accomplished by a 'fluttering' of the mouthparts in which fine particles are combed into the mouth and coarse particles rejected via the respiratory stream (Greenwood, 1972). Another method of feeding in hermits is to scrape organic deposits from shells or stones using stout serrated hairs on the ends of the endopods of the 3rd maxillipeds. In marine brachyuran crabs the commonest approach to deposit feeding occurs in the algivorous scrapers with their spoon-tipped chelae. These crabs often consume large quantities of detritus. This feeding method was probably practised by the ancestors of many of the crabs which are now commensals of coral colonies. Since then, however, some of these crabs have evolved a remarkable feeding method, part deposit and part carnivorous. An example is *Trapezia* which feeds by poking and scratching the polyps of its coral host with the spiny dactyli of its walking legs (Knudsen, 1967). The coral responds by secreting mucus which the crab scrapes up with special comb-like rows of hairs on its dactyli. These food-combs are cleaned by specialized maxillipeds and the mucus, along with any entangled detritus, is ingested. Most commensal coral crabs appear to feed on coral mucus and, although Knudsen regarded the behaviour of *Trapezia* as parasitic, it is possible that the coral benefits from the removal of deposited detritus (Patton, 1974).

Pride of place in deposit feeding crabs must, however, go to the semiterrestrial ocypodids, most of which feed on tidal sand or mut flats. These crabs emerge from burrows as the tide goes down and feed by scooping the top few millimetres of substratum up to their mouthparts with their spooned bristly chelae. Here it is rapidly sorted into fine and coarse fractions, the latter emerging from the mouthparts as pseudofaecal pellets. Feeding is continuous, alternate scoops constantly being supplied by the chelae, and rejected pellets appearing one after the other. The crabs walk slowly forward as they feed and deposit the pellets to one side or behind them so as not to sample the same substratum twice. Feeding is usually conducted along the radii of a circular area, the mouth of the burrow being at the centre. After feeding has finished lines of rejected pellets radiating from the burrow like the spokes of a wheel remain behind on the sand or mud. During feeding the burrow provides a refuge from predators and, since it often descends to the water table, trips down the burrow to replenish the water used in sorting are of fairly frequent occurrence.

This method of feeding is widely present amongst the ocypodids (Macrophthalminae, Ucinae, Scopimerinae) and has been most closely studied in *Uca* (Miller, 1961). The sorting process involves differential flotation in which the food is mixed with exhaled water and agitated by the mouthparts. Heavy inorganic particles accumulate towards the bottom of the mouth field where they go to form the rejected pellets. Fine particles are combed out of suspension and fed into the mouth. On sandy substrata where much of the organic matter is attached to the sand grains this relatively simple process is modified to allow some cleaning of the grains before they settle out of suspension. This is achieved by the development of spoon-tipped hairs (Fig. 28E) mostly on the inside edges of the 2nd maxillipeds. The sand grains are held by these hairs and swept across the outer faces of the 1st maxillipeds where short stiff bristles occur. This brushing action dislodges organic particles which can then be separated from the sand by flotation. Spoon-tipped hairs occur in several other ocypodids besides *Uca* and are always associated with sandy substrata; generally speaking the coarser the sand, the better developed the spoon-tips.

Much of the organic matter gathered by *Uca*, particularly in mangrove or salt marsh environments, is detritus derived from vascular plants. This material, although already quite finely divided, requires grinding and the teeth of the gastric mill, transversely ridged for this purpose (Fig. 28D), resemble those of specialized vascular plant eaters.

SUSPENSION FEEDERS

This specialized feeding method is not uncommon in anomurans, being found among porcelain crabs, mole crabs and in some hermit crabs. In all these forms setose appendages are used to collect small particles from the surrounding water. In porcelain crabs long plumose setae are developed on the ends of the endopods of the 3rd maxillipeds. These form a pair of scoop nets, one on either side, which are alternately swept through the water, folded and cleaned by the other mouthparts (Nicol, 1932). If a water current is present the maxilliped net may be cast stationary across it for a few seconds before being folded and cleaned. A similar situation occurs in the New Zealand hermit crab *Stratiotus setosus* except that here the 2nd antennae form the filtering nets (Greenwood, 1972). These long antennae, fringed on either side with plumose setae, are swept from side to side, turning through 180° at the end of each sweep so as always to face the direction of motion. Each antenna, after three or four sweeps, is cleaned by being drawn through the maxillipeds. These bear delicate plumed hairs with which to brush off the particles. Antennal filtering is also used by some mole crabs (Fig. 4B) but here the feeding current is produced not by moving the antennae but by spreading them in the path of the backwash of a wave.

Suspension feeding is hardly ever found in brachyuran crabs. The exceptions include the commensal coral gall crabs and some of the pea crabs referred to in the last chapter. In coral gall crabs, which are said to feed chiefly on phytoplankton, both the mandibles and the ossicles of the gastric mill are much reduced, the latter being setose rather than toothed; the pyloric filtering apparatus is also much simplified (Potts, 1915).

CRABS AS PREY

Despite their cryptic habits, tough armour and painful defence mechanisms, crabs are eaten by numerous predators. Apart from man, discussed in Chapter 11, and other crabs, described above, the most important predators are octopuses, fish, birds and mammals. Octopuses simply envelop crabs using the web of skin between the arms. They are then pressed to the jaws and bitten into pieces. Fish are voracious crab eaters both in the sea and in fresh water. Rays, wrasse, trout, the common eel *Anguilla* and the moray eel *Gymnothorax* have all been recorded as eating crabs. The latter even leaps out of the water to catch grapsids (Chave and Randall, 1971). Scavenging birds such as herring gulls or crows eat crabs if they find them. In India crows have been recorded as eating potamids, having first pulled them out of their burrows by their legs, shaken them onto their backs and pecked them on the underside until dead (Wagle, 1923). Birds are important predators of crabs which are active by day. These include most of the deposit-feeding ocypodids and many swamp-dwelling grapsids. Crane (1941) mentioned herons, sandpipers, curlews, herring gulls, grackles and egrets as being predators of *Uca* and also described the rapid retreat into the burrow which occurs in response to a bird flying within 7·5 m overhead (or to an aeroplane at 60 m). Several mammals are specialized crab eaters; there are, for instance, crab-eating seals and crab-eating racoons. Durrell (1953) experienced difficulty in feeding a specimen of the African giant water-shrew *Potamogale* until he tried living fresh water crabs; these were consumed with great relish at a rate of 20–25 per day.

7   Social behaviour

Much of the social behaviour of crabs would, if it occurred in human societies, be described as unfriendly. Crabs often avoid meeting each other; if they do meet they will probably threaten each other, they may fight, and eventually one will withdraw, having 'lost' the encounter. Very occasionally losers suffer more than loss of face: loss of limb and loss of life are not unknown and in such cases the victor will generally consume the spoils of its conquest. Social behaviour in the biological context, however, does not mean being nice to one's neighbours; rather it means acting or reacting to members of one's own species such that the order in the population is increased. At its simplest, such order may take the form of non-random dispersion, i.e. an aggregated or an even distribution; some control of population density also ranks as an increase in order. In complex cooperative societies a host of other factors may be controlled. All increases in order have to be paid for by an input of energy. Thus the advantage of each increase in order is carefully weighed by natural selection against the particular energy cost of the social behaviour which brings it about.

Crab societies tend to be competitive rather than cooperative. In most cases groups of individuals are organized into hierarchies in which each member learns its place. Alternatively, instead of competing for status in a hierarchy and thus directly defending their right to existence, individuals may transfer their interest from 'person' to 'property' and uphold their right to exist by defending a territory. Behaviour occurring during hierarchical and territorial encounters is usually termed agonistic. This term embraces both aggressive and defensive behaviour and includes threatening, fighting, submission and flight. It is an advantage to avoid injury to participants in such encounters and crabs, like many other animals, usually use signals rather than blows to sort out their differences.

The particular increases in order that crab societies gain probably include spacing out of the population and thus imposing a ceiling on population density. Such control might be important in ensuring an adequate supply of resources to all individuals, but the alternative hypothesis—that the population is limited directly by resources and/or predation—cannot be ruled out. A competitive social organization, however, conveys other advantages, at least to the successful participants. Individuals high in a hierarchy have important privileges: they can wander freely wherever they like, they can obtain for themselves the pick of the available food and it is likely that high status males can mate with more females than their rivals and thus promote their own genes. In the Mediterranean hermit crab *Dardanus arrosor* high status crabs do not allow low status crabs to carry the protective symbiotic anemone *Calliactis*; they take all the available anemones for themselves (Mainardi and Rossi, 1969). Such a society can survive hard times since it ensures that, whatever the state of the food supply, some individuals at least are fit and well fed and have a good chance of survival. Most of these advantages also accrue to a territorial society since territory is won by competition and, apart from being a resource in itself, has special sexual rights associated with its ownership.

Not all crab social behaviour is agonistic. The latter half of this chapter is given over to describing courtship and the few examples of communal behaviour which occur in crabs.

HIERARCHIES

A considerable amount of research has been carried out on agonistic behaviour in crabs and, although most of it has concentrated on advanced territorial forms, in particular on *Uca*, there still remains a moderate accumulation of knowledge on more conventional crabs. A variety of techniques have been used to study agonistic behaviour: observing groups of crabs in aquaria and analysing their interactions, analysing reactions to the presentation of models and matching groups of known crabs to assess the importance of such factors as size, sex and experience.

Encounter initiation and avoidance

Encounters are initiated between two crabs when one or both of them ceases to move and behave at random with relation to the other. The distance at which one crab reacts to the presence of another is called its individual distance, but this distance varies between individuals and within a single individual. One source of variation is the activity rhythm; crabs are more reactive during their active periods than during rest. Another source of variation is past experience: Hazlett (1975) found that in groups of hermit crabs maintained at relatively high population densities individual distance was less than in groups kept at relatively low density. One result was that high density crabs 'won' encounters with low density crabs more frequently than expected by chance. Hazlett explained this result by reference to the communicatory effect of 'doing nothing'. At a distance at which the low density crab reacted, the high density crab, its individual distance being smaller, did nothing. This lack of response, in particular a lack of withdrawal or of a defensive posture when faced with an approach, is liable to sow doubt in the mind of the low density crab and tip the balance slightly in favour of the other. A third source of variation in individual distance is the intensity of the stimulus given by the other crab. Hazlett (1975) found that a fast approach (attack) was reacted to by a Florida hermit crab *Clibanarius tricolor* at about 180 mm while for reactions to displays involving the legs and chelae the crabs needed to be much closer, about 14 mm apart. In other species reactions may occur at greater distances; responses to approach in *Callinectes* occur up to 30 cm away although 10 cm is the most usual response distance (Jackowski, 1974). In the mangrove crab *Goniopsis* I have observed reactions to approach occurring at a distance of between 30 and 100 cm. At less than 30 cm displays involving the legs and chelae may take place (Warner, 1970).

In the majority of encounters approach by one crab elicits withdrawal by the other; face to face encounters in which agonistic signals are exchanged are thus avoided. Avoidance is probably usually controlled by size, the larger crab advancing and the smaller retreating, but the relative development of the chelae and the physiological state of the participants may also play some part. Approach–withdrawal encounters are always won by the initiator since this is the crab that approaches; longer encounters that involve agonistic signals are also usually won by the initiator. Approaching and initiating encounters is much more commonly observed in larger crabs and consequently one would expect initiators normally to win (Lobb, 1972; Rubenstein and Hazlett, 1974; see also Hazlett, 1968b; Vannini and Sardini, 1971).

Agonistic signals

If an approach does not elicit a retreat by the other crab, then signals may be exchanged. These consist mainly of positions or movements by the legs and chelae. The raising of one or more walking legs is very common and the leg raised position so achieved may be held for a time. In the frontal approach commonly used by hermit crabs and spider crabs a pair of legs may be raised together to give the recipient a dramatic cross shaped display (Fig. 29A) (Hazlett, 1972a, b). In crabs which approach sideways the leg raise is usually directed towards the other, this occurs in the European hairy crab *Pilumnus hirtellus* and in the mangrove crab *Goniopsis* (Lobb, 1972; Warner, 1970). Judging from the reactions of recipients of the leg raise signal, it communicates the threat of attack. In *Pilumnus* and *Goniopsis*, advance–leg raise–advance is a common sequence of acts performed by a single individual. Lobb (1972) has suggested that the signal may have arisen by evolution from an exploratory movement performed as the prelude to locomotion. All communicatory signals must initially have evolved from non-communicatory acts and in the process, called ritualization, they become distinct and stereotyped such that they can be easily recognized and interpreted by the recipient (Huxley, 1966).

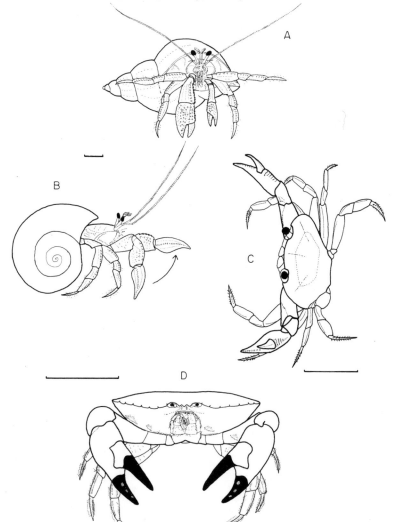

Fig. 29 Agonistic postures. A, front view of a hermit crab in a double leg-raise posture with chelae presented. B, side view of chelae extension in a hermit crab. C, view from above of the chelae outstretched posture in the Trinidadian fresh water crab *Kingsleya garmani*. D, front view of chelae extended in *Cancer pagurus*. C and D traced from photographs. Scale, A and B = 10 mm; C = 50 mm; D = 100 mm.

Leg raises in hermit crabs seem in general to be more stereotyped than in brachyuran crabs and Hazlett (1972b), by studying the reactions of crabs to models, has shown that in the frontal double leg raise of a Florida hermit *Calcinus tibicen* six features of the display are important for its correct interpretation. These features (1–6) are as follows: the raised legs on either side should form a line (1) which should be horizontal (2). The body forms an enlarged portion (3) which should be near the centre (4). White blotches (5) should be on the tips of the outstretched legs (6). Departure from any of these six features reduced the effectiveness of the model. The threatening effect of the model could be increased, however, by increasing the length of the model's outstretched legs. In real hermit crabs, leg length indicates size and in natural double leg raises it may be size that is being signalled. Another feature which can be signalled is the mood of the signaller. In leg raise displays and in those involving the chelipeds an increase in apparent size, and thus an increase in threatening effect, can be achieved by the crab raising itself up high on the tips of its legs (Hazlett, 1968a).

Cheliped displays are used in encounters which proceed beyond the leg raise stage. It is usually possible to distinguish three different signals transmitted by the chelae. Simplest is a submissive posture in which the chelae are held tightly against the front of the body, this posture is often combined with a low body position (decreasing apparent size) and with retreat. It has been observed in the hairy crab *Pilumnus* (Lobb, 1972) and similar behaviour is recorded for the blue crab *Callinectes* (Jackowski, 1974) and for the hermit crab *Pagurus* (Hazlett, 1966). The other two signals transmitted by the chelae are both threatening. Chela presentation in hermit crabs involves bringing the chelae forwards into a position in which the outer faces are displayed, the tips pointing directly down (Hazlett, 1966) (Figs. 29A, B). Threat is increased by chela extension in which the chelae are moved from presentation into a horizontal position with the tips pointing forwards (Fig. 29B). Two levels of threat can also be signalled by the chelae of brachyuran crabs (for reviews see Schöne, 1968; Wright, 1968). The lower level of threat in most brachyurans is shown by the chelae extended posture in which the chelae are moved out from the body such that the slightly opened fingers point forwards (Fig. 29D). The higher level is signalled by the outstretched posture in which the chelae are spread as widely as possible (Fig. 29C). In these displays the chelipeds are held more or less horizontal and are moved laterally (lateral merus displays—Wright, 1968). The cheliped displays of grapsid and some ocypodid crabs, however, depart from this typical brachyuran pattern and were called chela forward displays by Wright (1968). The lower level of threat in these crabs is signalled by a shield posture in which the chelae are held in front pointing downwards (frontispiece) (Warner, 1970). The higher level of threat is signalled in shield posturing crabs by various forms of mobile display. In the mangrove crabs *Goniopsis* and *Aratus* the chelae circle upwards and outwards, through the chelae outstretched position, down and back up into the original shield position (Warner, 1970). In *Aratus* the display is a smooth slow wave, but in the gaudily coloured *Goniopsis* it is a rapid movement, the brilliant red and white chelae flashing through the air above the glossy black body. The extent of outward circling in this display varies amongst the grapsids; in some, for instance the rock crab *Grapsus*, there is hardly any circling, the chelae simply being raised and then struck down again.

Chela presentation in hermit crabs and the shield position in grapsids and ocypodids look very much alike. Both groups often feed by scraping up material from the substratum and it seems not unlikely that, in both cases, the signal has evolved from the position used during feeding. Lateral merus displays, however, seem likely to have had antecedents which were more directly concerned with threat. Before grasping with both chelae the chelipeds must be spread wide and opened. These movements, and the position attained, are both so clearly attack intentions that it would be surprising if they had not evolved communicatory functions. That they do have such functions is evident from the behaviour of recipients. Indeed, this posture is such an obvious signal that it is widely used in interspecific encounters and against predators. The circling displays of grapsids may have evolved from the movements necessary in changing from the shield position to chelae outstretched.

The exchange of agonistic signals and associated advances or retreats is usually sufficient to sort out the differences between a pair of contestants. But visual signals may not be enough in evenly matched pairs and in these cases tactile signals may be employed. Touching the other crab with a walking leg or the tip of a chela (Vannini and Sardini, 1971; Lobb, 1972) is quite common and may be a gentle tactile signal. More forceful signals are provided by fighting. This activity takes many forms: *Goniopsis* push against each other using the outer faces of the chelae in a shield position; *Aratus* pushes against the opponent with interlocked chelae in the outstretched position (Warner, 1970). *Pilumnus* (Lobb, 1972) and the Italian river crab *Potamon fluviatile* (Vannini and Sardini, 1971) use both pushing and grasping, and striking with the tips of the chelae is seen in *Potamon, Callinectes* (Jackowski, 1974) and *Goniopsis*. Fighting in hermit crabs is unusual in that it does not generally involve contact between the bodies of the combatants. Shell fighting (Hazlett, 1966) is one of the commonest forms and takes place between individuals in poorly matched shells. Hermits are constantly on the look-out for a larger shell and if a crab (the attacker) finds such a shell occupied by a smaller individual then this shell is seized, manoeuvred and subjected to a series of raps delivered by the attacker's shell. This treatment results in the defending crab vacating its shell which is thus freed for occupation by the attacker. The defender usually ends up in the attacker's original smaller shell. According to Schöne (1968) fighting in brachyuran crabs is more formalized in grapsids and ocypodids than in most aquatic crabs and 'wild fights' are more liable to occur in the latter. Injury to either contestant is rare even in wild fighting. Fights end when one crab retreats, often adopting a submissive posture. In *Potamon* fights sometimes end in a manner reminiscent of human wrestling (Vannini and Sardini, 1971). The victor is the crab which succeeds in turning its opponent over onto its back, a feat which it accomplishes by twisting one of its opponent's chelae. Once overturned the vanquished crab is immediately released and the victor does not pursue its advantage; it stands nearby threatening while the loser rights itself and scrambles away.

Factors affecting status

The type of agonistic behaviour described above maintains hierarchies in which status is determined largely by size. Other factors, however, also affect status and in some species sex is the most important of these. Obvious structural differences between male and female crabs are that males are frequently larger than females and their chelae are usually larger than those of equal sized females (Fig. 32). Thus high ranking individuals tend to be male and even where females are amongst the largest crabs in a group males often dominate because of their larger chelae. The effect of chela size on status has been demonstrated in hermit crabs where the threatening effect of a model in the chela presentation position was greatly increased by the addition of supernormal chelae (Hazlett, 1969).

The importance of the chelae is also shown by comparisons between the behaviour of species which differ in the extent of the sexual dimorphism of their chelipeds. In *Goniopsis* the chelae of males are only slightly larger than those of equal sized females, but in *Aratus* the male chelae are much larger than those of females (Warner, 1970). *Goniopsis* females are often involved in agonistic behaviour and females may rank higher than similar sized males, in *Aratus* however, the females take little part in agonistic encounters and almost always behave in a subordinate fashion (see below). A situation similar to that in *Goniopsis* is found in *Pilumnus* where there is very little sexual dimorphism of cheliped size: females behave agonistically and may dominate (Lobb, 1972). Similar to *Aratus* are many of the territorial ocypodid crabs such as *Uca* and *Macrophthalmus* where males with their large chelae put far more effort into the maintenance of order in the population than do the females. Sexual dimorphism of cheliped size has two effects on the organization of populations. First, it creates two social classes in which role specialization can occur: males can maintain order by agonistic behaviour while females can feed and reproduce without being constantly involved in fights. Second, sexual dimorphism allows easy recognition of the opposite sex and this probably facilitates both the maintenance of a two-tier society and courtship (see below). Once large chelipeds become associated with courtship the extent of sexual dimorphism is likely to increase since sexual selection may take place. This is limited, however, by the other uses of the chelipeds. Where these limbs are used in predatory behaviour it may not be possible either for the males to develop huge chelae, since these might be too unwieldly for catching fast moving prey, or for females to develop very small chelae, since these might not be able to deal with the prey at all. Where the chelae are used merely to gather in the surroundings, however, it may not matter what size they are, and thus one finds the highest degree of sexual dimorphism amongst deposit feeding ocypodids, in herbivorous xanthids and in the omnivorous 'gathering' spider crabs. The most elegant solution to the problem is found in *Uca*: one type of chela is developed for signalling and another type for feeding. The result is the enormous status symbol of the male which must be close in size to its physical limit (Fig. 30).

Aggressiveness is another factor which helps to determine rank in a hierarchy. The behaviour of high ranking crabs contains more aggressive components (advance, threat, attack) than does the behaviour of lower ranking crabs and this behaviour is particularly prevalent in the dominant crab at the top of a hierarchy. Correlations between behaviour and rank have been demonstrated in *Potamon* by Vannini and Sardini (1971) and in *Pilumnus* by Lobb (1972). In *Potamon* dominant individuals grasped and fought far more frequently than did subordinates (all ranks beneath the dominant are grouped as subordinates). In *Pilumnus* dominants tended to advance with leg stretching, chelae outstretched postures were often adopted and fighting sometimes ensued. Subordinates on the other hand tended to withdraw with chelae folded in submission. Aggressive behaviour is usually correlated with size, producing a typical size determined hierarchy, but this is not always the case. In groups of juvenile *Potamon* Vannini and Sardini (1971) found that rank was correlated with size, but in adults there was no significant correlation. Similar, but less extreme, situations have been observed in other species where the winners of fights or the dominants of groups are usually larger—but not always.

Probably many factors contribute towards the aggressiveness of a crab. One factor is past experience (see below); another appears to be sex. Vannini and Sardini (1971) found that the incidence of grasping and fighting was higher in dominant males than in dominant females and that in male hierarchies there was greater separation between ranks one and two than in female hierarchies. In single-sex groups of a Mediterranean hermit crab *Diogenes pugilator* the largest is dominant, but in male–female pairs outside the breeding season the male always dominates regardless of size (Rossi, 1971). Initiators of encounters tend to win, but Lobb (1972) found that in male–female agonistic encounters in *Pilumnus*, male initiators lost 8 per cent while female initiators lost 23 per cent; in single-sex encounters initiators lost 10 per cent in both sexes. These observations suggest that female crabs may be less aggressive than males.

Maintenance of hierarchies — learning

There are two possible ways of maintaining a hierarchy: rank may be established *de nouveau* at every encounter or some memory of relative rank can be retained from one encounter to the next. The latter method carries the greater advantage since early recognition of rank should reduce the time spent in agonistic interactions. As hierarchies became older individuals would behave in ways which were increasingly appropriate to their ranks: agonistic encounters would become less frequent and shorter. Such a reduction in both number and violence of encounters has been observed by Lobb (1972) in *Pilumnus* and by Jackowski (1974) in *Callinectes*, but not by Vannini and Sardini (1971) in *Potamon*. Thus, although some species of crab appear to be able to learn their ranks in a hierarchy, others may lack this ability.

Recognition of rank can take two forms, one way is to be able to recognize individuals and to remember the outcome of previous encounters. Another method is to learn a pattern of behaviour appropriate to one's rank; a dominant crab might learn aggressive behaviour and a low status crab might learn submission. Lobb (1972) has investigated the effect of transferring *Pilumnus* individuals from established hierarchies, where they had learnt to recognize their ranks, into other established hierarchies where they were strangers. Dominant individuals transferred to hierarchies in which there were larger resident dominants behaved, to begin with, in typical dominant fashion as if they were still in their own hierarchies. Such inappropriately aggressive behaviour got these individuals into trouble — considerable increases in fighting were observed — but it also gained them slightly higher status than that predicted on size alone. Hierarchies to which a stranger had been added took up to a week to settle down; the stranger gradually learnt to accept its new rank and was accepted as such by the other individuals. When subordinates were transferred to hierarchies of smaller animals a similar situation occurred in that these crabs ended up with lower status than expected on the basis of size; their learnt subordinate behaviour apparently persisted to their disadvantage in the new group. Most interesting of all was an experiment in which an original dominant *Pilumnus* was repeatedly transferred from its own hierarchy to another in which it had a subordinate rank and back to its own again. It was observed that the time taken by this individual to adjust its behaviour following transference decreased with repeated transference, indicating that it had learnt, and could simultaneously retain memory of, its position in both hierarchies. It was shown that these memories lasted for up to two weeks. These results indicate that although the learning of appropriate behavioural sequences may be the main way of learning rank, some measure of individual recognition may also be important.

Hierarchies in nature

Memory of relative rank is most useful where individuals are not widely ranging and meet each other reasonably frequently. Jackowski (1974) suggested that *Callinectes* in the wild is a wide-ranging species and so unlikely to form stable hierarchies. *Carcinus* also goes in for fairly extensive movements (Edwards, 1958). Other species, however, may remain in the same area for considerable lengths of time. Marking and recapture of the mangrove crabs *Goniopsis* and *Aratus* showed that individuals stayed in the same general area for periods of several weeks or months (Warner, 1970). The same is broadly true of *Pilumnus* (Lobb, 1972). In a large Caribbean spider crab *Mithrax spinosissimus*, Hazlett and Rittschof (1975) have demonstrated the existence of home ranges; in males the mean maximum dimension of the home range was 57·5 m, but individuals usually had a centre of activity and often moved very little distance from day to day. It is likely that in populations of most species of fairly slow-moving non-territorial crab, individuals occur in loosely overlapping home ranges and probably do not move very far within their ranges from day to day. Thus reasonably stable hierarchical social organizations almost certainly exist in many species of crab in the natural environment.

TERRITORY

A territorial crab defends a space around its burrow. This space can vary in size from a few centimetres to more than a metre across, depending on the size and habit of the species. Such territories may be held by individuals for a number of weeks, a few days or for no more than an hour or two over a single low tide period, a different burrow being defended the following day. Most territorial crabs are ocypodids, familiar examples being fiddler crabs, *Uca*, and ghost crabs, *Ocypode*, but other burrowing crabs such as some grapsids and gecarcinids may also hold territories. Almost all known territorial crabs are semiterrestrial forms.

Territorial behaviour serves at least four functions. First, the burrow is a shelter providing protection from predators and a retreat from sun and tide. Each individual needs one and the burrow is therefore worthy of defence. Second, many territorial crabs are deposit feeders and use their territories as private pastures. Third, a territory provides a site for courtship; receptive females are attracted to the territory and copulation may take place there. Fourth, territories may be used as prizes in inter-individual contests, usually between males. As in hierarchical crabs, status is important and territory ownership appears to symbolize status.

The relative importance of these four functions varies between species. In lower shore crabs it appears that the burrow is less important as a shelter, probably owing to the proximity of the sea (Ono, 1965); such crabs may defend a particular burrow for no more than a few minutes. In species which do not feed in the immediate vicinity of their burrows the territory is unimportant as a feeding area; *Ocypode* falls into this category. The distinction between courtship and competition is difficult to draw. In the case of *Uca*, some workers concluded that territorial behaviour is entirely competitive between rival males. In contrast, others decided that courtship is the only function. Crane (1975) gave a variety of functions for inter-male, territorial combat and concluded that the status acquired was closely connected with the ability to court. In this section behaviour which appears to defend the territory, for whatever reason, is described. Courtship behaviour, which often takes place within territories, is described in the next section.

The occurrence of territorial behaviour

The daily behaviour of many intertidal burrowing crabs proceeds through a series of phases (Chapter 4). Emergence following the ebbing of the tide leads to burrow repair and feeding. In most crabs which feed around the mouths of their burrows, some territorial behaviour may occur during feeding. Neighbours which approach too closely may be warned off by threatening postures. This type of behaviour is not restricted to males, even female *Uca* with their tiny chelae are capable of threat postures (Crane, 1975). In the larger males, however, this maintenance phase sooner or later gives way to social phases in which some males defend territories while others wander about challenging them. Individual male *Uca* appear to pass through a wandering phase before developing true territorial behaviour (Crane, 1958) but at any one time both wanderers and territory holders may be found. This results from the fact that the daily phase sequence is superimposed on a longer term rhythm in which a single phase may dominate a crab's life for several days in a row (Chapter 4). Where there may be a generalized synchrony of particular phases within a population, there is sufficient individual variation for crabs in all phases to be present simultaneously.

Contests for territory involving both threat postures and more or less ritualized fighting takes place between burrow holders and wanderers and between neighbouring burrow holders. Victory in these contests depends both on size and on burrow ownership (Griffin, 1968), an owner having an advantage over a trespasser. Wanderers, of course, are always trespassers but losing does not normally seem to worry them and they continue to pick fights with burrow owners as they wander through the population (but see below in the case of *Uca*). If a wanderer happens to be successful in evicting a burrow owner, he may briefly defend his prize, but usually soon wanders off again to pick another fight. Crane (1975) suggested that in *Uca*, contests many serve to stimulate territoriality and courtship: behaviour during the aggressive wandering phase may stimulate the onset of the territorial and display phases, while for crabs already in these phases contests may serve to maintain their behaviour. Thus, as in hierarchical crabs where dominant status is correlated with aggressiveness, in territorial crabs the status of territory ownership is won through aggressive behaviour.

Threat postures and fighting in territorial crabs are often similar to those of hierarchical crabs. Fighting, however, may be more highly ritualized and extra components often appear. In *Dotilla* Tweedie (1950) described a typical encounter:

If ... a wandering male approaches the burrow ... its owner immediately engages in a wrestling or grappling contest with the intruder, the chelipeds of both being extended at full length. These contests are quite harmless and I do not think that the crabs are capable of inflicting injury on each other with their weak spoon-like claws. Soon, however, one, usually the intruder, gives ground and disengages, whereupon the victor executes a rather absurd looking dance of triumph, bouncing up and down on its long legs and drumming on the sand with his chelae.

In the soldier crab *Mictyris* rivals do not touch but posture in front of one another on extended legs with chelipeds stretched vertically and some walking legs stretched laterally and vibrating (Cameron, 1966). In *Macrophthalmus*, antagonists measure up to each other with chelae outstretched and indulge in mutual tapping of the tips (Griffin, 1968). In the land crab *Cardisoma* a burrow owner may defend his property by facing away from his opponent and adopting a chelae outstretched posture (Wright, 1968). Facing towards the intruder with chelae outstretched often leads to a fight but this reversed orientation appears to inhibit fighting.

The most studied, and probably the most complex, territorial behaviour is that of *Uca*. Taking all 62 species, Crane (1975) has described 14 threat postures or motions, 16 methods of probably social sound production, 13 components of combat — with 84 structures on the large chela of the male devoted to combat — and 18 components of waving display. Threat, combat and waving are sufficiently distinct to be dealt with separately.

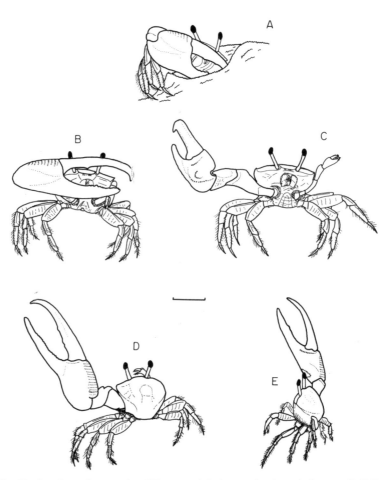

Fig. 30   Tracings from photographs of *Uca rapax* (♂). A, emerging from the burrow; B, C, D and E, display. C shows a sideways kick and D shows a lefthanded crab, populations are usually 50 per cent lefthanded. Scale = 10 mm.

Waving

Waving in *Uca* is only performed by territorial display-phase males. Such males often select a prominent burrow position towards the upper tidal limits of the population. Their coloration usually becomes more vivid than that of maintenance-phase crabs, polished white is not uncommon and red, yellow, orange, pink, blue and green occur in various species.

Standing conspicuously at the mouths of their burrows these males wave by alternate extension and flexion of the major cheliped. The wave takes many forms, each species having a characteristic wave pattern. In some species the cheliped is extended laterally, then raised and then flexed, the tip having described a circular path. In others the chela may be raised vertically as the limb is extended and may perform several circling movements before being flexed. The simplest waves are found in the primitive narrow-fronted species of *Uca* (Crane, 1957) and consist of a vertical raising and lowering of the chela, often without extension. Each wave may take less than a second, or, in some species, may last for ten or more seconds. I have watched *Uca rapax* waving in Jamaica (Fig. 30) and here the chela was extended in a series of jerks, five or six at about one second intervals being required for full extension. The walking legs were also progressively extended in synchrony with the jerks. Maximum extension was held for a second or so, then the crab would suddenly collapse into a flexed crouched position ready for the next wave.

Waving does not always require external stimulation and may take place when no other crabs, either male or female, are in sight. More commonly, however, displaying males have a clear sight of each other and they may even be crowded together, each territory being little more than standing room at the mouth of the burrow. The sight of other waving males probably helps to stimulate waving and amongst the particular events known to stimulate waving is the approach of another male (Crane, 1958). In this case waving is directed as a threatening display at a rival and is interpreted as such by non-aggressive wanderers and maintenance-phase males which avoid the territories of waving individuals. Non-receptive females ignore waving males or walk past them on extended legs, their threatening posture signalling lack of sexual interest (Crane, 1975). Waving may, therefore, be regarded as an advertisement of status and in this respect is at once a challenge to rivals, an attractive stimulant to receptive females and something to be avoided by maintenance-phase crabs.

Crabs other than *Uca* are known to wave. The circling displays of hierarchical grapsids are non-territorial waves performed with both chelae. In this case, however, the display is always directed towards another crab and not broadcast to the population at large. In other territorial ocypodids waving may approach more closely to the situation in *Uca*. Griffin (1968) described waving with both chelae in burrow holding males of *Heloecius cordiformis* and *Macrophthalmus latifrons*, both from eastern Australia and Tasmania. From his description it is clear that display may be directed at a particular individual (usually female), but often is not so directed. Griffin interpreted waving as courtship and while it clearly functions in this capacity it may also serve to defend territory from rivals.

Threat

Threat in *Uca* occurs in both maintenance- and social-phase crabs, but is much commoner and much better developed in the latter. Threatening postures are adopted by display-phase males in response to an intruder, or may be adopted by an approaching intruder. A common form is the raised-carpus in which the MC joint of the major chela is raised slightly from the resting position (Crane, 1958, 1975). Threat is intensified by the down-point in which the MC joint is further raised, the tip of the chela pointing down and the dactylus often opened. This posture is reminiscent of the shield position of hierarchical grapsids and, as in these crabs, may lead to combat. Other burrow defence postures used by *Uca* include the reversed chelae outstretched, described for *Cardisoma* above, and an odd series of postures described by Crane (1975) in which a burrow holder retreats into his burrow but leaves his major chela sticking out, either projecting or lying flat on the ground. This behaviour is perhaps analogous to that of the human householder who, in preference to time-consuming argument, shuts the door firmly in the face of the broom salesman!

In *Uca* and other crabs threatening sounds are often produced in the burrow in response to an intruder. Sounds include stridulation by rubbing the chela against the carapace or rubbing the walking legs together, and drumming with the major chela against the carapace or ground. The loudest sound producer is the ghost crab *Ocypode* which both stridulates and raps on the sand (p. 50). Stridulation in ghost crabs can be elicited by scratching the sand outside a burrow and in nature probably signals occupancy and warns off trespassers. Hughes (1966) described stridulation in east African *O. ceratophthalmus* as 'a series of three to seven short rasping sounds followed by a rapid rattle . . . Krr—Krr—Krr—Krr—Kirri Krr'. Stridulation and rapping may be heard by neighbours and may stimulate responses producing so called chorusing. Here each crab is proclaiming his ownership of a burrow, and through such behaviour, status and reproductive readiness may be maintained.

Combat

As in other crabs the majority of *Uca* encounters end without combat: one or both crabs take avoiding action or retreat in response to the threat of the opponent. When combat does take place it only occurs between neighbouring display-phase males or between a display-phase male and an aggressive wanderer. Combat in *Uca* is remarkable for its gentleness and high degree of ritualization (Crane, 1967; 1975). Antagonists measure up to one another and by a series of mutual rubs, pushes, taps, slides and interlockings of their major chelae they feel each others' tubercles and ridges. Usually a single bout includes only one or two of these components and lasts only a few seconds, but bouts of up to three minutes have been recorded (Crane, 1967). A typical bout was described by Crane (1975):

An instigator, whether wanderer or neighbour, approaches a burrow holder. A rub by one or both crabs, outer manus against outer manus, usually follows. Next the instigator sometimes holds perfectly still while his opponent slowly eases his chela into the actor's slide position; the two crabs may then reverse the role, the shift being accomplished slowly, without fumbling, and with the apparent cooperation of the crabs. In a few moments they may progress to a similar alternation of heel-and-ridging . . . when the actor breaks off, both crabs move apart and resume their pre-encounter activities.

Combat in *Uca* is not always gentle, however, and particularly in contests between a burrow holder and a wanderer, forceful components such as 'grips, flings and upsets' may occur (Crane, 1967). Unlike the situation in other crabs in most *Uca* combats the winner is not obvious. Occasionally, however, there is some alteration in the behaviour of one of the crabs: a reduction in aggressiveness in a wanderer or delay in the resumption of waving in a burrow holder, indicating a loser. Crane observed this result in about 25 per cent of combats in *Uca rapax*. As in other crabs, size and burrow ownership appear to increase a fiddler crab's chances of winning.

The frequent lack of a clear winner makes the function of combat in *Uca* more obscure than in other crabs where status is clearly the object. A likely function may be the stimulation and maintenance of territorial status and hence the ability to court. Combat may thus confirm the status of both contestants. In my opinion many human activities have similar functions; cocktail and stag parties for instance are often competitive but usually have no clear winners. Similarly many sports in which a winner can be discerned, provided one knows the rules, are nevertheless rewarding to the losers: it is sufficient merely to have taken part. It is possible that both of a pair of fiddler crabs gain, or at least maintain, status as a result of combat and thus they may prolong their display phases and the time that each has available for courtship. As in the human activities noted above observation suggests that combat is a rewarding occupation (Crane, 1967): 'Combat appears often to be in progress for its own sake'; 'these encounters give the strong impression that they provide one or both crabs with satisfactions that are not concerned in direct goals'; and 'occasionally a male even abandons an advanced courtship, attracted by a combat between two other males' (this last bears a startling resemblance to a stag party). However, the fact that occasionally a winner can be detected indicates that, as well as confirming status, combat may also function to demote crabs that are not in the right physiological state.

Other social activities

Apart from postures, movements, combat and sounds, there is evidence that certain structures built by crabs have social significance. In particular, the pyramids built by several species of *Ocypode* (Linsenmair, 1967; Jones, 1972; Lighter, 1974) and the porches built by some *Uca* species (Crane, 1941; 1975). The structures are only built outside the burrows of adult males and in *Uca* by display-phase males only. They probably signal the status of the owner and, like the neighbour's garden gnomes or his new car, sometimes arouse aggression in his rivals. The filling in of a neighbour's burrow and the flattening of his pyramid have been reported in *Ocypode*, and *Uca* is also occasionally guilty of pushing over a rival's porch. Such capricious behaviour is not uncommon in territorial crabs (Crane, 1975). In *Uca*, for instance, a burrow holder may retreat into his burrow leaving his chela sticking out as a threat, only to have it stamped on by an aggressive wanderer. A defending *Uca* may be pushed down his own burrow and sealed in. In contrast, in the New Zealand grapsid *Helice crassa* a resting burrow holder may be dug up and forced to defend himself (Beer, 1959). While a defending *Uca* is busy in combat a squatter may pop down his burrow and later must be evicted. This type of behaviour is difficult to interpret: it probably serves to test, stimulate and maintain status.

COURTSHIP

To achieve successful reproduction it is essential to have some method for bringing together sexually receptive females and sexually capable males. Agonistic behaviour would appear to oppose any such method. In fact agonistic behaviour itself is often used as a basis for courtship, the change being in the interpretation of agonistic signals by sexually capable crabs. Aggressive signals by males, interpreted as threatening by other males and by non-receptive females, are not so interpreted by receptive females. Such females react either by not retreating or by approaching the displaying male. This is excellent provided that the male also knows what is going on; he must be able to distinguish a receptive female from an aggressive male. Several factors enable him to do this. First, male and female morphology may differ (e.g. cheliped size) allowing the recognition of sex; second, anomalous behaviour (not retreating) allows the recognition of receptiveness; and third, in many aquatic crabs olfactory signals or pheromones are released by receptive females.

Aquatic crabs

Pheromones are probably of great importance in aquatic crabs. Their existence was first demonstrated in an Indo-Pacific swimming crab

Portunus sanguinolentus by Ryan (1966) who showed that the signal was released in the urine. Searching behaviour is elicited in males when water in which a receptive female has been kept is introduced to them (Rajula *et al.*, 1973; Eales, 1974). Several workers have claimed to have identified the sex pheromone— as the moulting hormone, crustecdysone (Kittredge *et al.*, 1971) and as 5-hydroxy tryptamine (5-HT) (Rajula *et al.*, 1973)— but considerable difficulty attaches to the idea of a sex pheromone common to all crabs; one can imagine the confusion caused amongst males by such a thing! Eales (1974) showed that the sex pheromones of *Carcinus* and the European *Macropipus holsatus* were different and this is probably the usual case. The searching behaviour elicited by crustec-dysone and 5-HT may, at least partly, be a search for food rather than for a mate. The involvement of these two substances in sexual behaviour probably arises because many crabs mate just after the female has moulted; the moulting hormone, at least, might be expected to escape in small quantities during the moult. However, Atema and Engstrom (1971), working with lobsters which also mate just after the female has moulted, showed that the reactions of a male to water in which a soft female (receptive) had been kept were quite different from the reactions of a male to water from a newly moulted male. Soft female water elicited sexual behaviour while soft male water produced aggression and feeding. Clearly, something other than, and in addition to, a newly moulted smell is released by the female. Soft female mating is characteristic of portunids and cancrids (Hartnoll, 1969). The male is attracted to the female a few days before the moult and carries her beneath his sternum until moulting. He may assist her during the moult and at all times is said to treat her very gently. Copulation takes place just after her moult and may last for a long time, several hours in *Carcinus*. After copulation the male carries and guards the female until her exoskeleton is partially hardened.

Aquatic crabs which copulate in the hard shelled state (e.g. most xanthids) probably also use pheromones. In the burrowing crab *Corystes* the female has hard opercula over her genital openings but these become flexible for 12–20 days to allow copulation and egg laying. The male is attracted to the female, probably by pheromones, and carries her about for a few days either clasped under his body or grasped in one of his extended chelipeds (Hartnoll, 1968). Hermit crab females may also be carried or dragged about for a few hours before copulation (Hazlett, 1968c). It is not known whether such pre-copulatory attendance serves as courtship in the sense of the male's behaviour producing compliance in the female, but there are some aquatic crabs in which courtship behaviour is more obvious. Male porcelain crabs of the genus *Petrolisthes* direct visual and tactile signals at receptive females (Molenock, 1975). These include maxilliped oscillations, chelae hunches, rocks and nudges, and antennal taps. The female responds to courtship by moving back and forth, turning and grooming. Males may defend breeding territories containing small harems of 1–4 females, but, 'During the ten days that one large male protected his territory, smaller males managed to get behind him and copulate with the females' (Molenock, 1975). In *Pachygrapsus crassipes* the male initially approaches the female in a threatening posture. If she is receptive the threat is transformed into a 'courtship dance' in which 'the pair moves in complete synchrony, chelae to chelae' forwards and backwards, and from side to side (Bovbjerg, 1960). Eventually the male rolls onto his back and the female moves over him into the characteristic copulation position for this species.

Just before copulation many crabs indulge in mutual stroking or tapping which may serve a courtship function. In the hermit crab *Pagurus bernhardus* the male begins by tapping the female's chelae with his own, she responds by stroking his chelipeds with her chelae and walking legs. Both crabs gradually ease out of their shells and copulation ensues (Hazlett, 1968c). In *Pilumnus* pre-copulatory behaviour can be initiated by either sex (Lobb, 1972). The initiator approaches sideways and taps the walking legs of the other crab with its walking legs, after this the crabs remain motionless for a few minutes touching one another before proceeding to copulation. In many crabs there is no apparent courtship: the male simply grasps the female and forcibly adjusts her to the appropriate position.

Semiterrestrial crabs

The best developed courtship behaviour is found in the semiterrestrial grapsids and ocypodids, almost all of which copulate in the hard shelled state. One reason for the complexity of courtship in these crabs may be that pheromones are less useful as sexual signals in air. The olfactory organs, the 1st antennae, are not adapted to work in air and in semiterrestrial crabs are often reduced. Sight, touch and hearing become more important and it is often the behaviour of the male which stimulates and attracts the female rather than the female's odour attracting the male. There are still some semiterrestrial crabs, however, which seem to lack courtship. In *Dotilla mictyroides*, for instance, females and immature males look alike and a mature male will attempt to capture any likely individual that comes near. If he succeeds, he carries his victim to his burrow and palpates it. Unsuitable crabs are released but others, presumably nubile females, are 'pushed down the burrow and followed by the male' (Tweedie, 1950). True courtship is found in the mangrove crab *Goniopsis* (Shöne and Schöne, 1963). Here the male directs waving displays towards the female. These appear identical to displays performed in agonistic contexts but the reactions of the female, if she is receptive, are different. A receptive female remains still, retreats slowly, or advances;

leg stretching towards the male is common. Eventually, when the pair is almost touching, the male leaps suddenly onto the female, embraces her and adjusts her for copulation.

Two types of copulation occur in *Uca*, on the surface and underground, and they result from different behaviour (Yamaguchi, 1971; Crane, 1975). In surface copulation in *Uca lactea* from Japan a display-phase male walks to the burrow of a neighbouring female and courts her by touching her with extended vibrating walking legs. If she has retreated into her burrow, his vibrating legs are inserted after her and often cause her to come out again. Copulation takes place at the mouth of her burrow. In underground copulation the female appears to be attracted to the burrow of a male by his waving. She approaches in a crouched position (Crane, 1975) and as she does so the male's waving increases greatly in tempo and extent, the chela being raised higher and waved through a wider arc. He may also introduce extra components: drumming on the ground with his major chela, kicking out sideways with his walking legs and curtsying before the female. If she approaches closely the male enters his burrow but continues his courtship by drumming just within the entrance. The female may enter after him and often remains with him over the next high tide. Copulation presumably takes place in his burrow. Salmon and Atsaides (1968) suggested that the porches of some display-phase *Uca* may act as sonic focusing devices, beaming the drumming sounds at the female and thus stimulating her to enter the burrow. Crane (1975) suggested that the porches may be visual stimulants emphasizing the burrow entrance and thus helping to maintain courtship in the visual absence of the male. The sand pyramids of *Ocypode* are also said to have a courtship function, advertising to receptive females the burrow of a high status, sexually able male (Linsenmair, 1967).

Several species of fiddler crab, especially those living in temperate climates where the breeding season is restricted, are also active at night. Under these conditions visual signals are no use and sounds are of major importance in territorial and courtship behaviour (Salmon and Atsaides, 1968). Display-phase males at night drum at the mouths of their burrows. The approach of another crab stimulates an increase in the rate of drumming, males being warned off and receptive females attracted and often enticed into the male's burrow. Night copulation may also occur at the surface; the male walks to the mouth of the female's burrow and attracts her up by drumming on the ground outside.

There is some evidence that surface copulation is commonest amongst primitive fiddler crabs, those with narrow fronts and simple vertical waving, while underground copulation is characteristic of the more advanced, broad-fronted lateral wavers (Crane, 1957). However, both methods may occur in a single species and in *Uca lactea*, a broad-fronted advanced species, surface copulation is much commoner than underground copulation (Yamaguchi, 1971). Surface copulation only lasts a few minutes, but there is far more time available underground. It is possible, therefore, that copulation underground may allow the transmission of more sperm and thus be the more effective of the two methods. If this is so, then the importance of underground copulation would be much greater than is suggested by its apparently rather low frequency in *Uca lactea*.

Visual, tactile and sonic courtship signals, like pheromones, need to be species specific if they are to avoid confusion. This is particularly important in *Uca* where considerable overlap between the ranges of species often occurs. Here different species have been shown to employ characteristic patterns and timing of both waving and sound production (Salmon and Astaides, 1968; see also Chapter 3) and confusion between species is minimal (Aspey, 1971).

Copulation

During copulation the ventral surfaces of the crabs are opposed, the male generally embraces the female with his chelipeds and walking legs. The abdomens are unfolded with the male's on the inside and his first pleopods are inserted into the genital openings of the female. Crabs may sit upright, or either the male or the female may be uppermost. In *Pilumnus*, Lobb (1972) has described two phases: the crabs first manoeuvre into position, then intromission occurs in which the male leans back and performs jerky movements with his chelipeds. He then releases the female but they may remain together grooming themselves for a few moments before proceeding with other activities. The duration of copulation in *Pilumnus* from initial embrace to release of the female is about 5·5 minutes with intromission lasting about 1·5 minutes.

COMMUNAL BEHAVIOUR

Although crabs almost always react agonistically to each other in non-sexual situations, there are some accounts of aggregation in which this behaviour is suppressed for communal ends. Easiest to interpret are the conical heaps of the European spider crab *Maia squinado* (frontispiece) which form a few metres below low tide mark during the summer and may remain stationary and intact for a few months (Carlisle, 1957; Števčić, 1971a). Heaps may be several feet high and Contain large numbers of crabs; Carlisle found 60–80 in one heap but Števčić cited fishermen's reports of 1000 or more. Heaps appear to be formed mainly by pubescent and adult crabs, the smallest sizes not being included. The larger crabs, especially the mature males, occur on top of heaps or around their edges while the smaller individuals are found within. Heaps are thus arranged to protect the smaller crabs and apparently function in this capacity against such predators as octopuses and lobsters (Stevčić, 1971a). Heaps offer particular protection to pubescent individuals which, in the English Channel, undergo their moults of puberty (p. 122) during the summer (Carlisle, 1957). Both males and females moult in the centres of heaps where they are best protected. Following the moult nubile females copulate with one of the hard-shelled mature males. In mid-August in a heap of 80 crabs Carlisle observed 6–8 pairs colpulating at any one time. Heaping thus appears to have reproductive as well as general protective functions.

Protection seems to be the main function of the heaps formed by juvenile king crabs *Paralithodes camtschatica* (Powell and Nickerson, 1965). These aggregations, termed pods, form fairly near shore and are described as spherical with the outermost crabs facing outwards. Each pod is composed of several layers of crabs and contains up to 3000 individuals. Crabs in pods are all quite small, 30–45 mm in carapace length, and mostly 2–3 years old. Younger individuals are solitary and hide in crevices or amongst algae as do small *Maia squinado*. Adult king crabs live offshore in deeper water, they are known to be gregarious but do not form pods. Pods disband from time to time for feeding, the crabs dismount layer by layer, the top layer first, lower layers waiting their turn. When disbanded, the crabs move as a herd, all in the same direction, grazing over the sea bed and probing the mud for food. Regrouping may result in a pod splitting into two, or two neighbouring pods may merge. After about a year, as the crabs grow, merging becomes more frequent and immense, elongated heaps may form containing up to 500 000 crabs. The function of podding must be largely protective, particular protection being provided for moulting individuals; moult frequency is highest in juveniles and at any one time 30 per cent of pod crabs showed evidence of a recent or imminent moult (Powell and Nickerson, 1965).

Many semiterrestrial crabs appear to live in colonies in the sense that individuals occurring over an apparently uniform habitat are clumped in their distribution. Such dispersion is implicit in much of the literature on *Uca* (e.g. Crane, 1975) in which coloniality and complex social behaviour are often considered to be closely linked (Salmon and Atsaides, 1968). Whatever the particular advantages of the social behaviour of *Uca*, it clearly wouldn't work over large distances; the crabs must be close together. Coloniality also occurs in some land crabs: *Cardisoma* may live in small colonies and can distinguish neighbours from strangers. A neighbour is ignored or greeted with ritualized postures, a stranger is unceremoniously chased away, neighbours sometimes aiding each other in this defence of group territory (Wright, 1966). Coloniality in burrowing crabs may serve a general protective function: during foraging many eyes are on the watch for predators instead of just two. But it probably also serves a variety of social functions, complex social behaviour in *Uca* and in-group behaviour in *Cardisoma* being just two examples.

In semiterrestrial crabs dense herding is sometimes found. The most spectacular example is provided by the marching armies of soldier crabs *Mictyris longicarpus* on the beaches of northern Australia (Cameron, 1966). Following emergence fairly high on the shore, these crabs trek to the lower levels where the substratum is damp and more suited to their sand-sifting feeding method. As the crabs feed they aggregate into groups and eventually huge armies containing many hundreds of crabs are formed. After a time an army will begin to move about the beach as a fairly disorganized crowd. The crabs keep close together, sometimes even scrambling over one another when the army changes direction. Armies may travel as much as 460 m during this phase. Marchers are mostly males but females sometimes join in. Eventually the army moves up the beach to the same level at which the crabs emerged, here they engage in burrowing and territorial behaviour before finally going underground. The functions of army wandering are obscure. Cameron (1966) suggested epideictic display—a population census providing feedback to the reproductive system and influencing reproductive output (Wynne-Edwards, 1962). Alternatively it may help in the systematic exploitation of the food. Feeding at random on an evenly distributed food source might reduce the quality of the entire area as a feeding ground. On the other hand, localized feeding followed by mass movement makes sure of an unexploited area at the next feeding and gives the first area time to recover. Army wandering does not seem to have a protective function. Several birds prey on armies and it appears that, unlike their reactions when in other phases, marching crabs do not try to escape. A similar type of aggregated wandering—droving—occurs in *Uca* (Crane, 1975). Droves may contain more than 1000 individuals, crabs of both sexes moving along close together nearly touching one another. They may move down to feed or may simply wander about. Very little is known of this behaviour in *Uca* but it is possible that, as in soldier crabs, the relative efficiency of group feeding may furnish a partial explanation.

8 Life histories

GROWTH

Growth is characterized by two main features. The first is the change in size with time, displayed by means of a growth curve. This generally shows a gradual reduction in growth rate during life. The second feature is the change in shape during growth. Shape changes are due to relative differences in the rates of growth of different parts of the body. A final growth phenomenon which is important in crabs is the regeneration of lost appendages.

Growth curves

One of the consequences of the possession of an exoskeleton is that growth proceeds in steps by a series of moults or ecdyses. This makes the study of crab growth under natural conditions quite difficult since it is rarely possible to mark individuals and successfully follow them through several moults. The result is that, for crabs, the question 'How old is it?' is often a difficult one to answer. Some of the work in this field is summarized in Table 1 which gives the measured or estimated ages of full grown males and shows considerable differences between the growth rates of different species. I have used 'full grown' here to describe a size that would be considered large but not maximum for the species in question.

The number of moults that a crab undergoes before becoming full grown depends on the increment at each moult and the frequency of moulting. The increment at each moult is generally expressed as a percentage of a premoult dimension such as carapace width. A common increment is 25 per cent, representing a doubling in volume at the moult — a considerable increase in size taking place in a very short time. However, increments in crabs vary between 3 and 44 per cent (Hartnoll, 1965) and within a species do not remain constant during growth: usually the growth increments become smaller as the crab becomes larger. For example, Hiatt (1948) found that in the lined shore crab *Pachygrapsus crassipes*, individuals of about 15 mm carapace width have a mean growth increment of 15 per cent; in 35 mm crabs, however, the mean increment is

TABLE 1

The ages of full grown male crabs (size is the carapace width in mm except in the case of *Paralithodes* in which carapace length is given).

Species	Size	Age years	Source
Halicarcinus australis	18	1	Lucas and Hodgekin, 1970
Cyclograpsus punctatus	20	2	Broekhuysen, 1941
Aratus pisoni	23	1·5	Warner, 1967
Rithropanopeus harisii	26	5	Turoboyski, 1973
Pachygrapsus crassipes	47	2·5	Hiatt, 1948
Carcinus maenas	65	4	Crothers, 1967
Callinectes sapidus	140	1–2	Tagatz, 1968
Paralithodes camtschatica	170	17	Hoopes and Karinen, 1972
Cancer magister	207	5	Butler, 1961
Cancer pagurus	250	15–20	Bennet, 1974

only 8 per cent. Hiatt also found variation within size groups: in small crabs variation in growth increment in excess of 400 per cent was recorded.

In older crabs not only does the growth increment decrease, the frequency of moulting also decreases. This decrease, however, is not as regular as the decrease in growth increment since the occurrence of a moult may be inhibited by a variety of factors. Regular moult inhibition (anecdysis, p. 64) occurs during winter outside the tropics. The attainment of puberty may also be marked by a reduction in moult frequency. Thus *Carcinus* may moult as many as twelve times to attain puberty in the summer of its first year. After this it may moult only once or twice a year for the next three years (Crothers, 1967). Sexual differences in growth rates show up after puberty: egg carrying in females produces temporary anecdysis and growth increments are usually less in mature females than in mature males. The result is that full grown males are generally larger than full grown females.

Crabs may either stop growing when full grown, entering 'terminal' anecdysis, or may continue growing with increasingly long intervals between moults. Members of several groups have been shown to enter terminal anecdysis: spider crabs, swimming crabs, the grapsid *Pachygrapsus*. Once in terminal anecdysis a crab's life is limited. This may be the result of a physiological ageing process: in the Australian estuarine crab *Halicarcinus* death at the end of its one year of life is the result of 'post-reproductive morbidity' (Lucas and Hodgekin, 1970). However, the inability to replace worn or damaged cuticle is, by itself, sufficiently disadvantageous to lead to death. Such senility makes way for the younger generation and also limits the species to within a particular size range. Size is often related to life-style and where this is the same for both young and old crabs it may be advantageous to place a limit on size.

In those species without terminal anecdysis, for example the Alaskan king crab *Paralithodes* and the edible crab *Cancer pagurus*, life may be very long and a considerable size range may be covered (Table 1). Frequently the juvenile and adult habitats are separate: *C. pagurus* juveniles are mostly intertidal while the adults are sublittoral (and see p.117 for *Paralithodes*). In large crabs and particularly in cold water growth may be very slow; Hoopes and Karinen (1972) estimated only one or two moults in nine years in one marked male king crab. A large crab has rather few predators, being well protected by its exoskeleton and chelae, but moulting is a dangerous process; the new exoskeleton is quite soft and may take several weeks to regain its previous strength. Consequently there is some advantage in cutting down the frequency of moulting. But the frequency cannot be cut down too much since, if left too long, the exoskeleton becomes worn and damaged. The condylic articulations at the joints get grains of sand stuck in them and no longer operate smoothly; numerous epifaunal animals such as barnacles and tube-worms settle on the skeleton and may become a heavy burden. Thus moulting retains some value as a periodic 'spring cleaning'. Death in these large slow-growing animals probably eventually occurs as a result of the disadvantages of long intermoult periods.

Relative growth

Growth of a part of the body (y) relative to another part, for instance carapace width, (x) is best expressed graphically and the relationship may take a number of different forms. In the simplest case there may be no change in the relative proportions of x and y and no change in shape with growth, the relationship is linear of the form $y=bx$ and growth is described as isometric. Alternatively there may be a constant difference between the growth rates of x and y producing a progressive change in shape with growth. This relationship has the form $y=bx^a$ where the exponent a is a measure of the difference in growth rates. The graph is an exponential curve and the type of growth is described as allometric, positive when $a<1$ (y increases in size relative to x) and negative when $a>1$. Lastly the relative growth of x and y may change during the growth of the crab, again producing changes in shape.

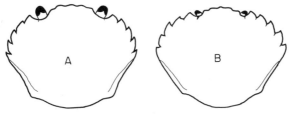

Fig. 31   The change in shape with growth of the carapace of the shore crab *Carcinus maenas*. A is the carapace of a juvenile crab 13mm wide, B is the carapace of a mature crab 66mm wide.

For examples it is worth looking first at relative growth of the carapace. When carapace length is plotted against carapace width the result is usually a straight line which passes through the origin; there is no change in shape and growth is isometric. In the case of several species of sentinel crabs *Macrophthalmus*, however, there is a change in shape during growth: the carapace becomes wider and shorter with increasing size (Barnes, 1968b). This change is of functional significance since these crabs are side-burrowers (p. 77). A straight line relationship obtains for most of the size range but the line does not pass through the origin indicating that a change in relative growth occurs at an early stage. Although in most crabs the overall shape of the carapace does not change, there may still be changes in the arrangement of the parts of the carapace. In *Carcinus*, Williams and Needham (1941) have demonstrated such changes: relative to the maximum carapace width the distances between the more anteriorly placed lateral teeth grow with negative allometry. The result is that the distance between the eyes becomes relatively less as the crab becomes larger (Fig. 31). Williams and Needham suggested that this might result in a relatively larger branchial cavity with a larger respiratory surface area which might compensate for the decrease in surface area to volume ratio in larger crabs.

Other important changes in shape are related to puberty (Hartnoll, 1974). Before sexual maturity the length of the first pleopods of the male (the intromittant organs) and the width of the abdomen of the female (the egg carrying organ) show positive allometric growth. The result is that at puberty these organs, which are small in juveniles, have attained the relative proportions which are proper to their adult functions. These pre-puberty changes take place in all crabs but the time-course varies between species. The organs may pass from the juvenile to the adult state over a number of moults or most of the relative growth may occur at a single moult—the moult of puberty. Subsequent growth of the width of the female abdomen is only slightly positively allometric—the abdomen must not outgrow the rest of the body. In the male pleopods post-puberty growth is slightly negatively allometric thus retaining the ability to fertilize small females.

A different change related to puberty obtains in the growth of the chelipeds (Hartnoll, 1974). These are often important as male status symbols (p.102). During pre-puberty, female chelipeds generally show slight positive allometric growth while male chelipeds show stronger positive allometric growth. At puberty the allometric growth of the chelipeds of males becomes even more strongly positive, but the chelipeds of females continue to grow at the pre-puberty rate. The change in growth rate of the male chelipeds may be abrupt, at the moult of puberty, or may be more gradual. In spider crabs the moult of puberty coincides with the terminal moult and the change in cheliped size over this moult is considerable. The result of the strong positive allometric growth of chelipeds in males is a marked sexual dimorphism of chela size (Fig. 32; see also p.103).

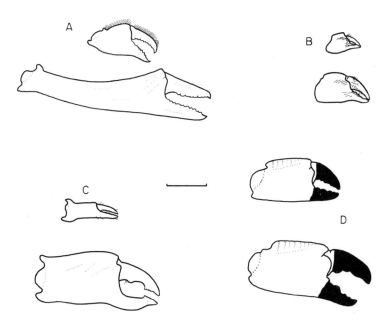

Fig. 32 Sexual dimorphism in crab chelae. A, *Corystes cassivelaunus*; B, *Aratus pisoni*; C, *Pisa tetradon*; D, *Xantho incisus*. The chelae are from large, but equal-sized, males and females in each species. The male chela (below) is larger than that of the female and is often different in shape. Scale = 10 mm.

Autotomy and regeneration

Autotomy is the voluntary shedding of a limb by snapping it off at the base. A preformed breakage plane occurs around the basi-ischium of each limb but is secured in an intact crab by a triangular cuticular plug which bridges the plane on the antero-dorsal side of the basi-ischium. To achieve autotomy this plug must be sheared away, a process accomplished by particular contractions in the levator muscles. There are two levators, anterior and posterior, the anterior levator being by far the larger. Normally both muscles act to lift the limb by pulling on the dorsal rim of the basi-ischium and rotating it about its joint with the coxa. In autotomy, however, a particularly strong contraction of the large anterior levator is suddenly focused onto the cuticular plug by the slipping of a catch-mechanism controlled by the posterior levator. The details of this process are fascinating and well worth describing (McVean and Findlay, 1976).

The anterior levator originates in the endophragmal skeleton and its long apodeme (Fig. 7B) makes two connections with the dorsal rim of the basi-ischium. One is its tough flexible insertion onto the cuticular plug which secures the breakage-plane; the other is an articulation, proximal to the insertion, between the hard cuticle of the apodeme head and a hard projection from the rim of the basi-ischium anterior to the cuticular plug.

During normal levation the pull of the muscle is transmitted to the basi-ischium through this articulation and not through the insertion to the cuticular plug. It is, of course, important that force should not be applied to the plug since this risks autotomy. Both anterior and posterior levator muscles help in this respect since particular parts of both muscles, during contraction, keep the abutting faces of the articulation pressed together. By preventing disarticulation, and the consequent transfer of stress to the plug, they act together as a safety catch. The posterior levator is a small muscle originating within the coxa and its apodeme inserts next to that of the anterior levator on the rim of the basi-ischium posterior to the plug. The posterior levator apodeme is set at an angle to that of the anterior levator and the heads of both apodemes are connected; this allows the contraction of the posterior levator to influence the operation of the anterior levator—acting as a safety catch in normal levation and springing the catch during autotomy. Catch-springing occurs as a result of contraction of a special part of the posterior levator which causes the head of the apodeme to rotate and to nudge the head of the anterior levator apodeme. The nudge disarticulates the apodeme and transfers stress to the plug.

The neural side of autotomy complements the mechanical side. Precise control is required and this is supplied by the CNS and the cuticular stress receptor organs (p.48). During autotomy a special motor unit is recruited and produces a particularly strong contraction in the anterior levator muscle. The resultant stress is transmitted, as in normal levation, through the articulation. The limb levates as far as possible but the stress is maintained and strains the articulation; the safety catch part of the posterior levator prevents disarticulation at this stage. The strain in the articulation produces mechanical deformation of the cuticular stress receptor which lies just anterior to the cuticular plug. When the strain is sufficiently great the stress receptor stimulates the CNS which responds by inhibiting the safety catch part of the posterior levator and stimulating that part which produces disarticulation. The strong force is suddenly transferred to the plug subjecting it to a strain-shock. This, combined with the elastic recoil of the adjacent articulation, is sufficient to shear the plug and the limb breaks off. It is likely that the sudden imposition of the various stresses is important since there is evidence that materials resist sudden strains less well than gradually applied ones (McVean and Findlay, 1976).

Crabs autotomize limbs which are badly damaged or seized by an attacker. The mangrove crab *Goniopsis* sometimes responds to a human attacker by pinching hard with a chela and then autotomizing the cheliped. The chela continues to pinch after autotomy and in one's haste to detach it one often lets the crab escape. Loss of body fluids following autotomy is prevented by an internal partition which remains behind as a seal over the stump. This is soon supplemented by clotted blood which accumulates to form a scab.

Autotomized limbs can only be replaced by moulting. Loss of limbs stimulates the onset of the next moult but may decrease the size increment since resources are diverted to the regenerating limbs. Regeneration starts soon after autotomy by the formation of a small limb bud (Adiyodi, 1972). The bud develops during intermoult (stage C, see below) into a tiny limb folded up inside a flexible sack which projects from the stump. During premoult (stage D) the bud grows rapidly and when the crab moults its length is about a quarter of the carapace width. Immediately after the moult the regenerated limb unfolds and expands but is still somewhat smaller than the other limbs. It regains its full size after the next moult. In the case of the chelipeds the form of the limb may change during regeneration. If a crab with dimorphic chelae (e.g. *Pilumnus*) loses its major cheliped it usually replaces it at the next moult by changing the morphology of the original minor to that of a major. The change is generally from righthanded (commonest) to lefthanded crabs. Probably the major cheliped is more important in feeding than the minor (p. 29) and this strategy results in it being replaced most rapidly. In male *Uca* in which the minor chela is most important in feeding (and is narrower anyway than most limb buds) the opposite situation obtains: a lost major is replaced by a regenerated major on the same side (Crane, 1975).

MOULTING

The modern concept of moulting in Crustacea dates from the work of Drach (1939) on crabs. Drach showed that ecdysis or casting of the old exoskeleton was only a part, and in terms of duration a very small part, of the full moult cycle. Ecdysis used to be thought of as a regular physical necessity which disrupted normal life for a short time. We now know that physical and physiological changes associated with moulting and growth take place throughout the interval between ecdyses. Ecdysis itself is simply one of the more obvious changes. The realization of this constant state of change led to a classification of stages in the moult cycle. This originated with Drach (1939) but has since been modified by a variety of authors. (For reviews see Passano, 1960; Lockwood, 1968.) In the following classification the characters of the exoskeleton (Chapter 1) which may be used to stage specimens in the field are based on the account given by Hiatt (1948) for *Pachygrapsus crassipes*. Events in the underlying physiological cycles are indicated but are described in more detail in the next section. Table 2 at the end of the classification gives the average duration of each stage in *Pachygrapsus*.

The stages of the moult cycle

Stage A. Newly moulted

A_1: the exoskeleton is a soft membrane. The legs are unable to support the body weight in water and the crab is inactive. Water absorption continues. Exocuticle mineralization begins.

A_2: the exoskeleton feels like parchment. The crab can support its weight and move about. Water content stabilizes at about 86 per cent. Endocuticle deposition and mineralization begin.

Stage B. Recently moulted

B_1: the exoskeleton is generally deformable without breaking.

B_2: parts of the exoskeleton become rigid, e.g. the chelipeds which now break rather than bend when force is applied. Feeding may start.

Stage C. Intermoult

C_1: the carapace is almost completely rigid but the branchiostegites, sternites, and the carpus and merus of the walking legs are still flexible. This is the main period of tissue growth.

C_2: the carapace is completely rigid. The branchiostegites, sternites and walking legs are barely flexible and crack if bent. Tissue growth continues.

C_3: the whole exoskeleton is rigid but endocuticle mineralization may still continue. The inner, membranous layer is not completed until the end of this sub-stage.

C_4: the exoskeleton is complete. The presence of the membranous layer can be judged by cracking and lifting a piece of the carapace or breaking off the dactylus of a walking leg: the membranous layer should remain attached to the epidermis. Tissue growth is complete and metabolic reserves accumulate. The water content is 61 per cent.

C_4T: terminal anecdysis. This is distinguished by the membranous layer adhering closely to the rest of the exoskeleton; it is not detectable except by histological examination. Crabs at C_4T are full grown and often show signs of age—the exoskeleton may be damaged and may support a sessile epifauna.

Stage D. Premoult

D_1: the epidermis separates from the membranous layer and secretes a new epicuticle. New spines develop within the cores of old ones, they are very soft but may be seen if a dactylus is broken off and the tissue withdrawn. Reserves are mobilized and glycogen builds up in the epidermal tissues.

D_2: new exocuticle secretion begins. The new spines are now firm and stand out from the tissue withdrawn from a broken dactylus. The old membranous layer degenerates to a gelatinous layer. Resorption of the old exoskeleton begins. Activity is reduced and feeding stops as the crab loses its muscle insertions.

D_3: the main period of old exoskeletion resorption; this is greatest at particular sites, e.g. the epimeral lines (Fig. 33), to allow splitting at ecdysis. Slight pressure on the epimeral line results in a precocious split.

D_4: resorption is complete. The old exoskeleton splits along the epimeral lines and water uptake begins.

Stage E. Ecdysis
The crab withdraws from the old skeleton and takes up water rapidly.

TABLE 2

The duration in days (unless otherwise stated) and the percentage durations of the stages of the moult cycle of *Pachygrapsus crassipes* (based on Hiatt, 1948)

	A_1	A_2	B_1	B_2	C_1	C_2	C_3	C_4	D_1	D_2	D_3	D_4	E
Duration	8–12 (hrs.)	1–2	1½–3	2½–4	4½–5	7–10	7½–11	15–22	3½–6	3½–6	1½–3½	12–15 (hrs.)	few mins.
% duration	1	2	3	5	8	14	15	30+	8	8	4	1	

Physiological cycles

Organic reserves are mainly stored in the hepatopancreas but reserves are also found in the blood and muscle. They reach a minimum level at C_1 following the major demands made by cuticle secretion during A and B. At C_1 full feeding activity recommences and no further depletion takes place. However, reserves do not accumulate during the first half of C since tissue growth occurs at this time. Tissue growth is complete by C_4 and during this stage, the longest of the whole cycle, the major build-up of organic reserves occurs. Drach (1939) found a threefold increase in the dry weight of the hepatopancreas between C_1 and D_1 in the edible crab *Cancer pagurus* and the spider crab *Maia squinado*. Most of the hepatopancreas reserves consist of lipids which often appear as droplets within the cells. Carbohydrates and proteins are also stored but it seems that in the case of the former the blood is a more important store than the hepatopancreas (p.16). Mineral reserves, mostly calcium and magnesium phosphates, also accumulate in the hepatopancreas during C_4.

During stage D mobilization of organic reserves occurs. The main demand is for the secretion of epicuticle and exocuticle which consist of protein and lipid, and chitin and protein respectively. Glucose derived from glycogen is polymerized to form chitin. This glucose may come from the glycogen which accumulates in the epidermis, or from the blood glycogen store. The glucose content of lobster blood increases by 35 per cent between C_4 and D_4 (Telford, 1971). Glycogen may also be derived from lipids in the hepatopancreas but this source is probably more important during endocuticle secretion during A and B.

Cuticular resorption is the most important change to take place during the later sub-stages of D. The old cuticle is broken down by the action of chitinase. The first part to go is the membranous layer which degenerates into a gelatinous layer. Exoskeleton resorption proceeds to different degrees in different species and generally more of the organic content than the mineral content is resorbed, for instance, *Carcinus* resorbs 79 per cent of the organic content but only 18 per cent of the inorganic content from the carapace. A considerable amount of the resorbed minerals may be excreted in the urine.

At ecdysis the large volume of sea water which is absorbed (mainly through the gut wall) disturbs the normal ionic balance of the haemolymph. Magnesium in particular is high and this may help to inhibit movement during A_1.

The major depletion of hepatopancreas reserves takes place during A and B. The exoskeleton is too soft to permit feeding and the crab must draw on its reserves to synthesize the endocuticle. This is the main layer of the exoskeleton and is composed of heavily calcified chitin. Much glycogen is required for chitin synthesis and probably also as an energy source during this time of high metabolic activity. This glycogen is derived from the breakdown of hepatopancreas lipids. Mineral reserves are depleted since the endocuticle is mineralized as it is secreted. However, a substantial part of the required inorganic ions are absorbed directly from the surrounding sea water.

When feeding starts again in late B_2 or C_1 the reserves are fully depleted. However, the crab has grown only in the sense that it has increased in size. Its exoskeleton is still thin and its tissues do not fill the space inside. A crab in this state, however large, is not a useful addition to any menu; the hepatopancreas is depleted and the muscles are atrophied and watery. The food intake in the first half of C is therefore utilized in tissue growth and only when this has caught up with the earlier exoskeleton growth does the crab set about accumulating its reserves once more.

Control

The moult cycle is probably largely under hormonal control and is modified via the central nervous system according to both internal and external environmental conditions. Moult initiation, however, is the only part of the control to be well understood (Passano, 1960; Lockwood, 1968). The X-organs—groups of neurosecretory cells situated in each eyestalk—produce a moult-inhibiting hormone which passes down the axons to the sinus glands (p. 62). Removal of both eyestalks, or of the X-organ/sinus gland complex, results in moult initiation; reimplantation of the organ complex delays the moult. The target organs of the moult-inhibiting hormone are the Y-organs which are situated at the front of the body beneath the branchiostegites, one on either side. These, when released from inhibition, produce a moulting hormone. The effect of the moulting hormone is to initiate premoult stage D. Removal of both eyestalks and Y-organs does not result in moult initiation, but reimplantation of the Y-organs alone leads to a moult. By stage D_2 moult initiation is irreversible; removal of Y-organs at this time does not delay the moult and neither is it accelerated by removal of the eyestalks. Thus the X- and Y-organs control the important transition from C_4 to D in the moult cycle. The control of the sequence of events from D_2 back to C_4 is less well understood. Each event up to C_4 may be triggered by the preceding event but it is likely that further hormonal control is involved.

Terminal anecdysis (C_4T) has been explained in terms of the X- and Y-organs by Carlisle (1957) who showed that there were different control mechanisms in *Maia* and *Carcinus*. In *Maia* C_4T is the result of degeneration of the Y-organs; eyestalk removal in C_4T does not produce moulting. In *Carcinus*, however, C_4T is achieved by constant release of moult-inhibiting hormone and removal of the eyestalks does produce moulting.

This dual control of moult initiation is similar to the situation found in insects except that in the latter group the release of moulting hormone is stimulated by a neurosecretion instead of being inhibited. A further similarity, which in this case links all arthropods, is that the chemistry of the moulting hormone—ecdysone—is similar in all groups and hormone extracts from one group can be used to initiate moulting in other groups (Krishnakumaran and Schneiderman, 1970). The crustacean moulting hormone is called crustecdysone.

An important part of the hormonal control of moulting is that, since the X-organs are part of the nervous system, the release of moult-inhibiting hormone is under nervous control. This provides a link between the moult cycle and the external and internal environments. The X-organs presumably stop secreting when sufficient metabolic reserves are present, when there are no reproductive duties such as egg carrying, and when external conditions are favourable. When conditions are unfavourable, however, the X-organs continue to secrete moult-inhibiting hormone. External conditions which tend to inhibit moulting are constant light, low temperature and crowding. In temperate regions mature females tend to moult in the autumn; moulting is inhibited by cold in the winter and by egg carrying during spring and summer. In mature males moulting is more common in the early summer; many species only copulate when the female is soft, just after a moult, and thus the males need to be hard-shelled in the autumn.

Ecdysis

Although of relatively short duration ecdysis is obviously one of the most important events in the moult cycle. Descriptions of ecdysis generally divide it into a passive phase followed by an active phase. The passive phase, which overlaps with D_4, is a time of swelling and splitting while the active phase involves muscular movements culminating in the withdrawal of the crab from the old skeleton. During both phases the crab is usually hidden away in a burrow or under a stone. It generally avoids members of its own species since most crabs have cannibalistic tendencies.

In the passive phase water uptake commences and a split develops from posterior to anterior along the epimeral line of each branchiostegite (Fig. 33) and between the back of the carapace and the first abdominal segment. The back of the old carapace gradually rises up revealing the new carapace underneath. This generally appears rather wrinkled but brightly coloured. Uptake of water and the consequent increase in haemocoel volume is no doubt responsible for these changes. The pericardial sacs (Fig. 7A) may be important here since they swell progressively during the passive phase and bulge from the branchial cavity under the new carapace (Watson, 1971). It is likely, however, that their main function is to store fluid displaced from the limbs during the active phase (Rao, 1968). Towards the end of the passive phase the epimeral split extends anteriorly almost to the mouth.

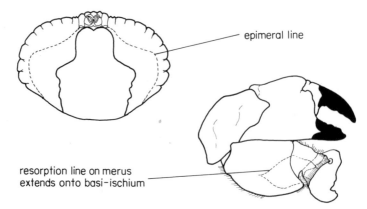

epimeral line

resorption line on merus
extends onto basi–ischium

Fig. 33   Ventral views of the carapace and chela of the edible crab *Cancer pagurus* showing resorption lines at which splitting occurs during ecdysis.

The active phase begins when the carapace has been raised 'like the lid of a box hinged at the anterior end of the animal' (Hiatt, 1948) to an angle of about 30°. Contractions of muscles attached to the leg bases commence and serve to loosen the limbs within the old skeleton. The outward sign of this activity is a rhythmic series of depressions appearing and disappearing on alternate sides of the new carapace (to which the leg muscles are ultimately attached). In *Pachygrapsus* each contraction lasts about 10 seconds (Hiatt, 1948) but in the much larger snow crab *Chionoecetes opilio* from northeast Canadian waters, each contraction lasts about 55 seconds (Watson, 1971). This loosening activity persists for a few minutes (*Pachygrapsus*) or a few hours (*Chionoecetes*). Eventually, however, beginning at the posterior end, the limbs are gradually withdrawn from the old skeleton. The pericardial sacs which are maximally swollen during the early part of the active phase now deflate as the fluid is redistributed to the emerging limbs. The crab then withdraws quite rapidly from the old skeleton, emerging backwards. The gelatinous layer between the old and new skeletons may lubricate withdrawal which has to be quick since as the gills are withdrawn the respiratory mechanism is temporarily put out of action. The chelipeds with their swollen distal ends present special problems but these are overcome by premoult breakdown of the cheliped muscle (Skinner, 1966) and by selective resorption and splitting along fracture lines on the basal podomeres which allow the bulky propodus to be withdrawn (Fig. 33). All parts of the old skeleton which have not been resorbed are left behind with the cast shell — endophragmal skeleton, apodemes, gastric mill, etc.

REPRODUCTION

The attainment of sexual maturity is marked by the growth of secondary sexual characteristics. These anatomical changes are paralleled by the development of the gonads. The growth of sexual characters is under hormonal control (Lockwood, 1968); the ovary produces a female hormone while a male hormone is produced by the androgenic gland, a group of cells lying along the vas deferens. As in the control of moulting it is likely that the output of these two organs is under neurosecretory control. Hormones probably also control the maturation of the gonads and sexual receptivity in the female.

Eggs

Females which become sexually receptive when hard shelled generally lay their eggs shortly after copulation. However, those which copulate just after moulting are in a depleted state and do not generally ovulate for some time. Sperm is stored by the female in the spermathecae; it can be retained through a moult and remains viable for a long time. Egg carrying is seasonal in crabs from temperate regions and tends to occur in spring and summer. In mature female *Cancer pagurus* ecdysis and copulation occur in September but egg laying does not take place until December of the following year, 14 months later (Pearson, 1908). The eggs are fertilized as they are laid since they pass through a spermatheca on their way out. New laid eggs are yolky and orange or khaki in colour; they adhere to the hairs on the pleopods and are retained and brooded in a mass under the broad abdomen of the female. Such females are described as ovigerous or berried. In *Cancer* the eggs hatch in July having been brooded for six months; a second batch may be laid the following December before the next ecdysis and copulation.

In tropical crabs breeding is often continuous throughout the year but may show a lunar rhythm in which egg hatching coincides with full or new moon (p. 63). In the mangrove tree crab *Aratus pisoni* the time from laying to hatching is only 16 days; more than one egg batch may be laid between consecutive ecdyses and an average of about six batches is laid per year (Warner, 1967). In terms of egg batches per year and the length of time taken for the eggs to develop, *Cancer* (large, temperate) and *Aratus* (small, tropical) probably represent two extremes.

The number of eggs in a batch is generally very large and varies with the size of the crab. *Aratus* of 16 mm carapace width lays about 5000 eggs and a 36 mm *Pachygrapsus* lays about 48 000 eggs. Large crabs like *Cancer pagurus* lay up to three million eggs when full grown. The size of a new-laid egg, however, is very small; they are generally slightly oval in shape with a maximum diameter of between 0·25 and 0·35 mm. The eggs swell as they develop so that by the time they are ready to hatch they are roughly double their new-laid volume. During development the colour of the egg changes through brown to grey as the yolk is used up and the outline of the embryo becomes visible. The eyes and pigment spots appear first, followed by the outlines of the abdomen and cephalothorax.

When the eggs hatch the larvae are released from beneath the abdomen of the female. Generally the female assists this process by wafting the abdomen to and fro and by digging into the egg mass with the chelae. In *Aratus* the female climbs down a mangrove root into the water and rapidly vibrates the abdomen back and forth releasing a cloud of larvae. In the northwest Atlantic spider crab *Libinia emarginata* unusual egg hatching behaviour involving the male has been described (Hinsch, 1968). Male *Libinia* can detect the presence of a female about to release larvae. They become very aggressive and fight for the possession of such a female. When a male has captured the female he positions her behind him with the backs of their carapaces touching and clasps his last pair of walking legs beneath her abdomen. Holding her in this 'obstetric' position he backs into a protected area and while the female releases the larvae by fanning her abdomen he drives away any other crabs that approach. After the larvae are liberated the female cleans the empty egg cases from her pleopods and the male then releases her.

The larval life of a crab is generally spent in the plankton. It may last from one to several months and during this time the larva moults several times before settling on the sea bed and moulting to the first crab stage. There are two larval forms, the zoea and the megalopa (or, in hermit crabs, the glaucothoë). There are between 2 and 6 (usually 4) zoeal stages and these are generally followed by one megalopa or glaucothoë stage.

Structure and development

The zoea larva hatches in an embryonic form as a prezoea but this quickly moults to the first zoea. These larvae are tiny shrimp-like animals (Figs. 34, 42), they have a full complement of functional head appendages but only the first two thoracic appendages, the 1st and 2nd maxillipeds, are developed and functional; the rest of the appendages are absent or present only as limb buds. The head appendages all appear to function as they do in the adult but the maxillipeds are used for swimming: the exopods bear long plumose setae and the zoea beats these against the water to achieve fairly fast but jerky progress.

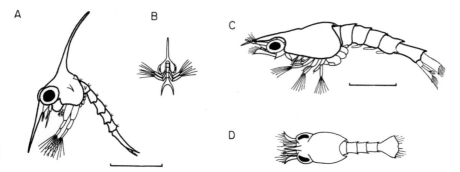

Fig. 34 Zoea larvae. A, side view of the third zoea of the swimming crab *Macropipus puber*. B, posterior view of the first zoea of *Carcinus maenas*. C, side view of the fifth zoea of the West Indian land hermit crab *Coenobita clypeatus*. D, dorsal view of the first zoea of the hermit crab *Pagurus bernhardus*. A and B after Lebour, 1928; C after Provenzano, 1962; D after MacDonald *et al.*, 1957. Scale = 1 mm.

Fig. 34 shows that hermit crab zoeae are more shrimp-like than brachyuran zoeae; this difference may reflect the greater degree of evolutionary change in the Brachyura away from the common ancestor

(Chapter 10). Further differences lie in the development of spines on the carapace and in the shape of the telson. In typical brachyuran zoeae the carapace bears a ventrally pointing rostal spine and a tall dorsal spine; lateral spines are also frequent. In the Anomura spine development is more variable. Hermit crab larvae and stone crab larvae (Lithodidae) usually have short spines and often only the rostral spine is developed; the zoeae of porcelain crabs and of squat lobsters have rather long carapace spines. However, in contrast to brachyuran larvae, anomuran larval spines are always orientated antero-posteriorly and contribute to the shrimp-like shape. The telson in brachyuran zoeae is usually forked whereas in anomuran zoeae it is often spade shaped and forms a tail fan. A list of the differences between brachyuran and anomuran zoeae was given by Williamson (1965).

At each moult the zoea grows and develops by adding setae to the existing appendages and adding appendages to the posterior half of the body. Addition of swimming setae to the exopods of the maxillipeds occurs in quite a regular fashion in brachyuran zoeae and can be used to 'stage' larvae. First zoeae almost always have 4 swimming setae on each maxilliped, this increases to 6 in the second zoea, usually 8 in the third zoea, and 9 or 10 in the fourth zoea. The development of other appendages in brachyuran zoeae is generally restricted to limb and pleopod buds. These usually appear first in the penultimate zoeal stage and by the last zoea (or metazoea, usually the fourth) they may bear a few hairs but are still non-functional. In contrast, in anomuran zoeae two other functional appendages are developed: 3rd maxillipeds used in swimming appear in the second zoea and functional uropods forming a wide tail fan with the telson are developed by the third zoea.

The megalopas and glaucothoës (Fig. 35) resemble the adult forms more closely than do the zoeae; indeed, they are often referred to as post-larval stages. There is a reduction in carapace armature and a complete set of functional appendages including chelipeds and walking legs is present. Locomotion is still largely by swimming but this is achieved by the pleopods borne on the extended abdomen and not by the maxillipeds. An interesting difference, apart from shape, between the megalopa and the glaucothoë is the presence in the latter of well developed uropods forming a tail fan with the telson; in the megalopa the appendages of the last abdominal segment take the form of pleopods and there is no tail fan.

Swimming

Zoeae usually swim backwards propelled by the anteriorly directed beating of the maxillipeds (Foxon, 1934). Brachyuran zoeae swim head downwards with the dorsal spine foremost and the abdomen trailing as shown in Fig. 36A. Anomuran zoeae, however, generally swim telson first

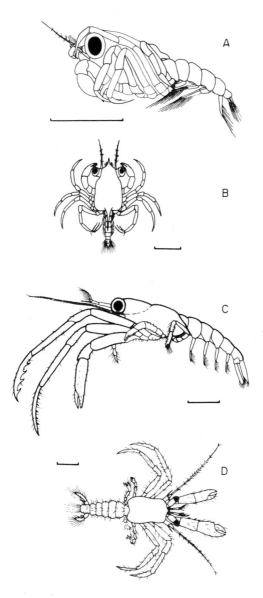

Fig. 35 The megalopa and glaucothoë. A, side view of the megalopa of *Carcinus maenas* in characteristic swimming position; after Atkins, 1954. B, dorsal view of the megalopa of *Cancer pagurus*; after Lebour, 1928. C, side view of the glaucothoë of the West Indian hermit crab *Petrochirus diogenes*; after Provenzano, 1968. D, dorsal view of the glaucothoë of the hermit crab *Pagurus bernhardus*; after MacDonald *et al.*, 1957. Scale = 1 mm.

with the abdomen extended and usually with the dorsal side uppermost. The direction of swimming, therefore, is along the axis of the spines in both types of larvae. The speed of swimming is generally 1–2 cm/s. Reversals or escape movements which occur on collision are effected in anomuran zoeae by tail-flips using the tail fan. In brachyuran zoeae, which lack a tail fan, there is no clear escape movement. When the larvae stop swimming they sink and the rate of sinking depends on the development of spines. Foxon (1934) showed that a narcotized zoea of the porcelain crab *Porcellana* sank in a horizontal posture at a rate of about 0·3 cm/s; *Porcellana* zoeae are characterized by the presence of enormously long carapace spines extending posteriorly and anteriorly. Narcotized brachyuran zoeae, however, with their globular carapaces and shorter spines, sank head first at a rate of about 1·2 cm/s. Thus one function of long spines may be to aid flotation and, indeed, anomuran larvae possessing long spines (Porcellanidae and Galatheidae) frequently rest in a horizontal position hardly sinking at all. Resting is rarely observed in brachyuran zoeae which remain in the same place by swimming constantly upwards. It is possible that short-spined zoeae gain the advantage of manoeuvrability; Foxon (1934) mentioned that *Porcellana* larvae had difficulty in turning but could change direction more quickly when the rostal spine was cut off.

The direction of swimming seems to involve responses to both light and gravity. Zoeae swim towards a light source and can perceive both direction and intensity of light. In the dark the normal swimming orientation is maintained indicating perception of gravity. However, in brachyuran zoeae control is lost in the dark (but not in the light) if the carapace spines are cut off (Foxon, 1934). Probably the spines bear hairs sensitive to water movement. These might distinguish relative water movements due to sinking and thus 'up' and 'down' could be perceived. Similarly differential water movements on either side of the spines during swimming could give directional information. In the light, visual cues could supplement or replace the information from the spines.

The megalopa and glaucothoë swim forwards with the dorsal side uppermost. The propulsive force is produced by the pleopods which beat backwards. In the megalopa during swimming the first two pairs of walking legs are tucked up underneath the body while the last two pairs are held above the carapace, the 3rd pair being extended forwards over the eyes (Fig. 35A). This disposition of the legs helps to streamline the animal. The megalopas and glaucothoës are the settlement stages and after a time swimming in the plankton they adopt a benthic existence. The glaucothoës take up residence in tiny empty gastropod shells while the megalopas walk about with their abdomens flexed under their bodies.

Feeding

Zoea larvae feed on a variety of planktonic organisms. Lebour (1928) cited diatoms and the larvae of echinoderms, molluscs and worms as being common food in nature. Rearing experiments, however, have shown that living and moving animal food is preferred to plant food. Indeed, animal food appears to be essential for the successful growth and development of crab larvae while plant food is not necessary. Living food must, of course, be of an appropriate size and since the larvae of other organisms fit this requirement they have frequently been used as food in rearing experiments. The larvae of sea urchins, oysters and copepods have successfully been used in this way. The most frequently used food in modern rearing experiments consists of the newly hatched larvae of the brine shrimp *Artemia*. This food appears to be suitable for all larval stages including the megalopa which, in nature, feeds on other decapod larvae, copepods and young fish (Gurney, 1942). The advantage of using brine shrimp larvae in preference to other food is mainly convenience: the eggs are remarkably resistant and can be kept in a bottle on the shelf for a long time; when placed in sea water they hatch within a few days.

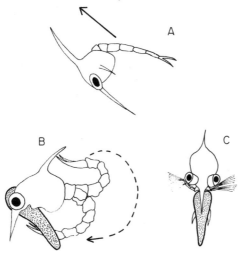

Fig. 36 Larval behaviour. A, the direction of swimming in a brachyuran zoea; after Foxon, 1934. B and C, feeding on *Artemia* larvae by the zoea of an American east coast fiddler crab *Uca pugilator*; after Herrnkind, 1968. B, food capture by tail lashing; C, position during food consumption.

It appears that food is taken by individual acts of capture. This has been described in *Uca* zoeae: the prey, *Artemia* larvae, were captured by lashing the abdomen backwards and forwards (Herrnkind, 1968). An individual *Artemia* larva is pinned between the forked telson and the rostral spine of the zoea and adjusted until the anterior end is in contact with the mandibles (Figs. 36B, C), it is then consumed. Tail-lashing was stimulated by the presence of *Artemia* larvae and can, therefore, be regarded as a behaviour particularly associated with feeding. Objects other than *Artemia* larvae which were captured by tail-lashing (other zoeae, sea urchin larvae) were rejected immediately indicating some sensory discrimination in feeding.

Megalopa larvae seize their prey with their chelae which often have hooked tips to prevent escape. Some glauchothoës capture prey with their long 1st and 2nd pairs of walking legs which stretch out anteriorly during swimming; in these forms the legs may be armed with teeth with which to grasp and hold the prey (Fig. 35C).

Effects of temperature, salinity and starvation

Temperature, salinity and the availability of food are three environmental variables which have received study during laboratory rearing experiments with crab larvae. Like most animals, crab larvae are able to survive under a range of environmental conditions; however, for each species there is generally an optimum area in the range of each variable within which survival, development, growth, etc. are at a maximum. These variables do not, however, act independently on survival; they are all part of the same environment and they tend to interact such that combinations of sub-optimal conditions usually, but not always, reduce survival to a greater degree than a single sub-optimal condition would do.

Within the temperature tolerance range, low temperature tends to slow development and prolongs the larval life. In the natural environment this probably leads to increased mortality from the chance causes of predation, disease, etc. A long larval life, however, should also lead to increased dispersal which, as argued below, may be advantageous. Conversely, high temperatures give rapid development and may lead to increased survival and less dispersal. In the case of low salinity it has been shown that the later larval stages are more tolerant than are the early larvae. This is a necessity for estuarine crabs in which the later larval stages must search out the habitat of the adults. The effects of starvation on crab larvae have shown up a partial independence of moulting and growth. When not enough food is available the larvae may continue to moult but may not grow and the larval life is prolonged. This may result in extra zoeal stages since it appears that metamorphosis to the megalopa or glaucothoë depends on the attainment of a certain bulk.

Combinations of temperature and low food show up the interactions of sub-optimal conditions. At low temperature, low food further prolongs the larval life. At high temperatures, with their attendant high metabolic rates (Chapter 9), low food may produce considerable mortality from starvation.

Reduction in larval life

In various groups of crabs there is a reduction in the number of larval stages or in the length of the larval life. In spider crabs, for instance, only two zoeal stages are found. This may lead, in tropical species, to a very short larval life of less than two weeks. In cooler regions, however, a larval life of about one month is more common even with only two zoeae.

Complete suppression of the larval life is very rare in marine crabs; it occurs in a few genera of the Dromiidae and Maiidae. In the fresh water Potamidae, however, direct development is the rule. The eggs are large and yolky and relatively few in number: a female potamid of 100 mm carapace width might carry about 200 eggs. There are no free larval stages and the eggs hatch directly into young crabs. Hatchlings of the potamid *Kingsleya* are about 6 mm in carapace width; they are called 'marsupial young' since they remain under their mother's abdomen for a time before venturing out on their own. Some fresh water grapsids also have reduced larval lives. One of these is the bromeliad crab *Metapaulus depressus* which lives in the water trapped in the leaf axils of epiphytic bromeliads in the mountain forests of Jamaica (Hartnoll, 1964). This crab lays relatively few large yolky eggs—about 100, each with a diameter of 1·5 mm, laid by a female of 18 m carapace width. There are two non-feeding zoeal stages lasting, together, for three days, and a megalopa lasting for six days. The suppression of the larval life in fresh water crabs has presumably evolved because fresh water is unsuitable for the dispersal of larvae. The same applies to land, but the land crabs of the family Gecarcinidae and the land hermit crabs have retained a full larval life. Land crabs, when the eggs are ready to hatch, may migrate considerable distances at night to liberate their larvae in the sea.

Function of larvae

Rough calculations of survival to various stages in the life cycle of the mangrove tree crab *Aratus* gave 0·041 per cent survival from egg to newly settled crab and 17 per cent survival from newly settled crab to an adult of 18 mm carapace width (Warner, 1967). Thus considerable mortality occurs during the larval life and this is almost certainly true for all marine animals with planktonic larvae. It is likely, therefore, that there is some particular advantage to be gained by releasing the young as an enormous number of tiny larvae rather than as a small number of young crabs. The existence of the latter state in potamids, although in this case an adaptation to fresh water life, shows that crabs are capable of evolving this system.

One advantage that is gained by species with a long planktonic larval life is dispersal. Larvae which drift in tidal and ocean currents are likely to settle some considerable distance away from their parents and may establish new populations in areas in which their species did not previously occur. Similarly, if a local population were to be wiped out by a temporary catastrophe—such as a very cold winter—rapid re-colonization from the plankton could occur. A difficulty attendant on dispersal is that a proportion of the surviving larvae may be transported to unfavourable environments and may not survive long after settling. This danger is to some extent avoided in many groups with planktonic larvae by delaying metamorphosis until the right environment is present. The ability of the megalopa and the glaucothoë to survive both in the plankton and on the sea bed indicates that some selection of the environment before metamorphosis may also occur in crabs.

A further possible advantage of a reproductive strategy which involves planktonic larvae derives from the fact that the vast majority of the primary production in the sea takes place in the plankton. This primary production, directly or indirectly, provides most of the food for the animals on the sea bed: the plankton is a net exporter of food whereas the sea bed communities are importers. In general, therefore, food must be more abundant in the plankton than elsewhere in the sea. Planktonic larvae may be able to exploit this abundance and grow more quickly than would be possible in other environments. There are, of course, exceptions to the generalization that food is more abundant in the plankton. The sea bed, being two dimensional, may accumulate food, as detritus and as resident organisms, to an extent that the local abundance of food exceeds that in the three dimensional plankton above it. However, as argued by Margalef (1963), the excess of production over consumption in the plankton should result in less competition for food, and less efficiency may be required to exploit the food than is necessary in an environment like the sea bed where production (imports) is more nearly balanced by consumption.

The huge mortality that occurs during the larval life is compensated for by the vast numbers of larvae produced and is, therefore, relatively unimportant. Some danger, however, lies in the variability in this mortality. Good years and bad years for larval survival are well known from fisheries studies (although their causes are not so well understood) and species with planktonic larvae must be able to survive a bad year as well as to take advantage of a good year. Dispersal helps in this context since the year may not be bad over the whole range of the species and settlement of larvae hatched in other areas may still occur. The relatively long length of life in most crab species also helps to reduce the danger of bad years; it is mainly the larvae which die, the adults survive to breed again.

9 Hostile environments

The sea experiences a remarkably constant climate. Temperature changes little and slowly; at the western end of the English Channel the mean annual temperature range on the sea bed is only 5°C. Other environmental factors also tend not to vary. Ionic concentrations remain almost constant and so do the quantities of dissolved gases. Even the currents, the winds of the undersea world, are predictable in a way that would put the weather forecasters out of work if they occurred on land. Thus, when crabs venture from the sea they encounter not just a new set of environmental levels, they find fluctuations far greater than any in the sea.

Where would a crab go if it left the sea? There are initially only two possibilities: shores and estuaries. From either of these environments it could climb out onto land or proceed up an estuary into fresh water. Once inland, movement between land and fresh water could occur in both directions. Crabs live in all four of these different environments.

What conditions do they face? Water and salt balance is one of the chief problems. Desiccation is a possibility both on shore and land. Another problem is oxygen availability. Reduced oxygen tensions frequently occur in estuaries, particularly in pools of standing water; and on land, although oxygen is plentiful, it is in gaseous form and not easily absorbed by the gills which are adapted to work best in water. Variable temperature often exacerbates these problems. High temperature increases a crab's metabolic rate thus making life more expensive in terms of energy. The energy cost of osmotic regulation may be harder to afford, and, to make matters worse, less oxygen dissolves in water at high temperatures. Low temperature, on the other hand, may make a crab torpid and easily captured by predators. Another problem, which applies particularly to life in air, is that of weight. Crabs weigh rather little in water, but once on land their full weight must be supported if they are to move about effectively.

One may wonder why, with all these problems, crabs inhabit these environments at all. The answer, as in all other environments, is that spare ecological niches, however hostile, tend to be exploited by those best able to do so. And crabs are remarkably pre-adapted to many of the problems referred to above. The tough exoskeleton and compact body can be used to limit diffusion and, on land, give some protection against desiccation. The gills are situated within capacious branchial chambers which require little modification to function as lungs. And the normal method of locomotion, walking, is the one best suited to carry the body weight on land. Once away from the sea, however, crabs face competition from terrestrial animals. Here the attributes which help them to survive probably include size, amphibious capabilities, armour and a low metabolic rate compared to homeotherms.

Nevertheless, despite all these points in their favour, crabs are not always wildly successful in these environments. To begin with, only in the tropics do they really do well on the shore, in estuaries, in fresh water and on land. One reason for this must be the relatively smaller temperature fluctuations encountered in the tropics. But even in the tropics they by no means dominate the fauna except in particular situations. They do well, however, in fresh water and in environments near the sea which are hostile to terrestrial animals. The mangrove swamp is one such environment and another is the sandy scrubland just landward of a beach. In both of these environments the water, if present, is often saline and thus not suitable for most terrestrial animals.

The aim of this chapter is to describe some of the adaptations which enable crabs to live on the shore, in estuaries, in fresh water and on land. It will be shown that many of these adaptations iron out of the effects of external fluctuations to produce, as nearly as possible, a state of internal homeostasis. In all four environments similar problems occur and consequently similar adaptations are required. I have therefore elected to arrange the chapter by the problems that the animals face rather than by the environments that they inhabit.

TEMPERATURE

Tolerance

The greatest temperature ranges are experienced by species which spend all, or part, of their lives exposed to the air. Miller and Vernberg (1968), discussing the temperature relations of fiddler crabs, cited air temperature ranges for the warmest and coldest weeks in Puerto Rico and North Carolina during 1961. These were 23–32°C and 20–28°C in Puerto Rico, and 23–32°C and −3–5·5°C in North Carolina. It may seem trite to point out that crabs can survive both the fluctuations and the extremes to which they are exposed, but what is less obvious is that many populations are living remarkably close to their limits of tolerance. Edney (1961), working with fiddler crabs from South African mangrove swamps, showed that the upper lethal temperatures of *Uca annulipes* was 42·1°C. This species inhabits sunny glades where, although air temperatures may be no higher than 30–32°C, the ground on which the crabs walk may be heated by the sun to 44–46°C. The level of the upper lethal temperature appears to be adapted to the particular habitat since Edney also found that *U. inversa*, which lives in more open areas, had an upper lethal temperature of 43·4°C, while that of *U. urvillei*, which prefers shady habitats, was 40·8°C. Similar results were obtained by Vernberg and Tashian (1959) who found that at 42° and 44°C, tropical *Uca* survived longer than temperate *Uca*. Temperature tolerance does, of course, depend on the length of exposure time as well as on the exposure temperature.

At the lower end of the temperature tolerance range a similar picture emerges. Tropical species are more sensitive to cold than temperate species. The distribution of *Uca* northward from Florida up the eastern coast of North America appears to be limited by low temperatures (Miller and Vernberg, 1968). *U. rapax*, a tropical species, is limited to Florida by its inability to survive cold: populations of crabs are killed off by severe winters at the northernmost end of its range. *U. pugnax*, a largely temperate species, extends just north of Cape Cod but further extension of its range may be prevented by sub-lethal effects of low temperature. Miller and Vernberg showed that moulting was greatly delayed in *Uca* at temperatures lower than 20°C and suggested that this effect might limit the northward spread of the genus.

Control of body temperature

Crabs do not simply sit in the sun or snow and equilibrate to the temperature of their surroundings. Like other terrestrial poikilotherms shore and land crabs have several methods of regulating their own body temperatures. Many of these methods are behavioural. At the upper end of the temperature range crabs may avoid the heat of the sun by being active only at night and remaining in their burrows or hiding under rocks during the day. Such behaviour also reduces desiccation and will be referred to in this context below. Crabs like *Uca*, which are active by day and thus exposed to the full heat of the sun, may pop down their burrows from time to time to cool off (Wilkens and Fingerman, 1965), but the main methods used to keep cool are transpiration and colour change. Transpiration is the evaporation of water from the body surface and acts in the same way as sweating in mammals. Wilkens and Fingerman demonstrated the effect in *Uca* by showing that in dry air at 37·5°C the body temperature of crabs was only 32°C; in saturated air it rose to the same temperature as the surroundings. Similarly, crabs could survive a much higher temperature in dry air than in moist air. In the natural environment Edney (1961) showed that live *Uca* in the sun had body temperatures which were higher than the surrounding air temperature but considerably lower than the (lethal) temperatures reached by the substratum and by similarly exposed, dead dried crabs. The role of colour change in the prevention of overheating involves the dispersion of white pigment at high temperatures (p. 62). Wilkens and Fingerman found that pale fiddler crabs exposed to sunlight had body temperatures 2°C lower than similarly exposed, dark crabs.

Land and semiterrestrial crabs avoid low temperatures by becoming inactive and remaining in their burrows. In temperate *Uca* this behaviour during winter is often called hibernation. Shore crabs like *Carcinus* which do not normally dig burrows seek sanctuary in the water and may move offshore during the winter.

Control of metabolic rate

Between the upper and lower lethal temperatures a progression of changes takes place in the metabolic rate. This rate may be measured as oxygen consumption per gram per hour and, as in other chemical reactions, it increases with temperature. However, metabolism is a very complex reaction and its rate does not always increase in a regular fashion. To live successfully over a range of temperatures animals must do something about their metabolic rates. It is disadvantageous to allow reserves to burn wastefully away at high temperatures and at low temperatures lengthy periods of torpor can lead to starvation. Further, metabolic rates are usually adapted to ways of life, being rapid in active animals and slower in more sluggish forms. Thus some control of metabolic rate is necessary for the maintenance of a particular life-style. In practice, poikilotherms have two ways of adjusting their metabolic rates to environmental temperature changes: long-term acclimation and short-term compensation (for reviews see Prosser, 1961c; Newell, 1969, 1973).

Acclimation is the means by which animals alter their metabolic processes to compensate for seasonal changes in temperature. It takes a week or two to occur when induced experimentally and its effect is to shift the position of the curve describing the increase in metabolic rate with temperature. The curve may shift in various ways but commonly is such that cold acclimated animals have higher metabolic rates than warm acclimated animals when these rates are measured at the same temperature. Thus animals exposed to cold can, with time, adaptively raise their metabolic rates, and the converse is true of those exposed to warmth. Acclimation, therefore, allows animals to maintain a relatively constant metabolic rate through seasonal fluctuations in temperature. It is of wide occurrence in crabs and was particularly clearly demonstrated in the shore crab *Pachygrapsus* by Roberts (1959). In *Callinectes* acclimation is particularly effective between 20° and 27°C (Leffler, 1972), but at low temperatures, reversed acclimation occurs:

metabolic rate is much less at 13°C in crabs acclimated to 13°C than in those acclimated to 20°C. Presumably at this low temperature a metabolic rate appropriate for the active life of this swimming crab cannot be maintained and it becomes advantageous to reduce metabolic rate as much as possible and enter a state of hibernation.

Acclimation has been extensively studied in *Uca* (Teal, 1959; Vernberg and Tashian, 1959; Vernberg, 1959a, b). Temperate fiddler crabs have a greater capacity for acclimation than tropical species, particularly at the cold end of the range. This result fits with the relative lack of seasonal temperature change in the tropics: acclimation is less useful to tropical crabs. Acclimation in *Uca*, and probably in other crabs, not only alters the metabolic rate, it also affects the temperature tolerance range. Edney (1961) found that the upper lethal temperatures of *Uca* in the summer were some 2°C higher than in the winter.

Short-term compensation is less common and involves the particular shape of the metabolic rate/temperature curve. In such curves plateaux are sometimes found where the increase in metabolic rate over particular temperature ranges is very slight. Increases over particular ranges can be compared by their Q_{10}'s. Q_{10} is the factor by which the rate would be expected to increase for a 10°C rise in temperature. (Q_{10}'s can, of course, be measured over smaller temperature ranges and are, perhaps, best visualized as the slopes of tangents drawn at particular places on the rate/temperature curve.) Within plateaux the Q_{10} may be close to one but in other parts of the rate/temperature curve much higher Q_{10}'s may be found. Thus within the temperature ranges spanned by plateaux animals can apparently control their metabolic rates. Newell (1969) has shown that in many intertidal animals these plateaux span the temperatures likely to be encountered on the shore during the low tide period. Most marine intertidal animals are inactive during low tide and it is the inactive, or standard, metabolic rate/temperature curve which shows the best development of temperature independent plateaux. During activity the metabolic rate is much higher; in large active *Carcinus* it is increased by 157 per cent (Wallace, 1972). Active rates, unlike standard rates, are usually temperature dependent, showing no plateaux. This is not a disadvantage to intertidal animals since, being active at high tide, they are active at uniform temperatures.

Short-term compensation has not been demonstrated for many crab species. In small *Carcinus* a wide plateau of temperature independence occurs in the standard metabolic rate between 10 and 30°C but in large crabs both standard and active rates are temperature dependent (Newell et al., 1972; Wallace, 1972). In *Uca* the problem is rather different: being active in air it is the active rather than the standard rate which is subjected to temperature fluctuations. Workers on *Uca* have not generally separated standard and active rates, but nevertheless some plateaux have been observed which appear to correlate with the environment (Vernberg, 1959a; Vernberg and Vernberg, 1966). In tropical species below 20°C, Q_{10}'s are often high, in some cases as high as 10–20; above 20°C, Q_{10}'s are generally lower (1–2) forming something of a plateau which extends to about 35°C, after which the Q_{10} may increase slightly. A similar but much less marked pattern appears to be present in temperate species. Fiddler crab activity generally takes place above 20°C and it is therefore advantageous for the slope of the rate/temperature curve to be less steep above this level.

Unfortunately for workers on temperature and metabolic rate, any patterns that are present are liable to be obscured by the large number of other variables which influence metabolism (Newell, 1973; Aldrich, 1975). These include the activity level, the time of day and state of tide (activity rhythms), environmental stresses (such as being put into a respirometer, but also including high temperature which can sometimes *depress* metabolism by switching the animal from the active to the standard rate!), the present level of feeding, the level of food reserves, the size (large animals respire more slowly per gram than small animals), and the temperature of acclimation. Clearly the subject is exceedingly complicated!

DESICCATION

This is a problem likely to be faced by almost all shore and land crabs. Accidental stranding away from a source of water is always a danger but some groups are particularly susceptible: small crabs, due to their high surface area to volume ratio, lose water by evaporation more rapidly than do larger crabs. This effect may limit the distribution of the smaller members of a species. In a Jamaican mangrove swamp I found that the smallest sizes of three crab species were restricted to the lower shore while the larger members of two of these species were commoner on the upper shore (Warner, 1969). Crabs which are exposed to the air by day when the temperature may be high and humidity relatively low are also particularly susceptible to desiccation. Fiddler crabs fall into this category but they exploit their susceptibility by using evaporation as a cooling system.

As a rule crabs are not good at preventing water loss by evaporation and in consequence are not generally found in very dry environments. They do not normally stray far from free water, or at least damp substrata, and use behavioural means to combat desiccation. The factor responsible for their lack of evaporation control is the permeability of the cuticle. Although land crabs have much less permeable cuticles than marine crabs (Fig. 37) they do not generally approach the degree of waterproofing achieved by true terrestrial anthropods such as insects and

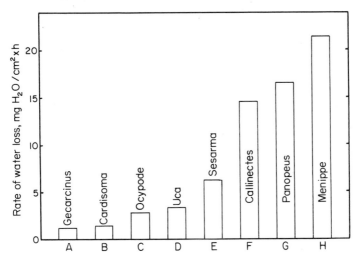

Fig. 37 The permeabilities of crab exoskeletons. A and B are land crabs; C, D and E are semiterrestrial crabs; F, G and H are aquatic crabs. In each case a piece of carapace was stuck over one end of a glass tube; water was put in and the tube was corked. Water can only be lost through the piece of carapace and the rate of water loss is a measure of permeability. After Herreid, 1969b.

spiders. Part of this inability must result from the lack of a waxy layer in the crab cuticle. Herreid (1969a) investigated the weight loss by evaporation in air of a range of crabs from marine to terrestrial environments. The tropical land crab *Gecarcinus* lost weight least rapidly while the most rapid weight loss occurred in aquatic species such as *Callinectes* and *Menippe*. Semiterrestrial crabs such as *Ocypode* and *Uca* were intermediate. In comparison with other terrestrial animals Herreid showed that *Gecarcinus* lost weight 3–5 times more rapidly than kangaroo rats and green iguanas; but a bull frog lost weight 7 times faster than the land crab. The semiterrestrial crabs lost weight 6–7 times faster than ordinary cockroaches, but at about the same rate as a species of cave cockroach. Herreid found that the weight loss of crabs at death was 12–25 per cent of body weight; land crabs did not appear to tolerate a greater weight loss than marine crabs. In a second series of experiments Herreid (1969b) showed that almost all the evaporative water loss occurred from the body and legs; very little was lost from the branchial chambers.

Behavioural mechanisms to combat desiccation include nocturnal activity and the burrow habit. Many land crabs such as *Gecarcinus* and *Cardisoma* are active chiefly at night when the temperature is lower and humidity higher than by day. The land hermit crab *Coenobita rugosus*, which lives on sand dunes near the sea in Somalia, spends the days buried in damp sand either beneath beach flotsam or under bushes (Vannini, 1975). Towards evening it emerges and, orientating by a combination of cues including sight of the seaward horizon and wind direction, it makes its way down to the beach where it forages and replenishes its water supply. At daybreak it returns to the dune, leaving the damp sand of the beach and crossing the dry sand of the upper shore. When it encounters damp sand again it digs in and buries itself. Such sand only occurs under flotsam or bushes and so this response ensures that the population finds shelter during the day. Vannini showed that the response was only switched on during the day and was influenced by the degree of dampness in the sand. Some digging was elicited at a dampness as low as one part of sea water per thousand of sand (%$_{oo}$) and 50 per cent of the experimental animals buried themselves at 5%$_{oo}$. Maximum digging occurred between 30 and 150%$_{oo}$ while above this level, although the sand was by no means waterlogged, crabs stopped digging and started to drink.

The commonest behavioural mechanism to combat desiccation in day-active crabs is to visit water regularly. This is particularly important in deposit feeders (e.g. *Uca*) which use water freely to sort their food. Three water sources may be available: the burrow, which frequently descends to the water table; standing pools; and a damp substratum. Many land and semiterrestrial crabs can absorb water from a damp substratum. Absorption depends on the presence of tufts of long unbranched hairs which attract water by capillarity and lead it up into the branchial chambers. Such tufts of hair are often found between particular legs guarding openings into the gill chambers. They are found in *Ocypode* on the coxae at the bases of the 2nd and 3rd walking legs and similar tufts occur in *Uca*. An unusual arrangement is found in *Dotilla* where the water absorbing setae are situated on the fourth segment of the abdomen (Hartnoll, 1973). Once within the branchial cavity the water is presumably led up to the gills, to moisten them, to be absorbed, or to be moved forwards for use in feeding. In *Gecarcinus* the conduction of water from the hairs (in this case situated between the bases of the 4th pair of walking legs and the base of the abdomen) into the branchial chamber is aided by the pericardial sacs which are very large in this species and project almost to the posterior border of the carapace (Bliss, 1963). The surface of the pericardial sacs is corrugated and leads water rapidly up to the posterior gills. These have lamellae which are set rather close together and water is sucked between them by capillarity. Copeland (1968) has shown that the epithelium of the posterior gill lamellae is well suited for the active transport of water and salts (see below) and it seems likely that the water taken up from the substratum by *Gecarcinus* is moved into the blood via the gills.

The size of the pericardial sacs in *Gecarcinus* is not just an adaptation for water conduction. Large pericardial sacs are found in many land and semiterrestrial crabs and are used to store water during moulting (Bliss *et al.*, 1966; Rao, 1968). Water is required to expand the new skeleton after moulting and in *Gecarcinus* and *Ocypode cordimana* (a particularly terrestrial ghost crab from the east coast of India) this water is stored in the pericardial sacs which swell progressively for several days before ecdysis. If a crab in premoult is not given access to damp sand the sacs do not swell and growth does not occur, indeed the crab may even shrink at ecdysis. Other less terrestrial species of *Ocypode* which have access to free water at the bottom of their burrows (*Gecarcinus* and *O. cordimana* do not) do not store water prior to ecdysis. The swelling of their pericardial sacs during ecdysis, as in marine crabs, is concerned with redistribution of fluid during withdrawal from the old exoskeleton (Rao, 1968).

SALINITY

Most animals maintain the concentration of their body fluids more or less constant; in the vast majority of crabs it is practically the same as that of sea water although the composition may be different. This concentration is not difficult to maintain in the sea since no osmotic gradients exist and the influx of water by diffusion equals the efflux. Concentration gradients for various ions exist and the resultant net movements are made good by ionic regulation often involving the excretory organs (p. 21). When a crab moves onto the shore or into an estuary, however, it meets fluctuating salinity. On the shore rainfall dilutes the available sea water while evaporation increases its concentration. In an estuary the salinity may always be somewhat reduced and tends to fluctuate with the tides. Mangrove swamps are often both shores and estuaries and are particularly susceptible to salinity fluctuations. One reason is that the seasons to which they are exposed are wet and dry rather than cold and warm. During the wet season heavy rain and floods may reduce the salinity of the swamp-water almost to zero while during the dry season pools of high salinity develop on the upper shore. In such places concentrations equivalent to 150 per cent of sea water (SW) are not uncommon. In saline pools above high tide level in Jamaica, the only water sources available to a large population of *Uca burgersi*, I obtained salinity measurements of 180–400 per cent SW. Some crabs, for instance *Callinectes sapidus*, avoid emerging onto the shore but proceed up estuaries into fresh water; they migrate back to the sea to breed. Others, such as the potamids, spend their entire lives inland, in or near fresh water, and never visit the sea.

Patterns of osmoregulation

Crabs which expose themselves to water in which the concentration is markedly different from that of the sea are exposing themselves to steep osmotic and ionic gradients. Unless they can do something about it, their body fluid concentration must change to that of the environment by a combination of osmosis and diffusion (for reviews see Potts and Parry, 1964; Lockwood, 1968). Most marine crabs (e.g. *Maia, Macropipus*) cannot do anything about it. In dilute sea water they gain weight rapidly by osmosis until external and internal concentrations are equal; then, more gradually, they lose weight as salts and water diffuse out of their distended bodies. These crabs die if the drop in concentration is more than about 25 per cent. Such crabs do not need to regulate their internal concentrations: they never encounter variable salinity in nature.

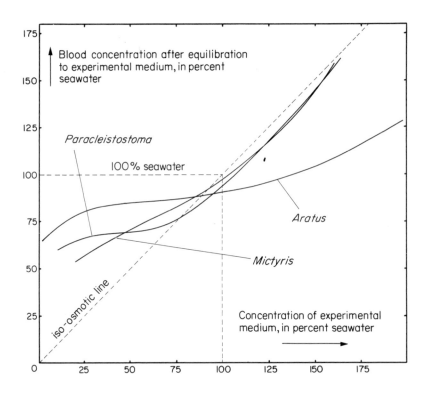

Fig. 38   Patterns of osmoregulation in three crabs. Data for *Paracleistostoma* and *Mictyris* from Barnes, 1967.

Crabs whose habits do take them into dilute sea water often behave quite differently. *Carcinus* gains little, if any, weight when placed in dilute sea water. Its blood concentration drops somewhat below the normal level but remains above that of its environment: it hyper-osmoregulates. Most semiterrestrial crabs (e.g. *Uca, Sesarma*), as well as being able to hyper-osmoregulate, can maintain their blood concentrations below that of the environment by hypo-osmoregulation. This ability is advantageous to species which may find themselves in strongly saline pools in the dry season. *Carcinus* and *Callinectes*, which rarely meet such conditions, have hardly any hypo-osmoregulatory ability. Fig. 38 shows osmoregulation in three species: two hyper-osmoregulators, one strong and the other weaker, and a mangrove crab capable of strong regulation in both directions. Osmoregulatory ability, as might be expected, is related to habitat; *Paracleistostoma*, the stronger of the two hyper-osmoregulators in Fig. 38, penetrates much further up the Brisbane River in northern Australia than does *Mictyris*, the weaker regulator (Barnes, 1967).

Fresh water and land crabs all appear to be excellent hyper-osmoregulators but the ability to hypo-osmoregulate may be lacking (it is difficult to be sure of the abilities of land crabs since they often drown when immersed). *Gecarcinus*, with a blood concentration of 80–90 per cent SW, cannot survive if given access to sea water only (Gross, 1964b). Similarly, some potamid fresh water crabs which have blood concentrations of about 50 per cent SW cannot survive in sea water (Shaw, 1959b). The lack of hypo-osmoregulation in these crabs is no disadvantage since, except for brief visits to the sea during egg hatching in *Gecarcinus*, they do not encounter saline environments in nature. Other land crabs, however, do meet these conditions. The land crab *Cardisoma* prefers damper environments than *Gecarcinus* and its burrows usually descend to the water table. It may live several miles inland where only fresh water is available, or it may occur close to the sea on the landward fringes of mangrove swamps. *Cardisoma* can regulate strongly in both directions and can even rehydrate from damp sand against a concentration gradient. Gross et al., (1966) put desiccated individuals on sand dampened with sea water and found that in 48 hours they had regained most of the weight lost during desiccation (about 10 per cent body weight) and reduced their blood concentrations by some 10 per cent SW to below that of normal sea water. Certain workers on osmoregulation in crabs have tried to link osmoregulatory ability with terrestrialness, but have had difficulty reconciling the differing abilities of land crabs. In general semiterrestrial crabs can regulate strongly in both directions while aquatic crabs either do not regulate at all (marine forms) or are capable of significant regulation only in dilute media (estuarine and fresh water crabs). The regulatory ability of land crabs depends on the habitat of each species. Thus Gross (1964b) concluded: 'Osmotic regulation and terrestrialness may have arisen independently but simultaneously in regions of varying salinity and high water temperature.'

Measures for reducing osmoregulatory problems

Fig. 39 summarizes the salt and water balance problems faced by crabs in

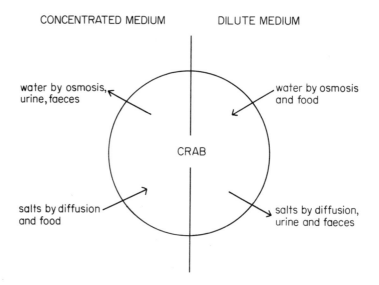

Fig. 39   The problems of osmoregulators. Without osmoregulation net movements of water and salts would occur as shown.

concentrated and dilute media. It may be seen that hyper-osmoregulators must remove water and gain salts while hypo-osmoregulators must do the opposite. It should also be clear, however, that all the problems can be much reduced by lowering the permeability of the cuticle to salts and water. Several comparative studies have shown that crabs which can osmoregulate have much lower permeabilities than non-regulators. The marine crabs *Cancer* and *Pugettia*, for instance, are about 20 times more permeable than the shore crab *Pachygrapsus* (Gross, 1957a). Adaptive reduction in permeability is also possible. Capen (1972), working with *Rithropanopeus*, found that in as little as half an hour after transfer from 75 to 10 per cent SW a reduction in permeability could be detected. Full reduction to a new steady state was completed in two days. Most of the water exchange, unlike evaporation in air, took place over the thin cuticle of the gills. Adaptive reduction in permeability is probably under hormonal control (Kato and Kamemoto, 1968) and may occur at the cuticle level by extra incorporation of lipids to aid waterproofing. Whitney (1974) has demonstrated an enhancement of phospholipid synthesis in the gills of *Callinectes* following transference from 100 to 50 per cent SW.

Other measures which help to reduce the problems include behavioural avoidance of high and low salinities and toleration of variations in body fluid concentration. Several crab species can detect concentration differences and, if given a choice, will select normal sea water (Gross, 1957b; Davenport and Wankowski, 1973). The raised oxygen consumption often seen in crabs exposed to osmotic stress may not be a result of energy expenditure on regulation but may simply indicate increased activity as the crab tries to escape (Gross, 1957a). Anomuran land crabs mainly use behavioural means to regulate their body fluid concentrations (Gross, 1964a; Gross *et al.*, 1966); they select pools of appropriate salinity from which to fill their shells or drink. These anomurans tolerate wide fluctuations in their body fluid concentrations: probably an adaptation to life on dry atolls where pools of appropriate salinity are not always available. In semiterrestrial and estuarine crabs the advantage of being able to tolerate a drop in body fluid concentration on exposure to dilute sea water or an increase when exposed to concentrated sea water is that it decreases the gradients which osmotic regulation must oppose. There is, of course, a limit to such tolerance since complete equilibration, although it would reduce the gradients to zero, would very likely kill the crab! Nevertheless, some crabs survive in habitats with wide salinity ranges by using toleration rather than regulation. An example is *Macrophthalmus setosus*, a very weak regulator, which Barnes (1967) found could survive between 30 and 170 per cent SW in the laboratory and which penetrates 21 km up the Brisbane River. The fresh water potamids with blood concentrations of about 50 per cent SW, face osmotic gradients which, considering the marine origin of these crabs, are much smaller than they might be. Most semiterrestrial crabs have followed the lead of the potamids in this respect and have natural body fluid concentrations between 70 and 90 per cent SW.

Internal methods of tolerance

Intracellular iso-osmotic regulation is the name given to one of the methods by which animals tolerate variations in their body fluid concentrations. The process operates to retain relatively constant ionic levels within cells despite variations in the overall osmotic concentration. There is, of course, no osmotic differential between the insides of cells and the body fluids surrounding them; but the levels of the various intracellular osmotic components are different from the levels of these components in the body fluids. A substantial intracellular osmotic component is a pool of free amino acids (70 and 35 per cent of the total osmotic activity in crab muscle and nerve cells respectively is due to free amino acids—Gerard and Gilles, 1972) and most of the intracellular accommodation to overall osmotic changes is carried out by varying the levels of these amino acids rather than by altering the levels of the intracellular ions. Gerard and Gilles (1972) showed that in *Callinectes* transferred from sea water to 50 per cent SW the intracellular amino acids in the muscles dropped by 34 per cent while the ionic levels dropped by only 20 per cent. In the nerves the drop in amino acids was 27 per cent and the ions dropped by 11 per cent. Amino acids were less important, however, in the osmotic accommodation of hepatopancreas and gill cells.

There are several possible ways in which intracellular amino acid levels can be altered. Their levels can be reduced by polymerizing them into proteins, by excreting them from the cell or by breaking them down and excreting the breakdown products. Equally, their levels can be raised by breaking down cell proteins, by absorbing them from the blood or by synthesizing them within the cell. Gilles and Schoffeniels (1969) showed that in the nerves of the Chinese mitten-handed crab *Eriocheir sinensis* downward osmotic accommodation was achieved by a mixture of excretion and breakdown while upward accommodation occurred through synthesis and uptake. Proteins did not appear to be involved. Siebers (1974), however, has presented evidence suggesting that in *Carcinus* in upward accomodation, metabolism of serum proteins may provide amino acids for uptake by cells. Lastly, on this subject, it is interesting to note that Shaw (1959a) found very limited intracellular iso-osmotic regulation in an African fresh water crab *Potamon niloticus* and correlated this with its inability to survive in sea water.

Methods of osmoregulation

To return to the overall problems: it appears that for hyper- and hypo-osmoregulation crabs must be able to move water and salts both into and out of their bodies. Most studies show that in dilute media water is removed by increasing the rate of urine production. Thus *Pachygrapsus* in normal sea water produces urine at the rate of 3·9 per cent body weight per day, but in half strength sea water the rate rises by 15 times to 58 per cent body weight per day (Gross and Marshall, 1960). In *Carcinus* the increase is less; 4·4 per cent body weight per day in sea water and four times faster in 50 per cent SW (Binns, 1969a). Unfortunately, crabs cannot excrete a urine which differs in concentration from the blood. This unusual disability (earthworms, crayfish and fresh water fish can) results in a considerable loss of ions with the urine when in dilute sea water — and this in addition to the loss by diffusion through the cuticle. Extreme impermeability can ease the problem somewhat: in potamids estimates of urine production in fresh water vary from 0·05–0·6 per cent body weight per day indicating tremendous impermeability. Nevertheless, sodium loss via the urine may be up to a not insignificant 12 per cent of the total sodium loss (Harris, 1975). The loss of salts by diffusion and in the urine is made good by salt uptake by the gills. In several strong osmoregulators epithelia apparently specialized for active transport have been found on the posterior gills (Copeland and Fitzjarrell, 1968; Dehnel, 1974; Storch and Welsch, 1975). These epithelia are much thicker than those concerned only with gaseous exchange and this results from the deeply folded nature of the inner and outer borders of the epithelial cells. The inner borders are the most deeply folded, the folds being packed with flattened mito-chondria and interdigitating with one another so as to leave very narrow sinuous fissures between them. These fissures are in communica-tion with the lumen of the gill. The mitochondria in the folds presumably supply the energy required for the active transport of salts against concentration gradients and the folds and fissures, common features of many transporting epithelia, may provide the framework for moving salts into the blood (see Berridge and Oschman, 1972).

Copeland and Fitzjarrell (1968) found that in *Callinectes sapidus* the proportion of the total gill area given over to transporting epithelia was adaptively variable. When transferred from normal to dilute sea water these crabs doubled their areas of transporting epithelia in 1–3 weeks. This observation, and the fact, mentioned above, that adaptive variations in permeability may also occur, suggests that osmoregulatory ability should improve with time: the two processes should provide for a measure of acclimation to osmotic stress. Acclimation has been demonstrated by Barnes (1968c) in *Macrophthalmus setosus* which, when transferred directly from sea water to a more dilute solution, is capable of only very limited osmoregulation. When acclimated by gradual transference over a number of days through a series of intermediate dilutions, however, the osmoregulatory ability of *M. setosus* almost doubles. Barnes pointed out that, in nature, gradual acclimation is possible since *M. setosus* individuals can insulate themselves from rapid environmental changes in salinity by burrowing into the muddy substratum of their estuarine habitat.

In hypo-osmotic regulation crabs must gain water and lose salts. Ex-cretion of monovalent ions such as sodium and chloride probably takes place over the gills (Greene *et al.*, 1959). The transporting epithelia in these crabs are presumably able to move salts in either direction. Very little salt is lost in the urine since its concentration is not different from that of the blood (Schmidt-Nielsen *et al.*, 1968) and its output decreases as the concentration of the medium increases. The excess of certain ions can be eliminated by this route, however, and magnesium is the most important of these. As the concentration of the medium rises, so too does the concentration of magnesium in the urine; in 150 per cent SW magnesium is 15 times more concentrated in the urine of *Pachygrapsus* than in the blood (Gross, 1959). There remains the problem of gaining water. In *Uca* water appears to be taken up by drinking the concentrated medium (Green *et al.*, 1959). Water and monovalent ions are presumably absorbed across the gut wall leaving behind the divalent ions like magnesium and sulphate. The excess ions absorbed with the water can be excreted over the gills. However, Gross *et al.*, (1966) working with *Cardisoma* in 150 per cent SW found no evidence of this method of water uptake and it is possible that other routes may exist. Likely candidates are the gills with their transporting epithelia; as in the insect rectum net water uptake may be possible here.

Nitrogen excretion

Problems of water balance, particularly on land, frequently affect the pattern of nitrogen excretion (for review see Prosser, 1961a). Most aquatic crabs produce ammonia as their chief nitrogenous excretory product. They find it unnecessary to reduce the toxicity of this substance by turning it into, for instance, urea, since it readily diffuses out through the cuticle and is never stored. In *Carcinus* only 3·2 per cent of the total nitrogen excretion goes out in the urine, and although urea and uric acid are present in the blood, 80 per cent of the total nitrogenous excretion is ammonia (Binns, 1969d). In an Indian fresh water crab *Paratelphusa hydrodromus* 92 per cent of the total nitrogenous excretion is ammonia, but when transferred to sea water (in which, unlike *Potamon niloticus*, it can survive) these crabs lower the proportion of ammonia to 28 per cent and increase their output of urea from 6·7 per cent of the total in fresh water to 59 per cent in sea water (Krishnamoorthy and Srihari, 1973). *Paratelphusa* transferred to sea water also increases the proportion excreted as uric acid from 0·4 to 9 per cent. It is not entirely clear why these crabs should change from ammonia excretion since ammonia should diffuse out as easily into sea water as into fresh water. However, fresh water crabs are notoriously impermeable and perhaps ammonia does not diffuse out readily through their cuticles. In fresh water it is probably removed during active sodium uptake by ammonium ions being exchanged for sodium ions over the gills. This removal route would be closed in sea water since active sodium uptake would almost certainly cease. In these circumstances urea and uric acid production might prevent a build up of toxic ammonia.

In land crabs excretion by diffusion is rarely possible, and they lack a plentiful supply of water to flush their excretory products out through the excretory organs. The solution to these problems in *Cardisoma* appears to be a compromise: toleration of high ammonia concentration in the blood, excretion of some ammonia into the gut, periodic immersion and the release of ammonia by diffusion, synthesis of urea and its release in the urine when on a high nitrogen diet, and synthesis and accumulation of uric acid in the tissues (Gifford, 1968; Horne, 1968). Uric acid, being insoluble, is particularly effective in water conservation and is the main excretory product in insects, reptiles and birds. *Cardisoma* appears unable to excrete concentrated uric acid as these other animals do, but it allows it to accumulate as a white precipitate in all the spare corners of the body — around the stomach, in the abdomen, around the edges of the carapace, behind the heart, in the dactyli of the chelae, etc. The amount of stored uric acid can rise to 16 per cent of the dry weight of the crab!

OXYGEN

Oxygen dissolves in water according to its partial pressure (pO_2) — about 20 per cent of an atmosphere or 155 mm Hg. At this pressure and at 20°C about 5·1 ml of oxygen will dissolve in a litre of normal sea water. Increasing temperature and increasing salinity both decrease the amount of oxygen in solution although they do not, of course, alter its partial pressure. Uptake of oxygen from water depends on the pO_2 gradient across the respiratory epithelium. To maintain a gradient both the blood and the respiratory water must be moving, preferably in opposite directions (p. 11). Even with movement, the thin layer of water in contact with the respiratory surface is rapidly depleted and the rate of diffusion through this depleted layer further limits the uptake of oxygen. In air the pO_2 is the same as in aerated water so the gradient across the respiratory epithelium is no steeper; but it is much easier to maintain. This is because air is far richer in oxygen — and so less easily depleted — and diffusion is more rapid in air.

Air-breathing adaptations

The problems encountered by a crab breathing air do not, therefore, concern oxygen availability; they are more concerned with anatomy. Gills are not suitable for extracting oxygen from air: they collapse and the lamellae stick together. To solve this problem, land and semiterrestrial crabs have reduced the number of their gills (only six pairs are present in *Sesarma* and *Ocypode*, but nine pairs in most marine crabs), reduced the number of lamellae per gill and strengthened the lamellae to prevent collapse. These measures have greatly reduced the surface area of the gills, a trend described by Gray (1957). Gray found gill surface areas (mm^2/g body weight) of about 1200 in aquatic portunids, 650 in aquatic spider crabs, 880 in intertidal xanthids, about 600 in semiterrestrial *Uca* and *Sesarma* and 350 in *Ocypode*. The trend is clearest when comparing the very active portunids with the equally active *Ocypode*; the relatively small gill areas of the spider crabs and xanthids relate to their sluggish life-styles. To replace the loss of respiratory gill surface in air-breathing crabs the branchial chambers of land crabs and of some semiterrestrial species (e.g. *Gecarcinus, Cardisoma, Birgus, Ocypode*) have been modified to function as lungs: the walls and ceilings are vascularized and often embellished with respiratory tufts (for reviews see Edney, 1960; Bliss, 1968). With this adequately large respiratory surface and with oxygen readily available, air-breathing crabs should not need to ventilate their branchial chambers as actively as aquatic crabs do. The available measurements tend to confirm this conclusion: the ventilation rate at rest of the air-breathing robber crab *Birgus* is 57 ml/kg/min, the rate for the aquatic *Cancer magister* is 625 ml/kg/min (Cameron and Mecklenburg, 1973; Johansen *et al.*, 1970).

Responses to low oxygen tension

Although when breathing air crabs do not generally face oxygen availability problems, aquatic crabs in certain environments can encounter reduced oxygen tensions (pO_2 in water). These conditions may be found in estuaries, mangrove swamps and salt marshes, and usually result from the bacterial decomposition of organic muds. Warm weather can aggravate the problems by increasing bacterial activity and decreasing the amount of oxygen in solution. Where plants are present oxygen tensions are often maintained by day, but may fall at night in such places as rock pools due to the combined respiration of the plant and animal inhabitants. Crabs which face these problems in nature have adopted several methods to maintain a constant rate of oxygen uptake despite the drop in external pO_2. They include increasing the ventilation rate, increasing the percentage extraction of oxygen, and opting out by changing to air breathing: *Carcinus* employs all three methods (Arudprugasam and Naylor, 1964).

Increasing ventilation helps to maintain oxygen tension gradients at the gills by moving depleted water rapidly on. Increasing the percentage of available oxygen that is extracted is clearly advantageous; normally in *Carcinus* ventilation rate and extraction are inversely proportional, but at low pO_2 both may increase indicating that they are under separate control. The combined effect of increasing ventilation and extraction in response to declining pO_2 is to make metabolic rate independent of pO_2 down to a certain critical tension; below the critical point metabolic rate declines in proportion to pO_2. Animals which do this are termed regulators while those in which metabolic rate is proportional to pO_2 over the whole range are called conformers (for review see Prosser, 1961b). Regulation is quite common in crabs: *Carcinus* regulates down to a critical tension of 30–40 mm Hg, *Cancer magister* down to 50 mm Hg, *Uca* in air down to 15 mm Hg, and in water to 50 mm Hg (Arudpragasam and Naylor, 1964; Johansen *et al.*, 1970; Teal and Carey, 1967). Some crabs, however, are conformers: *Panopeus* and *Menippe* (Leffler, 1973).

If the pO_2 drops below the critical level of a regulator then, to survive, it must adopt a new strategy. Below the critical pO_2 in *Uca* respiration continues anaerobically, lactic acid is produced and the crabs build up an oxygen debt which they repay fully on return to normal oxygen levels. Fiddler crabs can survive up to 40 hours without oxygen and this ability is very useful since, when their burrows are flooded, the pO_2 inside can drop almost to zero (Teal and Carey, 1967). The strategy adopted by *Carcinus* when the pO_2 in the water becomes critical is to breathe air instead. It does this by raising the front of the body above the surface and reversing the beat of the scaphognathites to draw air into the branchial chambers through the normally exhalant openings. The air bubbles out again at the bases of the chelipeds. Emersion occurs at external pO_2's between 20 and 60 mm Hg (12–17°C) and air breathing significantly increases the amount of oxygen in the arterial blood (Taylor *et al.*, 1973). *Carcinus* is not, of course, a typical air-breathing crab, its branchial chambers are not lungs and its air breathing in shallow water probably works simply by aerating the water around the gills. Nevertheless, the ability is a useful one: I have seen many *Carcinus* breathing air at night round the edges of weedy rock pools. *Carcinus* also possesses the ability to survive on air alone and is often stranded out of water at low tide. Large *Carcinus* can survive without cover in the shade for about seven days and under damp seaweed for as long as 60 days (Perkins, 1967), a remarkable achievement for this basically aquatic crab. When out of water *Carcinus* has a metabolic rate only 30 per cent less than the standard rate in water (Wallace, 1972); clearly the collapse of the gills which occurs in air does not severely impair its ability to take up oxygen.

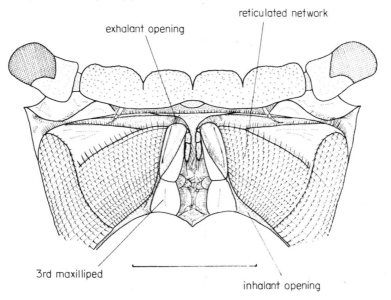

Fig. 40 View from the front of the mangrove tree crab *Aratus pisoni* showing the reticulated network on the branchiostegites. When the crab is out of water the respiratory stream, pumped from the exhalant openings, flows in a thin film over the network. Gaseous exchange takes place and the water is sucked back into the branchial chambers through the inhalant openings. Scale = 10 mm.

Mangrove swamp crabs are chronically exposed to low oxygen tensions in the available water and most of them use air in preference to water as the source of their respiratory oxygen. There are several records in the literature of upper-shore swamp crabs (*Uca, Sesarma,* the hermit crab *Coenobita*) climbing mangrove trees apparently to avoid being submerged by high spring tides or floods. Most mangrove crabs, however, have retained the ability to breathe water and, unlike some of the land crabs with their highly developed lungs, do not drown when submerged. Mangrove crabs use two methods for extracting oxygen from the air. First, the retention of some water around the gills which is aerated by periodic air breathing. In shallow water the mangrove crabs *Goniopsis* and *Ucides* breathe air in the same way as *Carcinus* by raising the front above the surface and reversing the direction of beat of the scaphognathites. This is the main method used by *Ucides* which has a well developed lung but lives in foul waterlogged burrows. *Goniopsis*, on the other hand, usually avoids being submerged and at high tide it climbs trees and rests, bubbling gently, just above water level. When out of water both *Goniopsis* and *Carcinus* beat their scaphognathites forward in the normal manner and bubbles of air appear above the mouth.

The second method of extracting oxygen from the air, is to recirculate the branchial water over the surface of the body. This method is characteristic of the grapsid sub-family Sesarminae but is also found in some other grapsids and in some ocypodids. In sesarmines the water is pumped from the exhalant openings and is distributed over a reticulated network of short hairs and ridges on the branchiostegites. It flows in a thin film over this network, picking up oxygen and losing carbon dioxide, and is sucked back into the branchial chambers at the bases of the legs (Fig. 40). The reticulated branchiostegites thus function as a type of inverted plastron. Alexander and Ewer (1969) showed that when water was available the recirculated fluid was changed periodically, no doubt to replace evaporative losses and to offset any increase in salinity due to evaporation. Water is released by raising the back of the carapace and opening a slit into the branchial cavities out of which the water flows, a fresh supply can be drawn up from a moist substratum by the use of the hair tufts at the leg bases.

The oxygen affinity of the blood pigment

A further line of defence against the effects of low environmental pO_2 lies in the oxygen affinity of the blood pigment (see p. 17). High affinity pigments continue to take up oxygen despite low external pO_2, the only disadvantage being that crabs containing such pigments must have metabolisms which work at lower pO_2's. Table 3 gives the pO_2 at half saturation (P_{50}) of haemocyanins of a variety of crabs and it is at once clear that those inhabiting well oxygenated environments, the marine crabs and the land crab *Gecarcinus*, have the highest P_{50}'s. Estuarine and mangrove crabs generally have lower P_{50}'s, but there are some exceptions and oddities. *Goniopsis* spends most of its time in air so its high P_{50} is not unexpected; but so does the tree crab *Aratus* which has a much lower P_{50}. Can it be that recirculating the branchial water, practised by *Aratus*, supplies oxygen to the gills at a lower pO_2 than does the air-breathing of *Goniopsis*? Or is it that *Aratus*, on its arboreal wanderings, spends longer away from water than *Goniopsis* and so runs a greater risk of losing its branchial fluid and of suffering gill collapse? The two measurements for *Callinectes* are rather different, but the population which yielded the very low P_{50} of 5·5 mm Hg was living in a salt pond thought to be particularly susceptible to low pO_2. It is likely (see below) that the oxygen affinity of the blood pigment can be adaptively varied and is yet another example of acclimation to environmental stress. It might be thought that *Cardisoma*, being a land crab, should be classed with *Gecarcinus* and thus be the greatest exception of all. In fact *Cardisoma* prefers to live near water, often near foul and muddy water. It enters water freely and, although equipped with lungs, does not drown. I have seen *Cardisoma* living 30 m below the surface of a fresh water limestone sink-hole some miles inland in Jamaica — hardly the habitat of a true land crab! Undoubtedly the very high oxygen affinity of its haemocyanin aids in the exploitation of its diverse habitats.

TABLE 3

P_{50}s in mm Hg of various crabs at environmental temperatures and physiological pH

Land crab	pH	P_{50}	Estuarine crabs	pH	P_{50}
Gecarcinus[1]	7·4	17	*Callinectes sapidus*[4]	7·4	5·5
			Callinectes sapidus[5]	7·5	12
			Carcinus[3]	7·9–7·5	7–13
Marine crabs			Mangrove crabs		
Cancer magister[2]	7·7	19·6	*Goniopsis*[4]	7·8	15·5
Cancer pagurus[3]	7·9–7·5	10–25	*Aratus*[4]	7·8	6·5
Macropipus[3]	7·9–7·5	16–30	*Cardisoma guanhumi*[4]	7·7	7·3
Xantho[3]	7·9–7·5	9–18	*Cardisoma guanhumi*[1]	7·4	4
Maia[3]	7·9–7·5	14–23			

1 Redmond, 1968	4 Young, 1972
2 Johansen *et al.*, 1970	5 Bonaventura *et al.*, 1974
3 Truchot, 1971b	

The oxygen affinity of haemocyanin is a convenient subject with which to draw together some of the threads running through this chapter. It should be clear that, although some fresh water and estuarine crabs do not suffer desiccation and some land crabs do not suffer oxygen lack, most of the inhabitants of hostile environments risk all four of the stresses which have been considered here. As was pointed out in the last chapter with reference to larvae, the effects of simultaneous stresses are not independent; obvious examples are the dependence of desiccation rate and metabolic rate on temperature — the addition of a second stress makes worse the effect of the first stress. In the case of haemocyanin it has been found that the oxygen affinity decreases with decreasing blood concentration, decreasing pH (the Bohr effect, p. 17) and increasing temperature. One would therefore expect increased temperature and decreased salinity (both of which make extra metabolic demands) to reduce the oxygen gradients at the gills and make it more difficult for crabs to take up oxygen. One would also expect this effect in air-breathing crabs since carbon dioxide, which escapes less easily into air, should accumulate in the blood and lower its pH. Truchot (1975a, b) observed all these effects in *Carcinus* but also showed that crabs could compensate for them and maintain a P_{50} close to 10 mm Hg over a wide range of environmental conditions. Compensation to temperature was by acclimation; it was found that the oxygen affinity of the haemocyanin was higher in crabs acclimated to high temperatures than in those acclimated to low temperatures (when both were measured at the same temperature and pH). In the case of reduced salinity, decreasing blood concentration was accompanied by a compensatory increase in pH, possibly partly caused by release of ammonia from the cells following breakdown of amino acids during intracellular iso-osmotic regulation (Weiland and Mangum, 1975). Concerning air-breathing, the expected rapid rise in blood CO_2 and drop in blood pH was found in *Carcinus* on emersion into air (Truchot, 1975a). This was followed by a slower, compensatory rise in bicarbonate. Buffering took four days to complete, rather longer than *Carcinus* might normally expect to be stranded, but half compensation was reached within 24 hours.

10 Evolution and systematics

Taxonomy need not be dry and dreary; when the object of one's endeavour is a natural classification which reflects the evolutionary history of a group it can become a fascinating study. Evidence can be drawn from all branches of biology and in the end an intellectually satisfying structure is built up which is of use to all those involved in studying the group. One passes from a collection of labels to an ordered system which reaches back through time and embodies an understanding of the intimate link between adaptation and life-style. Unfortunately, in the case of crabs, we have not yet reached the end of the path. Different authorities have built up different systems of classification, none of which is entirely satisfactory (see Glaessner, 1969; Števčić, 1971b). There are several reasons for this: first, the Brachyura is a fairly recent group which has undergone, and is undergoing, explosive adaptive radiation. Some groups of crabs have good fossil records extending back into the Jurassic and Cretaceous, but in others the record is scanty or absent (Table 5). It is particularly difficult to trace relationships in recently evolved groups since, although they are plentiful now, their ancestors were often scarce in comparison with the then dominant, more primitive groups. The job becomes almost impossible when the groups in question inhabit environments which are rarely preserved: rocky shores (Grapsidae), land (Gecarcinidae, Potamidae).

Another difficulty is the question whether to separate groups vertically or horizontally. Should the whole of an evolutionary line be grouped together (vertical) or should primitive survivors of an early divergence from one line be grouped with the primitive survivors of other lines (horizontal)? Clearly the vertical classification follows evolutionary history most closely—or does it? A primitive relict group may change little with time while the main stream from which it arose may change considerably. Thus relict groups from different stocks may end up with fewer real differences between them than exist between any one relict group and the descendants of its original stock. Who is to say which is the best approach; especially when one is not quite sure from which stocks the relict groups stem! The problem of separating stocks and stems is bedevilled by parallel evolution, a frequent occurrence in the descent of crabs. For example, one adaptation to life in deep water is to develop elongated legs to spread the weight over the soft substratum and, perhaps, to accommodate more vibration receptors — useful in this dark environment. Long legs are found in deep water crabs from several different groups: *Homolodromia* (Fig. 41C), *Paromola*, *Platymaia*, *Geryon*, *Palicus*. Long legs for climbing are also found in shallow water spider crabs (Fig. 26A). Adaptation to back-burrowing includes elongation of the carapace: *Emerita* (Fig. 4B), *Ranina* (Fig. 41B), *Corystes* (Fig. 25B): all from different groups. The taxonomist must try to look beyond superficial resemblances which result from similar ways of life; but how to decide which characters are superficial and which are not? Whole groups often arise because of the exploitation of similar life-styles (e.g. Portunidae, Pinnotheridae) and their resemblances indicate true relationships.

A final problem is administrative and results from the diverse nature of the Arthropoda. The Brachyura, despite containing more than a sixth of all crustacean species, is merely an infra-order of the class Crustacea, the seventh rank of crustacean classification. This puts a strain on the number of ranks which can be used to accommodate the diversity of crabs, since we begin to run out of titles for the ranks. Tribes and sub-tribes make their appearance in some classifications and a huge number of families and sub-families. Further splitting can be achieved only by inventing new names for the dispossessed higher ranks, and the same applies to lumping since the lumps must also be named. Table 4 is based on the classification published by Glaessner (1969) which he regarded as not being unduly contentious. Groups without fossil records (not covered by Glaessner) have been inserted according to Calman (1909) and Balss (1957). Table 5 which follows the classification is a summary of the fossil record and lists the numbers of genera known in each family in each geological period including the present.

The most primitive crabs, the Dromiacea, first appear as fossils in the lower Jurassic (Fig. 41A) and there is good palaeontological evidence for believing that they arose from within the Glypheoidea, a macruran group related to spiny lobsters (Palinura) (Glaessner, 1969). Other authors, however, have derived the Dromiacea from true lobsters (Astacidea) or from amongst the Anomura. There is little doubt that the Dromiacea are true crabs, but they sport a number of very primitive features (there have been attempts to place them in the Anomura rather than the Brachyura). The zoea larvae of the Dromiidae are distinctly anomuran (Fig. 42A): they have a shrimp-like shape, uropods and functional 3rd maxillipeds. The larvae of *Homola* possess the last two features but in other respects are more brachyuran (Fig. 42B). Adult Dromiacea have large numbers of gills, sometimes of a very primitive type with filaments rather than lamellae. The eyes may not arise from orbits and if they do, they may

TABLE 4

A classification of the Brachyura

All genera given as examples are referred to somewhere in the text. Asterisks indicate extinct taxa.

Section	Superfamily	Family	Genera
Dromiacea	Dromioidea	Eocarcinidae*	*Eocarcinus** (Fig. 41)
		Prosopidae	*Homolodromia* (Fig. 41)
		Dromiidae	*Dromidia* (Fig. 26)
		Dynomenidae	
	Homoloidea	Homolidae	*Homola* (Fig. 41), *Paromola*
	Dakoticancroidea*	Dakoticancridae*	
Oxystomata	Dorippoidea	Dorippidae	
	Calappoidea	Calappidae	*Calappa* (Fig. 25), *Hepatus, Matuta*
		Leucosiidae	*Ebalia, Iliacanthus, Persephona* (Fig. 25)
	Raninoidea	Raninidae	*Ranina* (Fig. 41), *Raninoides*
Oxyrhyncha		Maiidae	*Acanthonyx, Chionoecetes, Hyas, Inarchus, Libinia, Macropodia* (Fig. 26), *Maia* (frontispiece), *Mithrax, Pisa* (Fig. 26), *Platymaia, Pugettia, Stenocionops*
		Parthenopidae	*Daldorfia*
		Hymenosomatidae	*Halicarcinus*
Cancridea		Corystidae	*Corystes* (Fig. 25)
		Atelecyclidae	
		Cancridae	*Cancer* (Figs. 1, 29)
Brachyrhyncha	Portunoidea	Carcineretidae*	
		Portunidae	*Arenaeus, Callinectes* (Fig. 24), *Carcinus* (Fig. 31), *Macropipus* (Fig. 24), *Polybius* (Fig. 24), *Portumnus, Portunus, Scylla*
	Xanthoidea	Xanthidae	*Carpilius, Eriphia, Lybia, Menippe* (Fig. 22), *Panopeus, Pilumnus, Pseudocarcinus, Rithropanopeus, Trapezia, Xantho*
		Potamidae	*Kingsleya* (Fig. 29), *Paratelphusa, Potamon, Pseudotelphusa*
		Geryonidae	*Geryon*
		Goneplacidae	*Goneplax* (Fig. 25)
		Pinnotheridae	*Pinnotheres*
		Grapsidae	*Aratus* (Fig. 22), *Cyclograpsus, Eriocheir, Goniopsis* (frontispiece), *Grapsus, Helice, Metapaulus, Pachygrapsus, Sesarma*
		Gecarcinidae	*Cardisoma, Gecarcinus, Gecarcoidea, Ucides*
	Ocypoidea	Ocypodidae	*Dotilla, Heloecius, Macrophthalmus, Ocypode* (Fig. 22), *Paracleistostoma, Uca* (Fig. 30)
		Retroplumidae	*Retropluma*
		Mictyridae	*Mictyris*
	Uncertain	Palicidae	*Palicus*
		Hapalocarcinidae	*Cryptochirus, Hapalocarcinus* (Fig. 26)

TABLE 5

The fossil record of the Brachyura. The number of genera in each family found in each geological period (based on Chase, 1951; Balss, 1957; Glaessner, 1969). Asterisks indicate extinct taxa

	Jurassic	Cretaceous	Paleocene	Eocene	Oligocene	Miocene	Pliocene	Pliestocene	Recent
Length in millions of years	45	65	10	20	15	14	10	1	
Eocarcinidae*	1								
Prosopidae	6	7							4
Dromiidae			1	3	1	1	1	1	18
Dynomenidae	3	6	1	2					2
Homolidae	2	1			1				9
Dakoticancridae*		3							
Dorippidae		4		3	2	1	1	1	10
Calappidae		5	2	3	7	7	1	2	11
Leucosiidae				1	1	10	9	9	40
Raninidae		7	2	5	3	5	2	1	10
Maiidae				6	3	6	6	9	145
Parthenopidae				1	2	1	1	3	21
Hymenosomatidae									9
Corystidae									6
Atelecyclidae				2		3	2	1	13
Cancridae				1		3	1	1	5
Carcineretidae*		5							
Portunidae				10	9	9	4	7	38
Xanthidae		4	6	19	12	13	14	11	138
Potamidae						1	1		18
Geryonidae				2	2	4			3
Goneplacidae			3	9	7	8	2		54
Pinnotheridae				1	1	2			26
Grapsidae				3	2	1		3	40
Gecarcinidae							1		6
Ocypodidae				1		2	1	4	19
Retroplumidae				1			1		1
Mictyridae									1
Palicidae		2		1					5
Hapalocarcinidae									3

share them with the antennae. The female genital openings are on the coxae of the 2nd pair of walking legs (6th thoracic segment) not on the sternum as in most other crabs; and the spermathecae are quite unlike those of more advanced crabs, being simply cavities between the sternites rather than enlargements of the oviduct (Hartnoll, 1975). Last of the more obvious primitive features are the vestigial uropods found in adults of the Dromiidae. Nevertheless, the overall morphology of the Dromiacea is crab-like and they are clearly the ancestors of modern crabs. They are plentiful as fossils (Table 5) and reached their peak in the Jurassic and Cretaceous. Recent representatives of the Dromiacea survive by having specialized ways of life, some inhabit deep water while others creep about holding protective sponges or bivalve shells over their backs with their modified, dorsally positioned back legs (Fig. 23C).

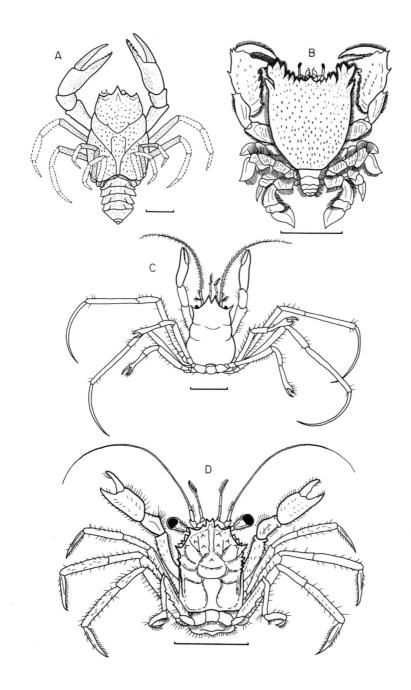

Fig. 41 Primitive crabs. A, *Eocarcinus praecursor*, lower Jurassic; B, *Ranina ranina* (♂), Indo-Pacific, Recent; C. *Homolodromia paradoxa* (♂), West Indies to East Africa, Recent; D, *Homola barbata* (♀), Atlantic, Recent. A, B and C after Glaessner, 1969; D after Rice and Provenzano, 1970. Scale, A, C, D, = 10 mm; B, = 100 mm.

The Oxystomata are characterized by elongated mouthparts and a triangular buccal frame. This development is certainly an adaptation to a back-burrowing life-style; the narrow upper end of the buccal frame and the elongated maxillipeds function as an exhalant channel (p. 76). Other burrowing adaptations in the Oxystomata include the elongated body and spade-shaped legs of the Raninidae (Fig. 41B) and the eye-hillocks of the Calappidae and Leucosiidae (Fig. 25). The Dorippidae possess the characteristic mouthparts of the Oxystomata, presumably inherited from burrowing ancestors, but their present life-style is more like that of the Recent Dromiacea. The last two pairs of walking legs are sub-chelate and held dorsally to grip a protective associate such as a sea anemone, or camouflage in the shape of a bivalve mollusc shell. The dorsal position of the posterior legs, a character of the Dromiacea, is a primitive feature which the Dorippidae share with the raninids (Fig. 41B). Another primitive feature — coxal female genital openings — is also found in these two groups: in the Raninidae and in a sub-family of the dorippids, the Tymolinae. This led Gordon (1963) to suggest that the Raninidae and the Tymolinae should be removed from the Oxystomata and grouped with the Dromiacea, a view criticised by Glaessner (1969) as an extreme application of horizontal classification. Raninids, however, have yet more primitive features: their zoea larvae possess uropods (Fig. 42C). Studying the larvae of primitive families Williamson (1965) found little relationship between raninids and the other Oxystomata and concluded that, as far as larval characters go, the inclusion of the Raninidae, Homolidae and Dromiidae within the Brachyura depended upon one's definition of true crabs. A narrow definition would exclude all three families but a wide definition would still exclude the Dromiidae. Table 5 shows the long fossil history of the Oxystomata; they first appear in the lower Cretaceous and one should not be too surprised to find primitive features within the group. They presumably originated as an early burrowing offshoot of the Dromiacea. Early raninids and calappids do not differ greatly, but the calappids 'advanced' while the raninids specialized. With the exception of the Leucosiidae, a later offshoot of the calappids, the Oxystomata appear to have undergone a slow decline from an early diversification in the Cretaceous (Glaessner, 1969).

The remaining groups of the Brachyura (the Oxyrhyncha, Cancridea and Brachyrhyncha) are grouped together in many classifications into the section Brachygnatha. All have a square buccal frame, distinct from the Oxystomata, and lack the combinations of primitive features found in the Dromiacea. A scattering of primitive features remains, however: in both the Retroplumidae and the Palicidae the last pair of legs is reduced and sub-dorsal. The section Brachygnatha is not used here since it seems highly likely to be a polyphyletic assemblage consisting of at least three separate offshoots from the early Dromiacea. The three groups are

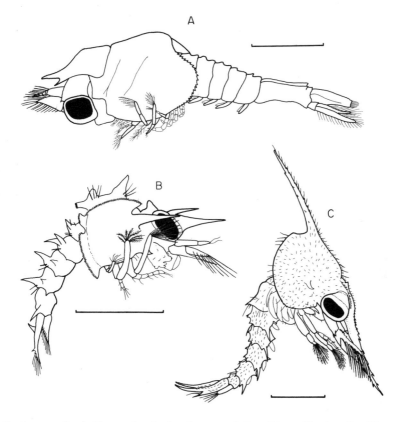

Fig. 42 Larvae of primitive crabs. A, fourth zoea of *Dromidia antillensis*; after Rice and Provenzano, 1966. B, third zoea of *Homola barbata*; after Rice and Provenzano, 1970. C, third zoea of *Raninoides benedicti*, tropical Pacific; after Knight, 1968. Scale = 1 mm.

similar because they are all advanced, not because they are closely related. The Oxyrhyncha is probably a natural group and is characterized by a rounded or triangular carapace, spiny or sculptured, and drawn out at the front into a rostrum, pointed or forked. The group does not have a long fossil record, but appears already diversified in the Eocene. Cancrideans have rounded or elongated carapaces, narrow fronts and a number of other minor characters in common which appear to separate them from the Brachyrhyncha. There is a general tendency to back-burrowing in the Cancridea, the Atelecyclidae and particularly the Corystidae (p. 77) are specialized back-burrowers while cancrids may partially bury themselves when at rest. Amongst the early Dromiacea the Dakoticancridae appear to constitute possible ancestors of the Cancridea (Glaessner, 1969).

The Brachyrhyncha contains a wide variety of families and the majority of living crabs. Its origin is obscure and the group may well be polyphyletic. The fossil records of the Portunoidea and the Xanthidae extend back into the upper Cretaceous, and the Palicidae first appear in the lower Cretaceous, but these fossils give few clues either to origins or to relationships within the Brachyrhyncha. The Portunoidea appear to have developed swimming quite early in their evolution since, in the Cretaceous Carcineretidae, the back legs already formed paddles. Within the Ocypoidea specialization is towards a semiterrestrial, deposit-feeding way of life. The predatory life-style of *Ocypode* may represent a primitive condition. The aberrant *Retropluma* is an Indo-Pacific deep water form.

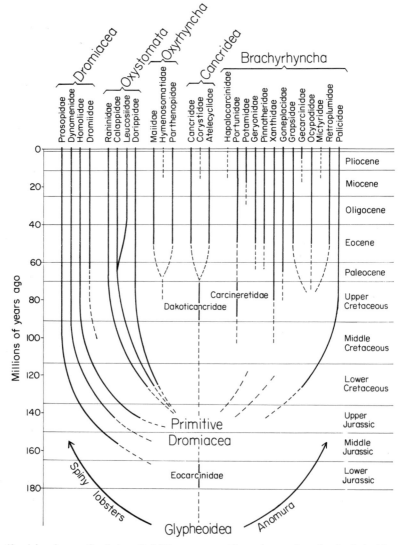

Fig. 43   A brachyuran family tree. Solid lines represent history known from fossils, dashed lines are assumptions. Probable relationships are indicated by convergences but juxtaposition of families does not necessarily indicate close relationship, e.g. the Dromiidae may have arisen from any group of the Dromiacea—Recent, fossil or unknown.

The coral gall crabs of the Hapalocarcinidae are so modified (Fig. 26E) as to make it almost impossible to trace their origins; Balss (1957) placed them in a separate section of the Brachyura.

The seven families of the Xanthoidea have all gone off in different directions: the xanthids as slow walkers, the potamids as fresh water crabs, the geryonids as deep water predators, the goneplacids as underwater side-burrowers (superficially similar to the ocypodids), the pinnotherids as commensals, the grapsids as scavenging shore crabs and the gecarcinids as land crabs.

There are some problems, however, associated with treating the seven families as a single superfamily. Fresh water crabs, for instance, are given only familial rank by Glaessner (1969) but other authors have raised them to super-familial rank. Bott (1970) separated fresh water crabs into three super-families: the Pseudotelphusoidea (tropical America, containing three families), the Paratelphusoidea (India, East Indies and Australia, containing three families) and the Potamoidea (Europe, Africa, Middle and Far East, containing five families). Fresh water crabs may be polyphyletic and the different groups may be of considerable age. Turning to another part of the Xanthoidea one finds that, in some classifications, the Grapsidae and the Gecarcinidae are grouped with the Ocypoidea and the whole assemblage referred to as the Grapsoidea. Grapsids, gecarcinids and ocypodids have broadly similar life-styles and a variety of anatomical features in common; on anatomical grounds the gecarcinid genus *Ucides* could easily be classified in the Ocypodidae. The Xanthoidea, therefore, may not be a natural group but one which serves, at present, as a taxonomical dumping ground for a variety of advanced brachyrhynchans.

Taken altogether, and despite the difficulties in sorting out relationships the evolution of the Brachyura is an excellent example of adaptive radiation (Fig. 43). First the Dromiacea, then the burrowing Oxystomata and now the diverse Oxyrhyncha and Brachyrhyncha, each family has taken a different life-style and, with an array of sub-families and species, exploited the numerous possibilities open to it.

A note on the Anomura seems in order here. This infra-order of crab-like crustaceans seems to have arisen somewhat earlier than the Dromiacea but from the same general stock: the spiny lobster stock, not the true lobster stock (Glaessner, 1969). Anomuran bodies differ from those of true crabs by being less thoroughly fused together: the epistome is not fused to the carapace and the last thoracic sternite is free. The abdomen is usually fairly large and the last pair of legs is reduced. The Anomura comprises four super-families: Thalassinoidea, Paguroidea, Galatheoidea and Hippoidea. The thalassinoids are lobster-like or shrimp-like and are first found as fossils in the lower Jurassic. Recent representatives which have survived from the Cretaceous are the burrowing prawns *Upogebia* and *Callianassa*. The Paguroidea also date from the lower Jurassic and include the hermit crabs and stone crabs (*Lithodes* (Fig. 4C) and *Paralithodes*). The Galatheoidea are first found in the middle Jurassic and contain the Galatheidae (squat lobsters) and Porcellanidae (porcelain crabs, e.g. *Porcellana* (Fig. 4D), and *Petrolisthes*). The Hippoidea (mole crabs, Fig. 4B) date from the Oligocene.

11 Crabs and man

The main use that man makes of crabs is to eat them. They are excellent food — boiled, roasted, curried, cold with salad and mayonnaise, hot with black pepper, cracked from their shells or eaten whole just after moulting — it is difficult in my opinion, unless one is allergic to them, to avoid being delighted by eating crabs. They are also very nutritious; the raw white meat (muscle) contains about 20 per cent protein, 1–2 per cent minerals, little fat and hardly any carbohydrate. Members of the following families are regularly consumed in various parts of the world: Lithodidae (Anomura), Maiidae, Cancridae, Portunidae, Xanthidae, Potamidae, Geryonidae, Gecarcinidae, Ocypodidae. These families contain the majority of large crabs; small crabs, although perfectly edible, are a bit fiddly to deal with.

The two commonest of the wide variety of crab catching methods are trapping and netting. A crab trap or pot is a baited cage which is lowered to the sea bed and left for a day or two attached by a rope to a buoy on the surface. Crabs are attracted by the smell of the bait (fish heads, etc.) and enter the pot through one or more entrance tunnels. These tunnels delve into the pot and open near the centre in mid-water so that, once in, it is difficult for crabs to find their way out. The size of the pot is tailored to the size of the crabs. For catching Alaskan king crabs *Paralithodes camtschatica* which may reach one metre or more in leg span, pots 2 metres square and 0·75 metres deep are used. In the early days of the king crab fishery, such pots when lifted after two or three days on the bottom were sometimes completely full of crabs, as many as 250 in a single pot! The return per pot is now far less; overfishing is all too easy in slow growing species (p.120). These huge heavy pots demand a sizeable investment for each fishing unit, as, indeed, does the rigour of the Alaskan climate and the fact that the fishing grounds are some distance offshore. Fishing boats are quite large, carry up to 150 pots, and have holding tanks on board capable of maintaining up to 12 000 live crabs (Idyll and Sisson, 1971). Such an investment is not necessary for crab fishermen of milder climes whose prey lives closer to shore. There are many fishermen in the English Channel who catch the edible crab *Cancer pagurus* from small boats, setting relatively few pots at a time. Large investments, however, are still profitable: off the east coasts of England and Scotland, where 80 per cent of the British crab catch is taken, most crabs are caught by large boats working 200–500 pots each. Pots are set in strings, 20–70 per string, buoyed at each end and lifted daily (Edwards and Early, 1972). Other important species taken in pots include the Dungeness crab *Cancer magister* along the western coast of North America, the blue crab *Callinectes sapidus* on the south-east coast of the USA, the Florida stone crab *Menippe mercenaria*, the red crab *Geryon quinquedens* at 170–400 fathoms off New England, and the large estuarine swimming crab *Scylla serrata* throughout much of the Indo-Pacific.

Nets are second to pots in importance but more varied in their form. Blue crabs, as well as being caught in pots, are captured by trawling. This type of fishing cannot be done in rocky areas and is therefore unsuitable for most crabs, but blue crabs swim up estuaries the muddy bottoms of which present few obstacles to the trawl. As in other types of bottom trawling the use of a tickler chain increases the catch. The chain drags along just in front of the net and disturbs the crabs from the bottom so that they are caught in the net. Tangle-netting is the method used by the Japanese and Russians to catch king crabs and snow or tanner crabs *Chionoecetes tanneri* (the snow or queen crab *C. opilio* is the north Atlantic representative of the genus). A typical tangle-net is 46 metres long, 2·5 metres high, and weighted and buoyed such that it forms a wall of netting resting on the sea bed. The spiky long-legged king and snow crabs get entangled in the nets as they try to move past them. Best catches are to be taken during the annual breeding migrations when the crabs move from deep to shallower water. The Russian and Japanese tangle-net fisheries are highly organized, there are separate net laying and net picking boats, and a factory ship to which each fleet is attached. Nets are linked together and set in lines 8 to 16 kilometres long; up to 20 such lines may be set parallel to one another and about a mile apart to form a 'field' covering some 400 square kilometres. A factory ship and its fleet of layers and pickers may tend ten fields at once. Crabs are cooked, picked and frozen or canned on board the factory ship (Idyll and Sisson, 1971).

A more rustic method of fishing for crabs (or fish or shrimps) found all over the world is the use of lift-nets. A lift-net is usually small enough to be operated by a single fisherman and consists of a piece of net lowered into the water in the form of a dish or bowl, baited at the centre. The net is lowered to where the prey is, to the bottom in the case of crabs, and the prey moves onto the net to get at the bait. The fisherman then hoists the net rapidly to the surface. *Scylla* and *Callinectes* may be caught in left-nets and in some areas the Dungeness crab is similarly caught in baited wire bowls, hauled every half-hour. Other types of net which catch crabs include seines used from the beach for *Scylla* and other portunids.

Trapping, tangle-netting and trawling are the only crab catching methods used in modern fishing industries. The host of other methods usually demand acts of individual capture and are therefore labour-intensive. They are practised widely by amateurs out for a free meal and by professionals in most underdeveloped coastal regions. Some methods require apparatus: baited lines (without hooks) can be used to draw crabs near to the shore so that they can be scooped out with a dip-net; this method is often used for *Scylla* and *Callinectes*. A curious bait is said to be used by Patagonians fishing for lithodid crabs; they lower a live sexually receptive (premoult) female crab into the water. Courting males cling so tightly to this glamorous bait that they can be hauled out and captured! Nicobar Islanders use spears to capture *Scylla* and *Portunus*, and hooked gaffs are widely used to pull crabs out of holes or from under rocks. The rock crab *Grapsus* is caught in Trinidad (for use as fish bait) by an interesting piece of apparatus consisting of a long stick with a fork at the end across which a cotton thread is stretched. The object of the exercise is to hook the thread over the eyestalks of the crab. Feeling something under its eye, the crab folds it into its socket, thus trapping the thread. The crab may then be lifted by its eyestalks and captured.

Perhaps the most common method of all is simply to catch crabs by hand. Several species are found on the shore at low tide sheltering under rocks: *Carcinus*, sold for food in London 100 years ago, and the velvet swimming crab *Macropipus puber*, eaten in the Channel Islands. In the tropics land crabs are caught at night when they come out of their burrows to forage for food. They are easiest to catch during breeding migrations to the sea. These take place on full moon nights and are times of great activity in the crab population as a whole. In the West Indies at such times groups of crab catchers go out with lanterns and sacks to spend an exhausting hour or two chasing about after these agile crustaceans (usually *Cardisoma*). In Trinidad an interesting method is practised for catching the large hairy mangrove crab *Ucides cordatus*. These crabs live in foul waterlogged burrows and come up periodically to breathe air (p.160). The fisherman's method is to make air-breathing impossible by blocking the mouth of the burrow with a clod of mud. After an hour or so he returns, removes the clod and easily catches the crab which is usually found sitting half asphyxiated beneath it.

TABLE 6

Landings in millions of kg of the commercially most important species of crab in the USA in the early 1970s (based on Holmsen and McAllister, 1974)

Year	King crab	Snow crab	Dungeness crab	Blue crab
1970	23·6	6·6	26·5	65·9
1971	31·9	5·7	19·3	65·7
1972	33·5	13·1	12·2	65·9
1973	34·4	27·7	5·5	61·1

Fisheries for crab are of small importance when compared with those for fish, but they are still quite big business. Table 6 shows the landings of the commercially most important species in the USA during the early 1970s. Stocks of Dungeness crab appear to be dwindling, but the total market is maintained by increasing catches of snow crab. Off southern England a supplement to the crab catch could be made by fishing the large spider crab *Maia squinado*, much prized by coastal communities further south. Unfortunately, there is no market for this species in Britain. Crab meat is sold canned or frozen or made into various concoctions such as crab paste, an important constituent of which is the brown meat (hepatopancreas). The crabs are cooked and the meat picked by hand from the skeleton; compressed air is sometimes used to blow the meat out of the legs. More spectacularly, crabs may be sold whole, live or cooked, or prepared for the table with the picked meat artistically packed into the carapace (dressed). In Trinidad piles of live *Cardisoma* may be seen at the market, their legs and chelae neatly tied with tough vines to prevent them escaping and injuring the customers. In the USA blue crabs are often sold and eaten as soft-shell crabs and fetch a higher price than the hard-shelled variety. Blue crab fishermen can recognize crabs which are about to moult ('peelers') and these are held alive until they do moult. They are then sent immediately to market. They must be sold and eaten quickly, since if left for more than a day or two they use up their reserves and become watery, and, of course, no longer soft-shelled (p.128). Soft-shell crabs are eaten whole, there being no wastage. In a hard-shelled crab the easiest meat to get at is the claw-meat and sometimes only the claws are marketed. In Portugal the large claw of male *Uca tangeri* is detached and the crab released, perhaps to grow another one; the claws are eaten as an hors-d'oeuvre. Similarly, the large claw of the Florida stone crab may be detached by fishermen and the crab released.

An alternative to fishing is to farm crabs. This is a common practice with *Scylla* in such places as Taiwan, Indonesia and the Philippines. In Taiwan in 1966 about 168 000 kg of crab were produced by pond culture, and production rate in Java is about 200 crabs/ha/y (Bardach *et al.*, 1972). *Scylla* is normally raised as a subsidiary crop in milk-fish culture. These fish are stocked in brackish water ponds fairly high on the shore, the water being retained by banks of mud. Some *Scylla* get in when the ponds are filled but more crabs are introduced as 'seed'—small crabs about 2 cm across collected in traps and lift-nets by fishermen and sold to farmers. The crabs feed on naturally occurring food in the ponds, probably mostly molluscs, but this can be supplemented by cheap fish and kitchen refuse. They can reach a marketable size in six months and are harvested by traps and lift-nets. Crab culture appears to be a casual procedure taking place mostly in poorly managed fish ponds; stocking and harvesting goes on at a low level throughout the year. Crabs are not stocked in well developed fish ponds since they are inclined to dig holes in the banks and let out the water. Elsewhere in the world crab culture is a popular subject for feasibility studies. These mostly show that crab culture is not a commercially attractive proposition because of the slow growth rates of the larger species, the expense of feeding and the frequency of cannibalism when stocked at high densities. Other, perhaps more attractive possibilities include the mass rearing of baby crabs for release in the sea to stimulate a declining fishery (greatest mortality occurs in nature during the larval life and this may be eliminated by culture; but whether mass release of babies has a significant effect on crab stocks has yet to be demonstrated), and the holding of crabs caught in season when the price is low in the hope of realizing a profit by selling them out of season when the price is higher.

Apart from being eaten, crabs impinge on human activities in a number of other ways. They can be agricultural and maricultural pests, vectors of human disease and they can provide entertainment. Fresh water potamids and, near the coast, the land crab *Cardisoma* can be very serious agricultural pests, rice being the main crop which they damage. They do it in two ways, first by eating the crop (they are particularly fond of the sprouting tips of young plants), and second by digging holes in the banks of the rice fields so that the water leaks out and the rice, exposed to the drying action of the sun, is killed. They do not confine their attentions to rice, however, and any crop grown near crabs is liable to damage. In the sea, crabs incur the odium of mollusc growers and gatherers. *Carcinus* has come in for particular blame in the USA as a predator of the soft-shell clam *Mya*, and in Britain cockles and mussels (*Cardium* and *Mytilus*) suffer from its attentions. Baby oysters may be attacked by *Carcinus* and other crabs while inside oysters, mussels and scallops the pea crab *Pinnotheres*, besides being an unwelcome addition to the meal, reduces the proportion of mollusc tissue which might otherwise go to man. Crab pests can be killed by the application of suitable poisons, often insecticides. Pea crabs in oysters can be controlled by spreading a mixture of sevin and chlorinate benzenes over oyster beds. Spreading poisons, especially in the marine environment, requires great care and detailed study since, amongst other hazards, it is not unlikely that valuable organisms such as blue crabs may be killed along with the pests (Loosanoff, 1965). Indeed, it is sometimes the case that the pest of one industry is the crop of another, *Callinectes* and *Scylla* both eat oysters.

The medical hazards of crabs come from potamids. In the Far East most species of fresh water crab act as intermediate hosts to the lung fluke *Paragonimus*. The primary intermediate host is a snail and the crabs are infected by cercariae. The encysted parasite is passed on to man when he eats the crab—raw with vinegar, curry or rice wine. The flukes encyst in the lungs producing symptoms not unlike tuberculosis. In Africa fresh water crabs are associaed with river blindness, a condition caused by the nematode *Onchocerca*. Here the association is less intimate than in the case of *Paragonimus*. *Onchocerca* is transmitted by the blackfly *Simulium*, and in some parts of Africa by *S. neavei*, the larvae of which are obligate ectocommensals of river crabs. Onchocerciasis is an unpleasant disease, the adult worms live beneath the skin in nodules of fibrous tissue and produce vast numbers of microfilariae which lie in wait in the skin ready to be picked up by the bite of a blackfly. The microfilariae cause itching in the skin and blindness when they get into the eyes. Control measures are concentrated on the blackfly and, in the case of *S. neavei*, on its unfortunate associate the river crab.

Crabs provide entertainment by racing and fighting. They are not, themselves, remotely interested in racing and must be coaxed or more likely frightened in the right direction. Racing crabs include *Cardisoma* and the land hermit *Coenobita*. In the latter species races are arranged in the bars of some West Indian hotels; the crabs are placed in the centre of a circle and the first one out of the circle is the winner. Crab fighting is practised in the Seychelles, the victims being *Ocypode*. The unfortunate creatures are induced to fight each other simply by confining them within their individual distances. The best entertainment to be had from crabs, however, is to eschew these functions and simply to watch them in their natural environments going about their daily lives.

References

Adiyodi, R.C. 1972. Wound healing and regeneration in the crab *Paratelphusa hydrodromus*. *Int. Rev. Cytol.* **32**: 257–89.

Aldrich, J.C. 1975. On the relationship between oxygen consumption and feeding levels in decapods. *Proc. 9th Eur. mar. biol. Symp.*: 407–18.

Alexander, R.McN. 1968. *Animal mechanics*. London: Sidgwick and Jackson.

Alexander, S.J., and Ewer, D.W. 1969. A comparative study of some aspects of the biology and ecology of *Sesarma catenata* Ort. and *Cyclograpsus punctatus* M. Edw., with additional observations on *Sesarma meinerti* de Man. *Zoologica Afr.* **4**: 1–35.

Alexandrowicz, J.S. 1972. The comparative anatomy of leg proprioceptors in some decapod crustaceans. *J. mar. biol. Ass. UK.* **52**: 605–34.

Allen, J.A. 1972. Recent studies on the rhythms of post-larval decapod crustaceans. *Oceanogr. mar. Biol.* **10**: 415–36.

Aréchiga, H., Huberman, A., and Naylor, E. 1974. Hormonal modulation of circadian neural activity in *Carcinus maenas* (L.) *Proc. R. Soc.* B, **187**: 299–313.

Arudpragasam, K.D., and Naylor, E. 1964. Gill ventilation volumes, oxygen consumption and respiratory rhythms in *Carcinus maenas* (L.). *J. exp. Biol.* **41**: 309–21.

Arudpragasam, K.D., and Naylor, E. 1966. Patterns of gill ventilation in some decapod crustaceans. *J. Zool. Lond.* **150**: 401–11.

Aspey, W.P. 1971. Inter-species sexual discrimination and approach–avoidance conflict in two species of fiddler crabs, *Uca pugnax* and *Uca pugilator*. *Anim. Behav.* **19**: 669–76.

Atema, J., and Engstrom, D.G. 1971. Sex pheromone in the lobster, *Homarus americanus*. *Nature, Lond.* **232**: 261–3.

Atkins, D. 1954. Leg disposition in the brachyuran megalopa when swimming. *J. mar. biol. Ass. UK.* **33**: 627–36.

Atkinson, R.J.A., and Naylor, E. 1973. Activity rhythms in some burrowing decapods. *Helgoländ. wiss. Meeresunters.* **24**: 192–201.

Atwood, H.L. 1967. Crustacean neuromuscular mechanisms. *Am. Zool.* **7**: 527–51.

Atwood, H.L. 1968. Peripheral inhibition in crustacean muscle. *Experientia* **24**: 753–63.

Atwood, H.L. 1973. An attempt to account for the diversity of crustacean muscles. *Am. Zool.* **13**: 357–78.

Atwood, H.L., and Johnston, H.S. 1968. Neuromuscular synapses of a crab motor axon. *J. exp. Zool.* **167**: 457–70.

Balss, H. 1957. Decapoda: Systematik. In H.G. Bronn, *Klassen und Ordnungen des Tierreichs.* **5**, pt 1. Crustacea, Bk 7, pp. 1505–1672. Leipzig: Akademische Verlagsgesellschaft.

Bardach, J.E., Rhyther, J.H., and McLarney, W.O. 1972. *Aquaculture. The farming and husbandry of freshwater and marine organisms.* New York: John Wiley and Sons Inc.

Barnes, R.S.K. 1967. The osmotic behaviour of a number of grapsoid crabs with respect to their differential penetration of an estuarine system. *J. exp. Biol.* **47**: 535–51.

Barnes, R.S.K. 1968a. On the evolution of elongated ocular peduncles by the Brachyura. *Syst. Zool.* **17**: 182–7.

Barnes, R.S.K. 1968b. Relative carapace and chela proportions in some ocypodid crabs (Brachyura, Ocypodidae). *Crustaceana* **14**: 131–6.

Barnes, R.S.K. 1968c. Gradual acclimation effects in *Macrophthalmus setosus* M. Edw. (Brachyura: Ocypodidae). *Life Sciences* **7**, No 4: 171–3.

Barnes, W.J.P., Spirito, C.P., and Evoy, W.H. 1972. Nervous control of walking in the crab *Cardisoma guanhumi*. II. Role of resistance reflexes in walking. *Z. vergl. Physiol.* **76**: 16–31.

Barnwell, F.H. 1968. The role of rhythmic systems in the adaptation of fiddler crabs to the intertidal zone. *Am. Zool.* **8**: 569–83.

Beer, C.G. 1959. Notes on the behaviour of two estuarine crab species. *Trans. R. Soc. N.Z.* **86**: 197–203.

Bennet, D.B. 1974. Growth of the edible crab (*Cancer pagurus* L.) off South-West England. *J. mar. biol. Ass. UK.* **54**: 803–23.

Berridge, M.J., and Oschman, J.L. 1972. *Transporting epithelia.* New York and London: Academic Press.

Binns, R. 1969a. The physiology of the antennal gland of *Carcinus maenas* (L.). II. Urine production rates. *J. exp. Biol.* **51**: 11–16.

Binns, R. 1969b. The physiology of the antennal gland of *Carcinus maenas* (L.). III. Glucose resorption. *J. exp. Biol.* **51**: 17–27.

Binns, R. 1969c. The physiology of the antennal gland of *Carcinus maenas* (L.). IV. The reabsorption of amino acids. *J. exp. Biol.* **51**: 29–39.

Binns, R. 1969d. The physiology of the antennal gland of *Carcinus maenas* (L.). V. Some nitrogenous constituents in the blood and urine. *J. exp. Biol.* **51**: 41–5.

Blatchford, J.G. 1971. Haemodynamics of *Carcinus maenas* (L.). *Comp. Biochem. Physiol.* **39A**: 193–202.

Bliss, D.E. 1963. The pericardial sacs of terrestrial Brachyura. In H.B. Whittington and W.D.I. Rolfe (eds.), *Phylogeny and evolution of Crustacea*, pp. 59–78. Cambridge, Mass.: Museum of comparative zoology, Special Publication.

Bliss, D.E. 1968. Transition from water to land in decapod crustaceans. *Am. Zool.* **8**: 355–92.

Bliss, D.E., Wang, S.M.E., and Martinez, E.A. 1966. Water balance in the land crab, *Gecarcinus lateralis*, during the intermoult cycle. *Am. Zool.* **6**: 197–212.

Bonaventura, C., Sullivan, B., Bonaventura, J., and Bourne, S. 1974. CO binding by haemocyanins of *Limulus polyphemus*, *Busycon carica* and *Callinectes sapidus*. *Biochem.* **13**: 4784–9.

Bott, R. 1970. Betrachtungen über die Entwicklungsgeschichte und Verbreitung der Süsswasser-Krabben nach der Sammlung des Naturhistorischen Museums in Genf/Schweiz. *Revue Suisse de Zoologie,* **77** Pt 2 No 24: 327–44.

Bouligand, Y. 1971. Les orientations fibrillaires dans le squelette des arthropodes. I. L'example de crabes, l'arrangement torsadé des strates. *J. Microscopie,* **11**: 441–72.

Bovbjerg, R.V. 1960. Courtship behaviour of the lined shore crab *Pachygrapsus crassipes* Randall. *Pacif. Sci.* **14**: 421–2.

Broekhuysen, G.J. 1941. The life history of *Cyclograpsus punctatus* M. Edw.: breeding and growth. *Trans. R. Soc. S. Afr.* **28**: 331–66.

Brown, F.A., Jr. 1972. The 'clocks' timing biological rhythms. *Am. Scient.* **60**: 756–66.

Bush, B.M.H. 1962. Peripheral reflex inhibition in the claw of the crab, *Carcinus maenas* (L.). *J. exp. Biol.* **39**: 71–88.

Bush, B.M.H. 1963. A comparative study of certain limb reflexes in decapod crustaceans. *Comp. Biochem. Physiol.* **10**: 273–90.

Bush, B.M.H. 1965. Proprioception by chordotonal organs in the mero-carpopodite and carpo-propodite joints of *Carcinus maenas* legs. *Comp. Biochem. Physiol.* **14**: 185–99.

Butler, T.H. 1961. Growth and age determination of the Pacific edible crab *Cancer magister* Dana. *J. Fish. Res. Bd. Can.* **18**: 873–89.

Calman, W.T. 1909. Crustacea. In E. Ray Lankester (ed.), *A treatise on zoology.* Part VII, Appendiculata, Pt 3. London: A.C. Black.

Cameron, A.M. 1966. Some aspects of the behaviour of the soldier crab, *Mictyris longicarpus*. *Pacif. Sci.* **20**: 224–34.

Cameron, J.N., and Mecklenberg, T.A. 1973. Aerial gas exchanges in the coconut crab *Birgus latro* with some notes on *Gecarcoidea lalandii*. *Respiration Physiology* **19**: 245–61.

Capen, R.L. 1972. Studies of water uptake in the euryhaline crab, *Rithropanopeus harrisi*. *J. exp. Zool.* **182**: 307–20.

Carlisle, D.B. 1957. On the hormonal inhibition of moulting in decapod Crustacea. II. The terminal anecdysis in crabs. *J. mar. biol. Ass. UK.* **36**: 291–307.

Case, J. 1964. Properties of the dactyl chemoreceptors of *Cancer antennularis* Stimpson and *C. productus* Randall. *Biol. Bull. mar. biol. Lab., Woods Hole* **127**: 428–46.

Chase, F.A., Jr. 1951. The number of species of decapod and stomatopod Crustacea. *J. Wash. Acad. Sci.* **40**: 370–2.

Chave, E.H., and Randall, H.A. 1971. Feeding behaviour of the moray eel, *Gymnothorax pictus. Copeia* 1971, pp. 570–4.

Clarac, F. 1968. Proprioceptor anatomy of the ischio-meropodite region in legs of the crab *Carcinus mediterraneus* L. *Z. vergl. Physiol.* **61**: 203–23.

Charac, F., Wales, W., and Laverack, M.S. 1971. Stress detection at the autotomy plane in the decapod Crustacea. II. The function of receptors associated with the cuticle of the basi-ischiopodite. *Z. vergl. Physiol.* **73**: 383–407.

Cohen, M.J. 1963. The crustacean myochordotonal organ as a proprioceptive system. *Comp. Biochem. Physiol.* **8**: 223–43.

Copeland, D.E. 1968. Fine structure of salt and water uptake in the land crab *Gecarcinus lateralis*. *Am. Zool.* **8**: 417–32.

Copeland, D.E., and Fitzjarrell, A.T. 1968. The salt absorbing cells in the gills of the blue crab (*Callinectes sapidus* Rathbun) with notes on modified mitochondria. *Z. Zellforsch. mikrosk. Anat.* **92**: 1–22.

Crane, J. 1941. Crabs of the genus *Uca* from the West coast of Central America. Eastern Pacific Expedition of the New York Zoological Society, XXVI. *Zoologica N.Y.* **26**: 145–208.

Crane, J. 1957. Basic patterns of display in fiddler crabs (Ocypodidae, genus *Uca*). *Zoologica N.Y.* **42**: 69–82.

Crane, J. 1958. Aspects of social behaviour in fiddler crabs, with special reference to *Uca maracoani* (Latreille). *Zoologica N.Y.* **43**: 113–30.

Crane, J. 1967. Combat and its ritualization in fiddler crabs (Ocypodidae), with special reference to *Uca rapax* (Smith). *Zoologica N.Y.* **52**: 49–77.

Crane, J. 1975. Fiddler crabs of the world (Ocypodidae: genus *Uca*). Princeton: Princeton University Press.

Crothers, J.H. 1967. The biology of the shore crab, *Carcinus maenas* (L.). *Fld. Stud.* **2**: 407–34.

Cutress, C., Ross, D.M., and Sutton, L. 1970. The association of *Calliactis tricolor* with its pagurid, calappid and majid partners in the Caribbean. *Can. J. Zool.* **48**: 371–6.

Davenport, J., and Wankowski, J. 1973. Pre-immersion salinity–choice behaviour in *Porcellana platycheles*. *Mar. Biol.* **22**: 313–16.

Dehnel, P.A. 1974. Gill tissue respiration in the crab *Eriocheir sinensis*. *Can. J. Zool.* **52**: 923–37.

Dennell, R. 1960. Integument and exoskeleton. In Waterman, T.H. (ed.), The physiology of Crustacea, I. pp. 449–472. New York and London: Academic Press.

Dennell, R. 1974. The cuticle of the crabs *Cancer pagurus* (L.) and *Carcinus maenas* (L.). *Zool. J. Linn. Soc.* **54**: 241–5.

Dikgraaf, S. 1956. Structure and function of the statocysts in crabs. *Experientia* **12**: 394–6.

Drach, P. 1939. Mue et cycle d'intermue chez les Crustacés décapodes. *Annls Inst. oceanogr. Monaco* **19**: 103–391.

Durrell, G.M. 1953. *The overloaded ark*. London: Faber and Faber Ltd.

Eales, A.J. 1974. Sex pheromone in the shore crab *Carcinus maenas*, and the site of its release from females. *Mar. Behav. Physiol.* **2**: 345–55.

Edney, E.B. 1960. Terrestrial adaptations. In T.H. Waterman (ed.), *The physiology of Crustacea*, I. pp. 367–93. New York and London: Academic Press.

Edney, E.B. 1961. The water and heat relationships of fiddler crabs (*Uca* spp). *Trans. R. Soc. S. Afr.* **36**: 71–91.

Edwards, E., and Early, J.C. 1972. *Catching, handling and processing crabs.* Torrey advisory note No 26. HMSO.

Edwards, R.L. 1958. Movement of individual members in a population of the shore crab *Carcinus maenas* (L.), in the littoral zone. *J. Anim. Ecol.* **27**: 37–45.

Evans, P.D. 1972. The free amino acid pool of the haemocytes of *Carcinus maenas* (L.). *J. exp. Biol.* **56**: 501–7.

Evoy, W.H., and Cohen, M.J. 1971. Central and peripheral control of arthropod movements. *Adv. comp. Physiol. Biochem.* **4**: 225–66.

Evoy, W.H., and Fourtner, C.R. 1973. Nervous control of walking in the crab *Cardisoma guanhumi*. III. Proprioceptive influences on intra and inter segmental coordination. *J. comp. Physiol.* **83**: 303–18.

Fingerman, M. 1960. Tidal rhythmicity in marine organisms. *Cold Spring Harb. Symp. quant. Biol.* **25**: 481–9.

Fingerman, M. 1965. Chromatophores. *Physiol. Rev.* **45**: 296–339.

Fingerman, M. 1966. Neurosecretory control of pigmentary effectors in crustaceans. *Am. Zool.* **6**: 169–79.

Foxon, G.E.H. 1934. Notes on the swimming methods and habits of certain crustacean larvae. *J. mar. biol. Ass. UK.* **19**: 829–49.

Gerard, J.F., and Gilles, R. 1972. The free amino acid pool in *Callinectes sapidus* (Rathbun) tissues and its role in the osmotic intracellular regulation. *J. exp. mar. Biol. Ecol.* **10**: 125–36.

Gibson-Hill, C.A. 1947. Field notes on terrestrial crabs. *Bull. Raffles Mus.* **18**: 43–52.

Gifford, C.A. 1962. Some observations on the general biology of the land crab, *Cardisoma guanhumi* (Latreille), in South Florida. *Biol. Bull. mar. biol. Lab., Woods Hole* **123**: 207–23.

Gifford, C.H. 1968. Accumulation of uric acid in the land crab, *Cardisoma guanhumi*. *Am. Zool.* **8**: 521–8.

Gilles, R., and Schoffeniels, E. 1969. Isosmotic regulation in isolated surviving nerves of *Eriocheir sinensis* Milne-Edwards. *Comp. Biochem. Physiol.* **31**: 927–39.

Glaessner, M.F. 1969. Decapoda. In R.C. Moore, (ed.), *Treatise on invertebrate paleontology*, Part R, Arthropoda 4, vol. **2**: 400–532. Boulder, Colorado: The Geological Society of America, Inc.

Gordon, I. 1963. On the relationship of Dromiacea, Tymolinae and Raninidae to the Brachyura. In H.B. Whittington, and W.D.I. Rolfe, (eds.), *Phylogeny and evolution of Crustacea*, pp. 51–7. Cambridge, Mass.: Museum of comparative zoology, Special Publication.

Gray, I.E. 1957. A comparative study of gill areas of crabs. *Biol. Bull. mar. biol. Lab., Woods Hole* **112**: 34–42.

Green, J.P., and Neff, M.R. 1972. A survey of the fine structure of the integument of the fiddler crab. *Tissue Cell* **4**: 137–71.

Green, J.W., Harsch, M., Barr, L., and Prosser, C.L. 1959. The regulation of water and salt by fiddler crabs, *Uca pugnax* and *Uca pugilator*. *Biol. Bull. mar. biol. Lab., Woods Hole* **116**: 76–87.

Greenwood, J.G. 1972. The mouthparts and feeding behaviour of two species of hermit crabs. *J. nat. Hist.* **6**: 325–37.

Griffin, D.J.G. 1968. Social and maintenance behaviour in two Australian ocypodid crabs (Crustacea: Brachyura). *J. Zool. Lond.* **156**: 291–305.

Grubb, P. 1971. Ecology of terrestrial decapod crustaceans on Aldabra. *Phil. Trans. R. Soc.* Ser. B **260**: 411–16.

Gross, W.J. 1957a. An analysis of response to osmotic stress in selected decapod Crustacea. *Biol. Bull. mar. biol. Lab., Woods Hole* **112**: 43–62.

Gross, W.J. 1957b. A behavioural mechanism for osmotic regulation in a semiterrestrial crab. *Biol. Bull. mar. biol. Lab., Woods Hole* **113**: 268–74.

Gross, W.J. 1959. The effect of osmotic stress on the ionic exchange of a shore crab. *Biol. Bull. mar. biol. Lab., Woods Hole* **116**: 248–57.

Gross, W.J. 1964a. Water balance in anomuran land crabs on a dry atoll. *Biol. Bull. mar. biol. Lab., Woods Hole* **126**: 54–68.

Gross, W.J. 1964b. Trends in water and salt regulation among aquatic and amphibious crabs. *Biol. Bull. mar. biol. Lab., Woods Hole* **127**: 447–66.

Gross, W.J., Lasiewski, R.C., Dennis, M., and Rudy, P., Jr. 1966. Salt and water balance in selected crabs of Madagascar. *Comp. Biochem. Physiol.* **17**: 641–60.

Gross, W.J., and Marshall, L.A. 1960. The influence of salinity on the water fluxes of a crab. *Biol. Bull. mar. biol. Lab., Woods Hole* **119**: 440–53.

Gurney, R. 1942. *Larvae of decapod Crustacea.* London: The Ray Society.

Hagen, H-O. v. 1970. Anpassungen an das spezielle Gezeitenzonen—Niveau bei Ocypodiden (Decapoda, Brachyura). *Forma Functio* **4**: 361–413.

Harris, R.R. 1975. Urine production rate and urinary sodium loss in the freshwater crab *Potamon edulis. J. comp. Physiol.* **96**: 143–53.

Hartman, H.B., and Boettiger, E.G. 1967. The functional organization of the propodus–dactylus organ in *Cancer irroratus* Say. *Comp. Biochem. Physiol.* **22**: 651–63.

Hartnoll, R.G. 1963. The biology of Manx spider crabs. *Proc. zool. Soc. Lond.* **141**: 423–96.

Hartnoll, R.G. 1964. The freshwater grapsid crabs of Jamaica. *Proc. Linn. Soc. Lond.* **175**: 145–69.

Hartnoll, R.G. 1965. Notes on the marine grapsid crabs of Jamaica. *Proc. Linn. Soc. Lond.* **176**: 113–47.

Hartnoll, R.G. 1967. The effects of sacculinid parasites on two Jamaican crabs. *J. Linn. Soc. (Zool.)* **46**: 275–95.

Hartnoll, R.G. 1968. Reproduction in the burrowing crab, *Corystes cassive-launus* (Pennant, 1777) (Decapoda, Brachyura). *Crustaceana,* **15**: 165–70.

Hartnoll, R.G. 1969. Mating in the Brachyura. *Crustaceana* **16**: 161–81.

Hartnoll, R.G. 1970. The relationship of an amphipod and a spider crab with the snakelocks anemone. *Rep. Mar. biol. Sta. Pt Erin* **82**: 37–42.

Hartnoll, R.G. 1971. The occurrence and significance of swimming in the Brachyura. *Anim. Behav.* **19**: 34–50.

Hartnoll, R.G. 1973. Factors affecting the distribution and behaviour of the crab *Dotilla fenestrata* on East African shores. *Estuarine and Coastal Marine Science* **1**: 137–52.

Hartnoll, R.G. 1974. Variation in growth pattern between some secondary sexual characters in crabs (Decapoda, Brachyura). *Crustaceana* **27**: 131–6.

Hartnoll, R.G. 1975. Copulatory structure and function in the Dromiacea, and their bearing on the evolution of the Brachyura. *Pubbl. Staz. zool. Napoli* **39**: Suppl., 657–76.

Hazlett, B.A. 1966. The social behaviour of the Paguridae and Diogenidae of Curacao. *Stud. Fauna Curaçao* **23**: 1–143.

Hazlett, B.A. 1968a. Communicatory effect of body position in *Pagurus bernhardus* (L.) (Decapoda, Anomura). *Crustaceana* **14**: 210–14.

Hazlett, B.A. 1968b. Size relationships and aggressive behaviour in the hermit crab *Clibanarius vittatus*. *Z. Tierpsychol.* **25**: 608–14.

Hazlett, B.A. 1968c. The sexual behaviour of some European hermit crabs (Anomura: Paguridae). *Pubbl. Staz. zool. Napoli* **36**: 238–52.

Hazlett, B.A. 1968d. Stimuli involved in the feeding behaviour of the hermit crab *Clibanarius vittatus* (Decapoda, Paguridae). *Crustaceana* **15**: 305–11.

Hazlett, B.A. 1969. Further investigations of the cheliped presentation display in *Pagurus bernhardus* (Decapoda, Anomura). *Crustaceana* **17**: 31–4.

Hazlett, B.A. 1971. Chemical and chemotactic stimulation of feeding behaviour in the hermit crab *Petrochirus diogenes*. *Comp. Biochem. Physiol.* **39A**: 665–70.

Hazlett, B.A. 1972a. Responses to agonistic postures by the spider crab *Microphrys bicornutus*. *Mar. Behav. Physiol.* **1**: 85–92.

Hazlett, B.A. 1972b. Stimulus characteristics of an agonistic display of the hermit crab (*Calcinus tibicen*). *Anim. Behav.* **20**: 101–7.

Hazlett, B.A. 1975. Individual distances in the hermit crabs *Clibanarius tricolor* and *Clibanarius antillensis*. *Behaviour* **52**: 253–65.

Hazlett, B.A., and Rittschof, D. 1975. Daily movements and home range in *Mithrax spinosissimus* (Majidae, Decapoda). *Mar. Behav. Physiol.* **3**: 101–18.

Herreid, C.F.II. 1969a. Water loss of crabs from different habitats. *Comp. Biochem. Physiol.* **28**: 829–39.

Herreid, C.F.II. 1969b. Integument permeability of crabs and adaptation to land. *Comp. Biochem. Physiol.* **29**: 423–9.

Herrnkind, W.F. 1966. The ability of young and adult sand fiddler crabs, *Uca pugilator* (Bosc), to orient to polarized light. *Am. Zool.* **6**: 298.

Herrnkind, W.F. 1967. Development of celestial orientation during ontogeny in the sand fiddler crab *Uca pugilator*. *Am. Zool.* **7**: 768.

Herrnkind, W.F. 1968. The breeding of *Uca pugilator* (Bosc) and mass rearing of the larvae with comments on the behaviour of the larval and early crab stages. (Brachyura, Ocypodidae). *Crustaceana* Suppl. **2**: 214–24.

Hiatt, R.W. 1948. The biology of the lined shore crab, *Pachygrapsus crassipes* Randall. *Pacif. Sci.* **2**: 135–213.

Highnam, K.C., and Hill, L. 1969. *The comparative endocrinology of the invertebrates.* London: Edward Arnold.

Hinsch, G.W. 1968. Reproductive behaviour in the spider crab, *Libinia emarginata* (L.). *Biol. Bull. mar. biol. Lab., Woods Hole* **135**: 273–8.

Holmsen, A.A., and McAllister, H. 1974. Technological and economic aspects of red crab harvesting and processing. *University Rhode Island Marine Technical Rep.* No 28/ *Ag. Exp. Sta. Bull.* No 413.

Holthius, L.B. 1968. Are there poisonous crabs? *Crustaceana* **15**: 215–22.

Hoopes, D.T., and Karinen, J.F. 1972. Longevity and growth of tagged king crabs in the Eastern Bering Sea. *Fish. Bull. Nat. Oceanic Atmos. Admin.* **70**: 225–6.

Horch, K. 1971. An organ for hearing and vibration sense in the ghost crab *Ocypode*. *Z. vergl. Physiol.* **73**: 1–21.

Horch, K., and Salmon, M. 1972. Responses of the ghost crab, *Ocypode*, to acoustic stimuli. *Z. Tierpsychol.* **30**: 1–13.

Horne, F.R. 1968. Nitrogen excretion in Crustacea. I: the herbivorous land crab *Cardisoma guanhumi* Latreille. *Comp. Biochem. Physiol.* **26**: 687–95.

Horridge, G.A., Ninham, B.W., and Diesendorf, M.O. 1972. Theory of the summation of scattered light in clear zone compound eyes. *Proc. R. Soc. B* **181**: 137–56.

Hoyle, G. 1968. Correlated physiological and ultrastructural studies on specialized muscles. Ia. Neuromuscular physiology of the levator of the eyestalk of *Podophthalmus vigil* (Weber). *J. exp. Zool.* **167**: 471–86.

Hoyle, G., and Burrows, M. 1973. Correlated physiological and ultrastructural studies on specialized muscles. IIIa. Neuromuscular physiology of the power stroke muscle of the swimming leg of *Portunus sanguinolentus*. *J. exp. Zool.* **185**: 83–96.

Hughes, D.A. 1966. Behavioural and ecological investigations of the crab *Ocypode ceratophthalmus* (Crustacea: Ocypodidae). *J. Zool. Lond.* **150**: 129–43.

Hughes, G.M., Knights, B., and Scammell, C.A. 1969. The distribution of pO_2 and hydrostatic pressure change within the branchial chambers in relation to gill ventilation of the shore crab, *Carcinus maenas* (L.). *J. exp. Biol.* **51**: 203–20.

Huxley, J.A. (ed.), 1966. A discussion on ritualization of behaviour in animals and man. *Phil. Trans. R. Soc. Ser. B*, **251**: 247–526.

Hyatt, G.W. 1975. Physiological and behavioral evidence for color discrimination by fiddler crabs (Brachyura, Ocypodidae, genus *Uca*). In F.J. Vernberg (ed.), *Physiological ecology of estuarine organisms*. pp. 333–65. Columbia, South Carolina: University of South Carolina Press.

Idyll, C.P., and Sisson, R.F. 1971. The crab that shakes hands. *Natn. geogr. Mag.* **139**: 254–71.

Jackowski, R.L. 1974. Agonistic behaviour of the blue crab, *Callinectes sapidus* Rathbun. *Behaviour* **50**: 232–53.

Jahromi, S.S., and Atwood, H.L. 1967. Ultrastructural features of crayfish phasic and tonic muscle fibres. *Can. J. Zool.* **45**II: 601–6.

Jahromi, S.S., and Atwood, H.L. 1969. Correlation of structure, speed of contraction, and total tension in fast and slow abdominal muscle fibre of the lobster (*Homarus americanus*). *J. exp. Zool.* **171**: 25–38.

Johansen, K., Lenfant, C., and Mecklenburg, T.A. 1970. Respiration in the crab, *Cancer magister*. *Z. vergl. Physiol.* **70**: 1–19.

Johnston, M.A., Davies, P.S., Elder, H.Y. 1971. Possible hepatic function for crustacean blood cells. *Nature* **230**: 471–2.

Jones, D.A. 1972. Aspects of the ecology and behaviour of *Ocypode ceratophthalmus* (Pallas) and *O. kuhlii* de Haan (Crustacea: Ocypodidae). *J. exp. mar. Biol. Ecol.* **8**: 31–43.

Kato, K.N., and Kamemoto, F.I. 1968. Neuroendocrine involvement in osmoregulation in the grapsid crab *Metopograpsus messor*. *Comp. Biochem. Physiol.* **28**: 665–74.

Kay, M.M. 1971. L-isoleucine: an inducer of the feeding response in decapod crustaceans. *Experientia* **27**: 103–4.

Kittredge, J.S., Terry, M., and Takahashi, F.T. 1971. Sex pheromone activity of the moulting hormone, crustecdysone, on male crabs (*Pachygrapsus crassipes*, *Cancer antennarius* and *C. anthonyi*). *Fish. Bull. US Dep. Commer.* **69**: 337–43.

Knight, M.D. 1968. The larval development of *Raninoides benedicti* Rathbun (Brachyura, Raninidae), with notes on Pacific records of *Raninoides laevis* (Latreille). *Crustaceana* Suppl. 2: 145–69.

Knudsen, J.W. 1967. *Trapezia* and *Tetralia* (Decapoda, Brachyura, Xanthidae) as obligate ectoparasites of pocilloporid and acroporid corals. *Pacif. Sci.* **21**: 51–7.

Krishnakumaran, A., and Schneiderman, H.A. 1970. Control of moulting in mandibulate and chelicerate arthropods by ecdysones. *Biol. Bull. mar. biol. Lab., Woods Hole* **139**: 520–38.

Krishnamoorthy, R.V., and Srihari, K. 1973. Changes in the excretory patterns of the fresh water field crab *Paratelphusa hydrodromous* upon adaptations to higher salinities. *Mar. Biol.* **21**: 341–8.

Krishnan, G. 1951. Phenolic tanning and pigmentation of the cuticle in *Carcinus maenas*. *Q. Jl Microsc. Sci.* **92**: 333–42.

Kuiper, J.W. 1962. The optics of the compound eye. In 'Biological receptor mechanisms'. *Symp. Soc. exp. Biol.* **16**: 58–71.

Lang, F., and Atwood, H.L. 1973. Functional morphology of nerve terminals and the mechanism of facilitation. *Am. Zool.* **13**: 337–55.

Lang, F., Sutterlin, A., and Prosser, C.L. 1970. Electrical and mechanical properties of the closer muscle of the Alaskan king crab *Paralithodes camtschatica*. *Comp. Biochem. Physiol.* **32**: 615–28.

Laverack, M.S. 1962a. Responses of cuticular sense organs of the lobster, *Homarus vulgaris* (Crustacea) — I. Hair-peg organs as water current receptors. *Comp. Biochem. Physiol.* **5**: 319–25.

Laverack, M.S. 1962b. Responses of cuticular sense organs of the lobster, *Homarus vulgaris* (Crustacea) — II. Hair-fan organs as pressure receptors. *Comp. Biochem. Physiol.* **6**: 137–45.

Laverack, M.S. 1963. Aspects of chemoreception in Crustacea. *Comp. Biochem. Physiol.* **8**: 141–51.

Lebour, M.V. 1928. The larval stages of the Plymouth Brachyura. *Proc. zool. Soc. Lond.* (1928), 473–560.

Leffler, C.W. 1972. Some effects of temperature on the growth and metabolic rate of juvenile blue crabs, *Callinectes sapidus*, in the laboratory. *Mar. Biol.* **14**: 104–10.

Leffler, C.W. 1973. Metabolic rate in relation to body size and environmental O_2 concentration in two species of xanthid crabs. *Comp. Biochem. Physiol.* **44A**: 1047–52.

Lighter, F.J. 1974. A note on the behavioural spacing mechanism of the ghost crab *Ocypode ceratophthalmus* (Pallas) (Decapoda, family Ocypodidae). *Crustaceana* **27**: 312–14.

Linsenmair, K.E. 1967. Optische Signalisierung der kopulationshöhle bei der

Reiterkrabbe *Ocypode saratan* Forsk. (Decapoda, Brachyura, Ocy-podidae). *Náturwissenschaften* **10**: 256–7.

Lobb, S.M. 1972. Aspects of the social behaviour, ecology and anatomy of the hairy crab *Pilumnus hirtellus* (L.). PhD thesis. University of Reading.

Lockwood, A.P.M. 1968. *Aspects of the physiology of Crustacea*. Edinburgh and London: Oliver and Boyd.

Lockwood, A.P.M., and Riegel, J.A. 1969. The excretion of magnesium by *Carcinus maenas. J. exp. Biol.* **51**: 575–89.

Loosanoff, V.L. 1965. Pesticides in sea water and the possibilities of their use in mariculture. In C.O. Chichester (ed.), *Research in pesticides.* pp. 135–46. New York, London: Academic Press.

Lucas, J.S., and Hodgekin, E.P. 1970. Growth and reproduction of *Halicarcinus australis* (Haswell) (Crustacea, Brachyura) in the Swan Estuary western Australia. *Aust. J. mar. Freshwat. Res.* **21**: 149–62.

MacDonald, J.D., Pike, R.B., and Williamson, D.I. 1957. Larvae of the British species of *Diogenes, Pagurus, Anapagurus* and *Lithodes* (Crustacea, Decapoda). *Proc. zool. Soc. Lond.* **128**: 209–57.

Macmillan, D.L., and Dando, M.R. 1972. Tension receptors on the apodemes of muscles in the walking legs of the crab, *Cancer magister. Mar. Behav. Physiol.* **1**: 185–208.

McVean, A., and Findlay, I. 1976. Autotomy in *Carcinus maenas*: the role of the basi-ischiopodite posterior levator muscles. *J. comp. Physiol.* **110**: 367–81.

Mainardi, D., and Rossi, A.C. 1969. La distribuzione delle attinie *Calliactis parasitica* in rapporto allo stato sociale nel pagro *Dardanus arrosor. Pubbl. Staz. zool. Napoli* **37** (Suppl. 2): 200–2.

Mangum, C.P., and Johansen, K. 1975. The colloid osmotic pressures of invertebrate body fluids. *J. exp. Biol.* **63**: 661–71.

Margalef, R. 1963. On certain unifying principles in ecology. *Am. Nat.* **97**: 357–74.

Mellon, D., Jr. 1968. *The physiology of sense organs*. Edinburgh and London: Oliver and Boyd.

Mill, P.J., and Lowe, D.A. 1972. An analysis of the types of sensory unit present in PD proprioceptor of decapod crustaceans. *J. exp. Biol.* **56**: 509–25.

Mill, P.J., and Lowe, D.A. 1973. The fine structure of the PD proprioceptor of *Cancer pagurus*. I. The receptor strand and the movement cells. *Proc. R. Soc. B* **184**: 179–97.

Miller, D.C. 1961. The feeding mechanism of fiddler crabs, with ecological considerations of feeding adaptations. *Zoologica N.Y.* **46**: 89–100.

Miller, D.C., and Vernberg, F.J. 1968. Some thermal requirements of fiddler crabs of the temperate and tropical zones and their influence on geographical distribution. *Am. Zool.* **8**: 459–69.

Molenock, J. 1975. Evolutionary aspects of communication in the courtship behaviour of four species of anomuran crab (*Petrolisthes*). *Behaviour* **53**: 1–30.

Muntz, L., Ebling, F.J., and Kitching, J.A. 1965. The ecology of Loch Ine. XIV. Predatory activities of large crabs. *J. Anim. Ecol.* **34**: 315–29.

Muramoto, A., and Tamasige, M. 1971. Reflex mechanism of pinching a soft or solid body with the claw of the crayfish. *J. Fac. Sci. Hokkaido Univ. series VI*, **18**: 32–44.

Naylor, E. 1958. Tidal and diurnal rhythms of locomotor activity in *Carcinus maenas* (L.). *J. exp. Biol.* **35**: 602–10.

Naylor, E. 1963. Temperature relationships of the locomotor rhythm of *Carcinus*. *J. exp. Biol.* **40**: 669–79.

Naylor, E. 1976. Rhythmic behaviour and reproduction in marine animals. In R.C. Newell (ed.), *Adaptation to environment: physiology of marine animals*. pp. 393–429. London: Butterworths.

Naylor, E., Atkinson, R.J.A., and Williams, B.G. 1971. External factors influencing the tidal rhythm of shore crabs. *Proc. 2nd int. Interdisc. Conf. Cycle Res.* **2**: 173–80.

Naylor, E., and Williams, B.G. 1968. Effects of eyestalk removal on rhythmic locomotor activity in *Carcinus*. *J. exp. Biol.* **49**: 107–16.

Newell, R.C. 1969. Effect of fluctuations in temperature on the metabolism of intertidal invertebrates. *Am. Zool.* **9**: 293–307.

Newell, R.C. 1973. Factors affecting the respiration of intertidal invertebrates. *Am. Zool.* **13**: 513–28.

Newell, R.C., Ahsanullah, M., and Pye, V.I. 1972. Aerial and aquatic respiration in the shore crab *Carcinus maenas* (L.). *Comp. Biochem. Physiol.* **43A**: 239–52.

Nicol, E.A.T. 1932: The feeding habits of the Galatheidae. *J. mar. biol. Ass. UK.* **18**: 87–106.

Ono, Y. 1965. On the ecological distribution of ocypodid crabs in the estuary. *Mem. Fac. Sci. Kyushu Univ.* series E, **4**: 1–60.

Palmer, J.D. 1967. Daily and tidal components in the persistent rhythmic activity of the crab *Sesarma*. *Nature, Lond.* **215**: 64–6.

Palmer, J.D. 1973. Tidal rhythms: the clock control of the rhythmic physiology of marine organisms. *Biol. Rev.* **48**: 377–418.

Passano, L.M. 1960. Moulting and its control. In T.H. Waterman (ed.), *The physiology of Crustacea, I*. pp. 473–536. New York and London: Academic Press.

Patton, W.K. 1974. Community structure amongst the animals inhabiting the coral *Pocillopora damicornis* at Heron Island, Australia. In W.B. Vernberg (ed.), *Symbiosis in the sea*. pp. 219–43. Columbia: University of South Carolina Press.

Pearson, J. 1908. *Cancer*. Liverpool Marine Biological Committee Memoirs on typical British marine plants and animals. **16**: 1–209. London: Williams and Norgate.

Perkins, E.J. 1967. Some aspects of the biology of *Carcinus maenas* (L.). *Trans. J. Proc. Dumfries. Galloway nat. Hist. Antiq. Soc.* 3rd ser., vol. XLIV: 47–56.

Potts, F.A. 1915. *Hapalocarcinus*, the gall forming crab, with some notes on the related genus *Cryptochirus*. *Publs Carnegie Instn.* **212**: 33–69.

Potts, W.T.W., and Parry, G. 1964. *Osmotic and ionic regulation in animals*. Oxford: Pergamon Press Ltd.

Powell, G.G., and Nickerson, R.C. 1965. Aggregation amongst juvenile king crabs (*Paralithodes camtschatica*, Tilesius) Kodiak, Alaska. *Anim. Behav.* **13**: 374–80.

Prosser, C.L. 1961a. Nitrogen excretion. In C.L. Prosser and F.A. Brown, Jr., *Comparative animal physiology*, 2nd Ed., pp. 135–52. Philadelphia and London: W.B. Saunders Co.

Prosser, C.L. 1961b. Oxygen: respiration and metabolism. In C.L. Prosser and F.A. Brown, Jr., *Comparative animal physiology*, 2nd Ed., pp. 153–97. Philadelphia and London: W.B. Saunders Co.

Prosser, C.L. 1961c. Temperature. In C.L. Prosser and F.A. Brown, Jr., *Comparative animal physiology*, 2nd Ed., pp. 238–84. Philadelphia and London: W.B. Saunders Co.

Provenzano, A.J., Jr. 1962. The larval development of the tropical land hermit *Coenobita clypeatus* (Herbst) in the laboratory. *Crustaceana* **4**: 207–28.

Provenzano, A.J., Jr. 1968. The complete larval development of the West Indian hermit crab *Petrochirus diogenes* (L.) (Decapoda, Diogenidae) reared in the laboratory. *Bull. mar. Sci.* **18**: 143–81.

Rajula, S.G., Santhanakrishnan, E., and Shyamalanath, S. 1973. Nature of the sex attractant pheromone in a crab *Paratelphusa hydrodromus* (Crustacea). *Curr. Sci.* **42**: 467–8.

Rao, K.R. 1968. The pericardial sacs of *Ocypode* in relation to the conservation of water, moulting and behaviour. *Am. Zool.* **8**: 561–7.

Rasmussen, E. 1973. Systematics and ecology of the Isefjord marine fauna. *Ophelia* **11**: 1–495.

Redmond, J.R. 1968. Transport of oxygen by the blood of the land crab, *Gecarcinus lateralis*. *Am. Zool.* **8**: 471–9.

Rice, A.L., and Provenzano, A.J., Jr. 1966. The larval development of the West Indian sponge crab *Dromidia antillensis* (Decapoda: Dromiidae). *J. Zool. Lond.* **149**: 297–319.

Rice, A.L., and Provenzano, A.J., Jr. 1970. The larval stages of *Homola barbata* (Fabricius) (Crustacea, Decapoda, Homolidae) reared in the laboratory. *Bull. mar. Sci.* **20**: 446–71.

Ripley, S.H., Bush, B.M.H., and Roberts, A. 1968. Crab muscle receptor which responds without impulses. *Nature, Lond.* **218**: 1170–1.

Roberts, J. 1959. Thermal acclimation of metabolism in the crab *Pachygrapsus crassipes* Randall. II. Mechanisms and the influence of season and latitude. *Physiol. Zoöl.* **30**: 243–55.

Ross, D.M. 1974. Evolutionary aspects of associations between crabs and sea anemones. In W.B. Vernberg (ed.), *Symbiosis in the sea.* pp. 111–25. Columbia: University of South Carolina Press.

Ross, D.M., and Sutton, L. 1961a. The response of the sea anemone *Calliactis parasitica* to shells of the hermit crab *Pagurus bernhardus*. *Proc. R. Soc. B* **155**: 266–81.

Ross, D.M., and Sutton, L. 1961b. The association between the hermit crab *Dardanus arrosor* (Herbst) and the sea anemone *Calliactis parasitica* (Couch). *Proc. R. Soc. B* **155**: 282–91.

Rossi, A.C. 1971. Dominance—subordinance relationships in the hermit crab *Diogenes pugilator* (Anomura, Paguridae). *Rev. Comp. Anim.* **5**: 153–62.

Rubenstein, D.I., and Hazlett, B.A. 1974. Examination of the agonistic behaviour of the crayfish *Oronectes virilis* by character analysis. *Behaviour* **50**: 193–216.

Ryan, E.P. 1966. Pheromone: evidence in a decapod crustacean. *Science, N.Y.* **151**: 340–1.

Salmon, M. 1971. Signal characteristics and acoustic detection by fiddler crabs, *Uca rapax* and *Uca pugilator*. *Physiol. Zoöl.* **44**: 210–24.

Salmon, M., and Atsaides, S.P. 1968. Visual and acoustic signalling during courtship by fiddler crabs (genus *Uca*). *Am. Zool.* **8**: 623–39.

Salmon, M., and Horch, K. 1972. Acoustic signalling and detection by semiterrestrial crabs of the family Ocypodidae. In H.E. Winn and B.L. Olla (eds.), *Behaviour of marine animals*, **1**: 60–96. New York: Plenum Press.

Sandeman, D.C., and Okajima, A. 1972. Statocyst induced eye movements in the crab *Scylla serrata*. *J. exp. Biol.* **57**: 187–204.

Schäfer, W. 1954. Form und Funktion der Brachyuren-Schere. *Abh. senckenb. naturforsch. Ges.* No 489: 1–65.

Schmidt-Nielsen, B., Gertz, K.H., and Davis, L.E. 1968. Excretion and ultrastructure of the antennal gland of the fiddler crab *Uca mordax*. *J. Morph.* **125**: 473–81.

Schöne, H. 1968. Agonistic and sexual display in aquatic and semiterrestrial brachyuran crabs. *Am. Zool.* **8**: 641–54.

Schöne, H., and Schöne, H. 1963. Balz und andere Verhaltenweisen der Mangrovekrabbe *Goniopsis cruentata* Latr. und das Winkverhalten der eulitoralen Brachyuren. *Z. Tierpsychol.* **20**: 641–56.

Scott, S., and Mote, M.I. 1974. Spectral sensitivity in some marine Crustacea. *Vision Res.* **14**: 659–63.

Shaw, J. 1959a. Solute and water balance in the muscle fibres of the East African freshwater crab *Potamon niloticus* (M. Edw.). *J. exp. Biol.* **36**: 145–56.

Shaw, J. 1959b. Salt and water balance in the East African freshwater crab *Potamon niloticus* (M. Edw.). *J. exp. Biol.* **36**: 157–76.

Shelton, R.G.J., and Laverack, M.S. 1968. Observations on a redescribed crustacean cuticular sense organ. *Comp. Biochem. Physiol.* **25**: 1049–59.

Shelton, R.G.J., and Mackie, A.M. 1971. Studies on the chemical preferences of the shore crab, *Carcinus maenas* (L.). *J. exp. mar. Biol. Ecol.* **7**: 41–9.

Sherman, R.G., and Atwood, H.L. 1972. Correlated electrophysiological and ultrastructural studies of a crustacean motor unit. *J. gen. Physiol.* **59**: 586–615.

Shoup, J.B. 1968. Shell opening by crabs of the genus *Calappa*. *Science, N.Y.* **160**: 887–8.

Siebers, D. 1974. Mechanisms of intracellular isosmotic regulation: fate of ^{14}C-labelled serum proteins in the shore crab *Carcinus maenas* after changed environmental salinity. *Helgoländ. wiss. Meeresunters.* **26**: 375–81.

Skinner, D.M. 1966. Breakdown and reformation of somatic muscle during the moult cycle of the land crab, *Gecarcinus lateralis*. *J. exp. Zool.* **163**: 115–24.

Snow, P.J. 1973. Ultrastructure of the aesthetasc hairs of the littoral decapod, *Paragrapsus gaimardii*. *Z. Zellforsch. mikrosk. Anat.* **138**: 489–502.

Snyder, A.W., Menzel, R., and Laughlin, S.B. 1973. Structure and function of the fused rhabdome. *J. comp. Physiol.* **87**: 99–135.

Spirito, C.P. 1972. An analsis of the swimming behaviour of the portunid crab *Callinectes sapidus*. *Mar. Behav. Physiol.* **1**: 261–76.

Spirito, C.P., Evoy, W.H., and Barnes, W.J.P. 1972. Nervous control of walking in the crab, *Cardisoma guanhumi*. I. Characteristics of resistance reflexes. *Z. vergl. Physiol.* **76**: 1–15.

Spirito, C.P., Evoy, W.H., and Fourtner, G.R. 1973. Consideration of proprioception and neuromuscular integration in crustacean locomotion. *Am. Zool.* **13**: 427–34.

Števčić, Z. 1971a. Laboratory observations on the aggregations of the spiny spider crab (*Maja squinado* Herbst). *Anim. Behav.* **19**: 18–25.

Števčić, Z. 1971b. The main features of brachyuran evolution. *Syst. Zool.* **20**: 331–40.

Storch, V., and Welsch, U. 1975. Ueber Bau und Funktion der Kiemen und Lungen von *Ocypode ceratophthalmus* (Decapoda: Crustacea). *Mar. Biol.* **29**: 363–71.

Tagatz, M.E. 1968. Biology of the blue crab *Callinectes sapidus* Rathbun in the St. Johns River, Florida. *Fishery Bull. Fish Wildl. Serv. US* **67**: 17–33.

Taylor, E.W., Butler, P.J., and Sherlock, P.J. 1973. The respiratory and cardiovascular changes associated with the emersion response of *Carcinus maenas* (L.) during environmental hypoxia at three different temperatures. *J. comp. Physiol.* **86**: 95–115.

Teal, J.M. 1959. Respiration of crabs in Georgia salt marshes and its relation to their ecology. *Physiol. Zoöl.* **32**: 1–14.

Teal, J.M., and Carey, F.G. 1967. The metabolism of marsh crabs under conditions of reduced oxygen pressure. *Physiol. Zoöl.* **40**: 83–91.

Telford, M. 1971. Changes in blood sugar composition during the moult cycle of the lobster *Homarus americanus*. *Comp. Biochem. Physiol.* **26**: 917–26.

Truchot, J.P. 1971a. Fixation d'oxygène par le sérum de *Carcinus maenas* (L.) (Crustacé Décapode Brachyoure). *C. r. hebd Séanc. Acad. Sci., Paris* (D.) **272**: 984–7.

Truchot, J.P. 1971b. Etude comparée de la fixation de l'oxygène par le sérum de cinq espèces de Crustacés Décapodes Brachyoures. *C. r. hebd. Séanc. Acad. Sci., Paris* (D) **272**: 2706–9.

Truchot, J.P. 1975a. Blood acid–base changes during experimental emersion and reimmersion of the intertidal crab *Carcinus maenas* (L.). *Respiration Physiology* **23**: 351–60.

Truchot, J.P. 1975b. Factors controlling the *in vitro* and *in vivo* oxygen affinity of the hemocyanin in the crab *Carcinus maenas* (L.). *Respiration Physiology* **24**: 173–89.

Turaboyski, K. 1973. Biology and ecology of the crab *Rithropanopeus harrisii* ssp. *tridentatus*. *Mar. Biol.* **23**: 303–13.

Tweedie, M.W.F. 1950. Notes on grapsoid crabs from the Raffles Museum. *Bull. Raffles Mus.* **23**: 310–24.

Vannini, M. 1975. Researches on the coast of Somalia. The shore and dune of Sar Uanle. 5. Description and rhythmicity of digging behaviour in *Coenobita rugosus* Milne-Edwards. *Monitore Zool. Ital.* **11**: 233–42.

Vannini, M., and Sardini, A. 1971. Aggressivity and dominance in river crab *Potamon fluviatile* (Herbst). *Monitore Zool. Ital.* **5**: 173–213.

Vermeij, G.J. 1975. Marine faunal dominance and molluscan shell form. *Evolution,* **28**: 656–64.

Vermeij, G.J. 1976. Interoceanic differences in vulnerability of shelled prey to crab predation. *Nature, Lond.* **260**: 135–6.

Vernberg, F.J. 1959a. Studies on the physiological variation between tropical and temperate zone fiddler crabs of the genus *Uca*. II. Oxygen consumption of whole organisms. *Biol. Bull. mar. biol. Lab., Woods Hole* **117**: 163–84.

Vernberg, F.J. 1959b. Studies on the physiological variation between tropical and temperate zone fiddler crabs of the genus *Uca*. III. The influence of temperature acclimation on oxygen consumption of whole organisms. *Biol. Bull. mar. biol. Lab., Woods Hole* **117**: 582–93.

Vernberg, F.J., and Tashian, R.E. 1959. Studies on the physiological variation between tropical and temperate zone fiddler crabs of the genus *Uca*. I. Thermal death limits. *Ecology* **40**: 589–93.

Vernberg, F.J., and Vernberg, W.B. 1966. Studies on the physiological variation between tropical and temperate zone fiddler crabs of the genus *Uca*. VII. Metabolic–temperature acclimation responses in southern hemisphere crabs. *Comp. Biochem. Physiol.* **19**: 489–524.

Wade, B.A. 1967. Studies on the biology of the West Indian beach clam *Donax denticulatus* Linné. I. Ecology. *Bull. mar. Sci.* **17**: 149–74.

Wagle, P.V. 1923. *Land crabs as agricultural pests in western India.* Bull. No 118 of 1924, Department of Agriculture, Bombay.

Wald, G. 1968. Single and multiple visual systems in arthropods. *J. gen. Physiol.* **51**: 125–56.

Wallace, J.C. 1972. Activity and metabolic rate in the shore crab, *Carcinus maenas*. *Comp. Biochem. Physiol.* **41A**: 523–33.

Warner, G.F. 1967. The life history of the mangrove tree crab *Aratus pisoni*. *J. Zool. Lond.* **153**: 321–35.

Warner, G.F. 1969. The occurrence and distribution of crabs in a Jamaican mangrove swamp. *J. Anim. Ecol.* **38**: 379–89.

Warner, G.F. 1970. Behaviour of two species of grapsid crab during intraspecific encounters. *Behaviour* **36**: 9–19.

Warner, G.F., and Jones, A.R. 1976. Leverage and muscle type in crab chelae (Crustacea: Brachyura). *J. Zoo. Lond.* **180**: 57–68.

Watson, J. 1971. Ecdysis of the snow crab, *Chionoecetes opilio. Can. J. Zool.* **49**: 1025–7.

Weiland, A.L., and Mangum, C.P. 1975. The influence of environmental salinity on haemocyanin function in the blue crab, *Callinectes sapidus. J. exp. Zool.* **193**: 265–74.

White, Q., and Spirito, C.P. 1973. Anatomy and physiology of the swimming leg musculature in the blue crab *Callinectes sapidus. Mar. Behav. Physiol.* **2**: 141–53.

Whitear, M. 1962. The fine structure of crustacean proprioceptors. I. The chordotonal organs in the legs of the shore crab *Carcinus maenas. Phil. Trans. R. Soc.* Ser. B **245**: 291–324.

Whitear, M. 1965. The fine structure of crustacean proprioceptors. II. The thoracic-coxal organs in *Carcinus, Pagurus* and *Astacus. Phil. Trans. R. Soc.* Ser. B **248**: 437–56.

Whitney, J.O. 1974. The effect of external salinity upon lipid synthesis in the blue crab *Callinectes sapidus* Rathbun and in the spider crab *Libinia emarginata* Leach. *Comp. Biochem. Physiol.* **49A**: 433–40.

Wicksten, M.K. 1975. Observations on decorating behaviour following moulting in *Loxorhynchus crispatus* Stimpson (Decapoda, Majidae). *Crustaceana* **29**: 315–16.

Wiersma, C.A.G. 1959. Movement receptors in decapod Crustacea. *J. mar. biol. Ass. UK* **38**: 143–52.

Wiersma, C.A.G. 1961. The neuro-muscular system. In T.H. Waterman (ed.), *The physiology of Crustacea* II, pp. 191–240. New York and London: Academic Press.

Wilkens, J.L., and Fingerman, M. 1965. Heat tolerance and temperature relations of the fiddler crab, *Uca pugilator*, with reference to body coloration. *Biol. Bull. mar. biol. Lab., Woods Hole* **128**: 133–41.

Williams, B.G., and Naylor, E. 1967. Spontaneously induced rhythm of tidal periodicity in laboratory-reared *Carcinus*. *J. exp. Biol.* **47**: 229–34.

Williams, G., and Needham, A.E. 1941. Metric variations in populations of *Carcinus maenas*. *J. mar. biol. Ass. UK* **25**: 261–81.

Williamson, D.I. 1965. Some larval stages of three Australian crabs belonging to the families Homolidae and Raninidae, and observations on the affinities of these families (Crustacea: Decapoda). *Aust. J. mar. Freshwater. Res.* **16**: 369–98.

Wright, H.O. 1966. Comparative studies of social behaviour in grapsoid crabs. PhD thesis, University of California, Berkeley.

Wright, H.. 1968. Visual displays in brachyuran crabs: field and laboratory studies. *Am. Zool.* **8**: 655–65.

Wynne-Edwards, V.C. 1962. *Animal dispersion with relation to social behaviour.* Edinburgh and London: Oliver and Boyd.

Yamaguchi, T. 1971. Courtship behaviour of a fiddler crab *Uca lactea*. *Kumamoto J. Sci.* (B.2) **10**: 13–37.

Young, R.E. 1972. The physiological ecology of haemocyanin in some selected crabs. II. The characteristics of haemocyanin with relation to terrestrialness. *J. exp. mar. Biol. Ecol.* **10**: 193–206.

Glossary

ACCESSORY FLEXOR MUSCLE   A small muscle which flexes the leg at the MC joint. It is in two parts, proximal and distal, and inserts on a long thin apodeme in the merus (Fig. 19).

ANTENNAE   The appendages of the 2nd and 3rd head segments are the 1st and 2nd pairs of antennae respectively. The 1st antennae are secondarily biramous (Fig. 3). Both pairs of antennae are sensory.

APODEME   A cuticular, usually calcified invagination upon which muscles insert and which, itself, inserts by means of tough flexible cuticle onto that part of the skeleton which is moved by its muscles (Figs. 12, 13).

ARTHIODIAL MEMBRANE   Tough flexible cuticle occurring between skeletal elements and allowing relative movement.

ARTHROPHRAGM   A cuticular calcified invagination, usually in the form of a plate, which provides a rigid origin for muscles.

BASI-ISCHIUM   The second podomere from the base of a limb, formed from the fusion of the basis and the ischium of the primitive appendage (Figs. 1, 2).

BENDER MUSCLE   The muscle which bends a leg forwards at the CP joint.

BIRAMOUS   Having two branches, as in the basic appendage (Fig. 2).

BRANCHIOSTEGITES   The anterior and lateral margins of the carapace extend ventrally on either side forming the walls of the cephalothorax and enclosing the branchial chambers (Fig. 1).

CARAPACE   A sheet of cuticle extending back from the head to enclose the dorsal and lateral parts of the thorax; the 'shell' of a crab (Fig. 1).

CARPUS   The 3rd podomere from the tip of the endopod of a limb (Figs. 1, 2).

CB   The junction between the coxa and the basi-ischium (Fig. 12).

CEPHALOTHORAX   The body of a crab; formed from the fusion of the head and thorax, enclosed dorsally and laterally by the carapace and ventrally by the sternum.

CHELA   A pinching claw composed of a movable finger, the dactylus, and a fixed finger, a distal extension of the propodus (Fig. 1). If a pair of chelae differ in size the larger is called the major chela and the smaller the minor.

CHELIPED   A limb bearing a chela. In crabs this limb is borne on the 4th thoracic segment (Fig. 1).

CLOSER MUSCLE   The muscle which moves the dactylus downwards relative to the propodus (Figs. 12, 13).

COXA   The basal podomere of a limb (Fig. 1).

CP   The junction between the carpus and the propodus (Fig. 12).

DACTYLUS   The terminal podomere of the endopod of a limb (Figs. 1, 2).

DEPRESSOR MUSCLE   The muscle which moves the limb downwards by rotating it about the CB joint.

ENDOPHRAGMAL SKELETON   An internal skeleton composed of arthrophragms arising from the sternites and supporting the muscles of the leg bases (Fig. 7B).

ENDOPOD   The inner of the two branches of the primitive appendage (Fig. 2).

EPIPOD   A lateral extension from the base of an appendage (Fig. 2).

EPISTOME   A broad strongly calcified plate in front of, and above, the mouth. It represents the fused sternites of the 3rd and 4th segments.

EXOPOD   The outer of the two branches of the primitive appendage (Fig. 2).

EXTENSOR MUSCLE   The muscle which extends the leg at the MC joint (Fig. 19).

FLEXOR MUSCLE   A muscle which flexes the leg at the MC joint (Fig. 19).

GASTRIC MILL   The structures responsible for grinding food within the stomach (Fig. 10).

HAEMOCOEL   Composed of the blood-filled spaces mainly on the venous side of the circulatory system which fill all gaps between tissues and organs.

HEPATOPANCREAS   The main organ of digestion and of the storage of reserves. It arises on either side of the mid-gut as a much branched diverticulum and occupies a considerable proportion of the space within the body cavity (Fig. 7).

IM   The junction between the basi-ischium and the merus. It is called IM rather than BM because the junction is with the ischium end of the basi-ischium (Figs. 2, 12).

LEVATOR MUSCLE   A muscle which moves the limb upwards by rotating it about the CB joint.

MANDIBLES   The appendages of the 4th head segment. They form a pair of jaws which bite from side to side across the mouth.

MAXILLAE   The appendages of the 5th and 6th head segments are the 1st and 2nd pairs of maxillae respectively (Fig. 3). Both pairs are included in the mouthparts and the 2nd maxillae bear the scaphognathites.

MAXILLIPEDS   There are three pairs of maxillipeds borne on the first three segments of the thorax; all three pairs are included in the mouthparts. Maxillipeds are biramous and bear epipods (Fig. 3).

MC   The junction between the merus and the carpus (Fig. 12).

MERUS   The 4th podomere from the tip of the endopod of a limb (Figs. 1, 2).

MILNE-EDWARDS OPENINGS   The main inhalant respiratory openings; one on either side between the base of the cheliped and the lower edge of the branchiostegite.

MOUTHPARTS   A collective term for the appendages around the mouth which are concerned with feeding: mandibles, maxillae and maxillipeds.

OPENER MUSCLE   The muscle which moves the dactylus up relative to the propodus (Figs. 12, 13).

ORBIT   The socket at the front of the carapace in which the eye is situated and into which it can be folded.

PD   The junction between the propodus and the dactylus (Fig. 12).

PLEOPOD   An appendage of any one of the first five abdominal segments.

PODOMERE   A segment of an appendage joined to the body or to adjacent podomeres by joints and capable of independent movement.

PROMOTOR MUSCLE   The muscle which moves the leg forwards by rotating it about the TC joint.

PROPODUS   The 2nd podomere from the tip of the endopod of a limb (Figs. 1, 2).

REMOTOR MUSCLE   The muscle which moves the leg backwards by rotating it about the TC joint.

SCAPHOGNATHITE   A lateral flap on the 2nd maxilla which, by beating within a narrow pump chamber, draws a respiratory stream of water through the branchial chamber (Figs. 3, 10).

SETA   A cuticular hair arising from the outside of the exoskeleton.

SINUS   A blood-filled space on the venous side of the circulatory system.

STERNITE   A calcified plate on the ventral side of a segment between the bases of the appendages.

STERNUM   The calcified underside composed of fused sternites.

STRETCHER MUSCLE   The muscle which bends the leg backwards at the CP joint (stretches the cheliped).

SUB-CHELATE   The state of a limb in which the dactylus can be closed so as to bite against the propodus. Unlike the case in a true chela, a fixed finger is not developed and the dactylus bites either against an enlarged edge of the propodus or against projecting spines (Figs. 23B, C).

TC   The junction between the thorax and the coxa (Fig. 12).

TELSON   The terminal part of the body which bears the anus; it articulates with the last (6th) abdominal segment.

UNIRAMOUS   Composed of a single branch. When used with reference to an appendage, it usually implies the loss of the exopod, as in a walking leg.

UROPOD   An appendage of the last (6th) abdominal segment.

Index

Page references in italic refer to line drawings